VICTIMS OF THE REVOLUTION

NATHANAEL BLAKE

Victims of the Revolution

How Sexual Liberation Hurts Us All

With a Foreword by Ryan T. Anderson

IGNATIUS PRESS   SAN FRANCISCO

Cover photo ©iStock/BiancameveMoSt

Cover design by Enrique J. Aguilar

© 2025 by Ignatius Press, San Francisco
All rights reserved
Foreword © 2025 by Ryan T. Anderson
ISBN 978-1-62164-770-6 (PB)
ISBN 978-1-64229-343-2 (eBook)
Library of Congress Control Number 2024951806
Printed in the United States of America ∞

For Julie—wife, mother, and subeditor

"Across the pale parabola of joy"

CONTENTS

FOREWORD

by Ryan T. Anderson

The sexual revolution has been a disaster. More than fifty years since the so-called Summer of Love, the victims are all around us: Unborn babies who never got to see the light of day. Kids who grew up without a father. Women who were used and abused by men for sexual gratification and then abandoned, left to fend for themselves. Men who are addicted to pornography and unable or at least unwilling to commit, thus missing out on one of life's greatest joys: marriage and fatherhood. And now a cohort of kids who don't feel comfortable as boys or girls, with irreversible damage being inflicted on their bodies and minds by adults who should know better. The sexual revolution is built on a series of lies about the human person. And there are human costs to getting human nature wrong.

Consent—that was the guiding principle of the sexual revolution. And consenting adults should be free to do whatever they want sexually—free in the legal sense from any restrictions or penalties, but also free in the cultural sense from any social opprobrium, from any cultural norms that might suggest a more humane approach to our sexual lives. Of course, consent alone cannot make an ethic; at the very least one needs something deeper in order to know when and where and how and why to consent. This is what traditional marital vows and norms provided. And, of course, what started as consenting adults quickly became

applied to minors. Consenting teens should be free to ...
And consenting preteens ... And it didn't just stay restricted
to sexual acts; it eventually progressed to sexual identities as
well. If I should be free to engage in sex however I want,
why shouldn't I be free to *be* whatever sex (gender identity)
I want? There is a certain debased logic to it all.

But where has this train of logic taken us? Now three
generations into the sexual revolution, we see more and
more Americans who have gone along with its consenting-
adults mantra and the ensuing erosion of marital norms—the
rise of cohabitation and the hookup culture, the normal-
ization of premarital sex and nonmarital childbearing, the
introduction of no-fault divorce laws and the more than
doubling of divorce rates, and a marriage rate that has fallen
by 65 percent since 1970. Compared to the pre-revolution
'60s, we're left with fewer marriages, more divorce, fewer
kids, and more atomized adults. The kids we do have are
often growing up without dads, and many of our elderly are
aging without spouses or adult children to care for them.
Why now, when we have the best medical care in history,
with the best pain management ever, do we think we need
to kill our elderly with assisted suicide? The sexual revolution has not just attacked the transmission and beginnings of
life but has also destroyed the matrix of love and care and
support that the family provides throughout the life cycle,
from birth to death.

And this has brought profound unhappiness. The sexual
revolution is fundamentally opposed to marriage and the
virtue that makes marriage possible, chastity. The sexual
revolution says there's nothing unique or special about
marriage—at best, it's simply one of many acceptable ways
to "consent" to sex, and at worst it's an outdated, overly
restrictive institution of repression. But marriage is meant
to bring together a man and a woman as husband and wife,

committed to each other permanently and exclusively, so that any children their union may produce will have the love and care of both their mother and father. By ensuring a man and a woman commit to each other before engaging in the act that could produce new life, marriage helps guarantee that a mother and father will be committed to that new life. In other words, the way that you get fathers to commit to their kids is by first getting them to commit to their (future) children's mother. We now have decades of social science research that confirms what every one of our grandparents knew because of the law written on the heart: that marriage is the best institution for the bearing and rearing of children. It protects against child poverty and increases the odds for social mobility; it decreases the rates of delinquency and crime while increasing the rates of graduation and employment. These goods—social justice, limited government, care for the poor, and the protection of freedom—are all better served by a healthy marriage culture than by the government picking up the pieces of a broken marriage culture.

But it's not just these secular metrics of poverty and crime and employment that marriage affects. Marriage and family and children are the source of many of life's deepest fulfillments and happiness. And yet millions of our neighbors now have missed out on these great goods. Perhaps that is the deepest form of victimization caused by the sexual revolution: the people who have gladly bought into its ideology and lived out its mantras, thinking they were being liberated from oppressive and outdated strictures, when in reality they were enslaving themselves to lives spent chasing fleeting dopamine and oxytocin hits. Consent plus condoms does not make people happy (or safe). No one on his deathbed looks back on his life and thinks of all his various and sundry orgasms. He does think of the love built up in a decades-long relationship with his spouse and in relationships with his children and grandchildren—something the sexual revolution simply can't compete with.

And yet we have to be formed (and informed) to pursue such long-term, true fulfillment, especially in the face of the sexual revolution's seductions for immediate gratifications. To a certain extent the entire point of civilization is to help people navigate the temptations for immediate satisfaction that come at the expense of long-term happiness. Cultures cultivate. That's true of horticulture and agriculture just as much as it is of human culture. Good cultures cultivate natural capacities to their proper ends—in this case, our sexual capacities toward chaste marriage. But we've been living in a bad sexual culture for generations, and there's been little sustained focus on combatting its corrupting lies.

The root cause of virtually all our social problems is the collapse of marriage and family following the sexual revolution. Yet so little sustained, organized, strategic effort has gone into responding to this collapse. We must think it through: How can we reach ordinary people who don't know what the word "anthropology" means and help them reject the lies of the sexual revolution? How can we help people live the virtue of chastity? How can we help people get married and stay married? This is a daunting task. But if the real root causes of our suffering and loneliness and social malaise are the sexual practices that Americans have habituated for generations, then we need institutions that will combat the sexual revolution with the same sophistication with which conservatives have fought for judicial reform, regulatory reform, and economic reform.

And this is particularly urgent in our post-*Roe*, post-*Dobbs* world. I've spent the past two years running myself ragged trying to persuade people of the need to engage in our immediate battles (winning ballot initiatives, passing legislation, electing pro-life officials) without ignoring what should be our long-term priority. I use two statistics to illustrate that long-term goal, statistics about who gets an abortion and who gets aborted: 4 percent of babies conceived in marriage will be aborted, compared to 40 percent of children conceived outside marriage; and 13 percent of women who have abortions are married, while 87 percent are unmarried. Nonmarital sex is the main cause of abortion. Marriage is the best protector of unborn human life. As long as nonmarital sex is expected, large numbers of Americans will view abortion as necessary when contraception fails. As long as marriage rates are declining and the average age of marriage is delayed—though the human sex drive persists—abortion rates will remain high. Our primary task is not to persuade people of the humanity of the unborn—anyone who has ever seen an ultrasound knows all about that—but to change how people conduct their sexual lives. We have a pro-life movement, but could anyone seriously suggest that we have a pro-marriage or pro-chastity movement? New institutions and new initiatives must turn their attention to the real battlefield. But few people want to. Who wants to be viewed as a professional prude?

Nathanael Blake, that's who. He has written a radical book. Radical not in the political sense of extreme or incendiary but in the etymological sense of *radix*, or root. Nathanael goes to the root of the sexual revolution and is therefore willing and able to tell the entire truth, including certain politically incorrect and momentarily unpopular truths that many "influencers" shy away from. Indeed, we live in an age when many sexual revolutionaries themselves are trying to contain the effects of the revolution they helped set in motion. The very people who pushed for the legal redefinition of marriage now object to the legal redefinition of sex as gender identity; the very people who deny biological reality in the womb rush to defend the biological reality of sex. But should we be surprised that the logic of "my body, my choice" is now being applied to gender identity? The conclusion follows naturally from the premise. Can we insist on the biological reality of sex while denying the biological reality of the unborn child? "This far and no further" has its limits. We should make tactical partnerships in the battles that can be won today. But we shouldn't allow tactical alliances to cloud our vision of the truth. The revolution will eat its own, which is why we need someone like Nathanael who is willing to go all the way to the roots. He has written a profound book. May you profit by reading it and be inspired to become a counterrevolutionary.

PREFACE

This book began in Ryan Anderson's living room. My family was visiting his farm, and over dinner and a few drinks, an idea for a book was conceived and a promise made to write a foreword if it was carried through.

That is enough backstory; this volume is not about where books come from but where babies come from. It is a book about sex and how our culture has gone wrong regarding it.

This is a Christian book written to Christians first, but it is not a work of theology, nor is it a Bible study. It is certainly not a personal testimony. And though I have noted areas where believers and churches may act, I have kept the suggestions brief—for example, this is not a guide for how pastors can prepare young men for marriage.

This book is a social critique grounded in the Christian natural law tradition. The argument, in its simplest form, is that Christian sexual morality is not arbitrary but directs us toward our good and that of others. Departing from it harms self and society. Christian sexual mores have always been imperfectly observed, but they are now scorned and derided. The sexual revolution has won, but its promises were empty.

This raises a point of terminology. Throughout the book I refer to the sexual revolution, sexual liberation, and sexual liberalism. These are related, but I try to use them distinctly. In succinct terms, the sexual revolution was an event (or ongoing series of events) staged in the cause of sexual liberation to establish a regime of sexual liberalism.

This book was written because the time is ripe for a counterattack. There are sorties in this direction—and not all from Christian conservatives, as seen in the recent trio of books by Christine Emba, Louise Perry, and Mary Harrington criticizing the sexual revolution. These books are good, even excellent, in many ways, but they are also insufficient. They leave much untouched and struggle to articulate a basis for how we should live.

In writing this book I have relied heavily on sources such as *The Atlantic* and *The New York Times*—when criticizing the world of sexual liberalism, it may help to use sources it trusts and to represent it with those it identifies with. Of course, given the nature of this project, there were inevitably some less prestigious sources. As I told my wife one day when she asked why I was reading a tawdry *Daily Mail* article, "Because I'm writing a book about this".

Here is that book.

INTRODUCTION

After Sleeping with the Devil ...

The devil may offer the world, but he'd rather give people hell.

Rejecting Satan and all his empty promises is not just a rhetorical flourish in traditional baptismal vows. The blandishments of sin are deceptive. The immediate enjoyment rarely lives up to the hype, and in the long run we find ourselves, in the words of C. S. Lewis' wily devil Screwtape, ruled by an "ever increasing craving for an ever diminishing pleasure".[1]

This is why the sexual revolution's promises of freedom, authenticity, and happiness were empty indeed. The revolution's ethos of sexual liberalism triumphed in the United States, insofar as people are now free to hop in and out of beds, relationships, marriages, and even genders as they wish. The acolytes of sexual liberation won with a half century of abortion on demand as a constitutional right, and a ferocious commitment to abortion in many states even after the Supreme Court corrected that error. They won by framing religious objections to, and opt-outs from, this new order as bigotry. The sexual revolution has conquered institutions from academia to Wall Street, which observe its holidays, fly its flags, and repeat its creeds. But though the new regime of sexual liberalism reigns almost unchallenged, it has failed on its own terms. It has not made Americans happy, or even sexually satisfied, let alone fixed the problems that its advocates claimed it would solve.

It wasn't supposed to be this way. We were assured that ditching traditional norms, obligations, and loyalties would allow people to be their authentic selves, liberated from the unwanted bonds and baggage of the past. People would be free to be who and what they want to be, to love whom and how they want, to enjoy what they want when they want it. This freedom would make us happy and eliminate, or at least reduce, the causes of social strife and oppression.

Yet we need only look around to see the failures of sexual liberation, from the social to the personal. At the civilizational level, Americans, along with much of the world, are increasingly unmarried and childless, with birthrates well below the replacement rate. Apparently, having babies is one of those jobs that Americans won't do.

There is something wrong with a culture that cannot fulfill the imperative of pairing enough men and women to beget and raise its next generation—a civilizational ailment manifest in an aging, often lonely population.

Supporters of sexual liberation might reply that this chosen childlessness is a feature, not a bug. After all, the point of the sexual revolution was to give people more sexual and relational freedom, and so getting married and having children should be personal choices, not civilizational duties encouraged by social expectations and legal norms. So what if voluntary sterility has become normal and birthrates are declining throughout the world—especially in rich, developed nations?[2] Those who view the pressure to settle down and have kids as an imposition will shrug and say that's the price of freedom. And they might add that though an aging, shrinking population poses challenges to everything from the economy to immigration, it is at least better for the environment.

Childlessness has been rebranded as a certified-green "child-free" lifestyle. And if this means more Americans live alone as they age, well, they will have the satisfaction of environmental virtue, as seen in a sympathetic 2021 *New York Times* piece profiling those choosing not to have children because of worries about the climate.[3] And these Americans will enjoy lives lived on their own terms, without the inconveniences imposed by dependents. Consider, for example, a 2022 *New York Times* piece in which Frank Bruni extolled living alone—oh, the bliss of an uninterrupted morning coffee routine![4]

This ode to solitude would be more persuasive if sexual liberalism were delivering on its promises of happiness—if the declines in marriage, childbearing, and family stability correlated with increased personal happiness. The truth is the reverse. Married people are, on average, happier than their unmarried peers. The same is true for churchgoers compared to the nonobservant and nonbelieving. And though they may be denounced as miserable puritans or hateful bigots, conservatives are generally happier than liberals.[5] As Musa al-Gharbi wrote in a 2023 article for *American Affairs*, "The well-being gap between liberals and conservatives is one of the most robust patterns in social science research.... Conservatives report significantly higher levels of happiness, meaning, and satisfaction in their lives as compared to liberals. Meanwhile, liberals are much more likely to exhibit anxiety, depression, and other forms of psychic distress."[6]

This happiness gap is at least partly due to conservative resistance to the sexual revolution. As University of Virginia sociologist Brad Wilcox and his colleagues reported in 2021, liberals are happier when they get married, go to church, and have children. These habits of life used to be nonideological, but after the sexual revolution they are increasingly perceived as conservative. Thus, even those on the Left who personally live in these ways are reluctant to preach what they practice, and so Wilcox observed that "the very institutions that might improve liberals' happiness are increasingly viewed negatively by liberals."[7] Ideological commitment to the sexual revolution is impeding happiness by discouraging the pursuit of better ways of life.

Sexual liberalism produces unhappiness because it is inimical to relationships and practices that offer us profound meaning and joy in life. Deep relationships require deep commitments, but sexual liberation requires that every romantic relationship (and therefore also every parental relationship) be severable. Thus, the sexual revolution doubly cheats its disciples. Not only does its ethos of pursuing immediate pleasure injure the commitment that is needed for lasting and fulfilling relationships, but it also provides far less sexual gratification than promised.

Rising singleness is not the result of Americans having too much fun to want to settle down. Rather, Americans are increasingly alone, depressed, and anxious, with fewer children than they say they want, and these lonely people are not filling their lives with great sex. Indeed, we are in the midst of a sex recession, as *The Atlantic* labeled it in a much-discussed 2018 story by Kate Julian. This reduction in the amount of sex Americans are having is not the result of a return to chastity but of people, especially younger people, struggling to pair up in a hookup culture. After all, for most people, having a regular sex life requires a committed partner. As Julian blandly put it, "People who live with a romantic partner tend to have sex more than those who don't."[8]

Thus, as much as men may want it, the old *Playboy* dream of a tall blonde today, a petite brunette tomorrow, a curvy redhead next week, and a sexual world tour next month is unattainable for most. Marriage, or the "marriage lite" of a long-term relationship, is still the most reliable way for the average person to have sex; as these pairings decline, so does the amount of sex people are having.

This is why, contrary to the expectations of sexual liberalism, married churchgoers are having more, and more satisfying, sex. As Brad Wilcox and Wendy Wang noted in a 2024 *First Things* essay, "Churchgoing couples report more sex than non-religious couples. Specifically, about two-thirds of husbands and wives who attend religious services together have sex at least once a week, compared to less than half who do not regularly attend together or at all," and "couples who attend religious services together also report the greatest sexual satisfaction."[9] This is probability, not certainty—getting married and going to church is not a sure ticket to sexual paradise—but it is still a marked contrast to the likes of Julian's "sex recession" reporting, which depicted a generation that is delaying marriage and children to an unprecedented degree without enjoying the sexual liberation it was given in exchange. As she observed, "I was amazed by how many 20-somethings were deeply unhappy with the sex-and-dating landscape; over and over, people asked me whether things had always been this hard."[10] And it is not just that forming and maintaining stable relationships is difficult but that the sex is often terrible.

If there was one thing the sexual revolution was supposed to deliver, it was lots of great sex. Yet it is failing to do so, in part because the casual sexual encounters it encourages are not conducive to satisfying sex. Hookups are a bad sexual teacher. They provide little opportunity or incentive to become a good lover, in large part because strangers don't know how to please each other and aren't going to stick around long enough to learn. And pornography is training people, especially young men, to be bad in bed. As Julian reported, "In my interviews with young women, I heard too many iterations to count of 'he did something I didn't like that I later learned is a staple in porn.'"[11] These unwelcome sexual habits range from uncomfortable to humiliating to outright violent. That such behaviors are becoming normal should be horrifying, but it is to be expected when almost every teenage boy is given a smartphone that provides immediate access to an endless supply of porn videos that shape his sexuality.

Sexual liberation cannot offer the rewards of virtue, and it is increasingly stingy with the pleasures of vice. Thus, in recent years, a noticeable unease about the sexual revolution has emerged even in the high, holy places of sexual liberalism, such as *The Atlantic* and *The New York Times*. For example, a piece in the latter by Nona Willis Aronowitz complained that even though "women's right to sexual satisfaction is taken as much more of a given ... extracting what we actually want from a mess of cultural and political influences can still sometimes feel like an impossible challenge."[12] Michelle Goldberg, a columnist at the same paper, has likewise wondered how sexual liberation has produced so much misery and oppression. She admitted that "as sex positivity went mainstream and fused with a culture shaped by pornography ... [it] became a cause of some of the same suffering it was meant to remedy."[13] Elsewhere, she wrote that our "dating culture appears to be an emotional meat grinder whose miseries and degradations can't be solved by ever-more elaborate rituals of consent".[14]

Liberal feminists writing in flagship liberal publications are acknowledging that the sexual revolution has failed to provide good sex and that it regularly makes men and (especially) women unhappy. And all the faithful Christians said "Amen!"—and maybe also "I told you so." Christians predicted these evils and saw that each successive victory of the sexual revolution would lead to more radical demands. Recognition of the now-undeniable harms of the sexual revolution should lead to further questions, such as whether this wretched sexual and relational landscape explains why a multitude of young women are suddenly fleeing being female and embracing transgender or non-binary identities. Or these writers (and the many others who think as they do) might wonder whether this culture of terrible sex and unhappy relationships is really worth the hundreds of thousands of abortions it demands each year.

But answering these questions might require curtailing, or even condemning, the sexual revolution, which few are willing to do. Rather than admit they have been badly wrong, they insist that just a little more liberation will do the trick. Goldberg concluded that women just need to be more assertive, both in bed and in the dating market, to realize their desires. In her view, sex should be treated as a negotiation between self-interested actors who must reach a mutually satisfactory settlement. Sex, in this view, is undertaken between partners, not necessarily of any more significance to each other, and possibly of less, than partners in any business transaction. Women, Goldberg argued, are "*too* willing to act in what they believe to be their partners' best interests rather than their own". They "are still embarrassed by their own desires, particularly when they are emotional, rather than physical". She suggested that women just need to get better at the art of the relational and sexual deal—to be more aware of what they want and more assertive in trying to get it from their partners.[15] Willis Aronowitz was even more committed to staying the course, declaring that "reaching for more sexual freedom, not less—the freedom to have whatever kind of sex we want ... is still the only way we can hope to solve the problems of our current sexual landscape."[16] If hookups and kink are not satisfying, the solution must be more and kinkier hookups.

This doubling down is the mindset of an addict chasing the dragon of a better high, even as lives crumble, relationships collapse, and flesh decays. It is how, as Screwtape put it, the devil seeks to "get the man's soul and to give him nothing in return."[17] In the end there is no longer even much pleasure, just desperate and despairing appetite—a wretched Gollum clutching the Ring in the miserable darkness, year after year.

A Revolution in More Than Morals

Of course, lust and obstinance in its service are as old as mankind. History, including that of self-consciously Christian cultures and peoples, is filled with examples of these sins—just consider the debauchery of regency England. Even the history of the Church provides many examples of sexual sins being indulged and tolerated no matter how much they conflicted with Christian teaching. What sets the modern sexual revolution apart is that it has gone beyond disobedience or even defiance of Christian sexual ethics to supplant them at the civilizational level. It has been a genuine revolution, abolishing the old moral order and replacing it, thereby altering everything from religion to family life to our view of what it means to be human.

Like many revolutions, the sexual revolution was sparked by changing material conditions as well as changing ideas; it triumphed because it was an idea whose technological time had come. The material prosperity and technological developments of the twentieth century promised freedom from the consequences of sexual indulgence. The most relevant of these innovations were advances in preventing pregnancy and in avoiding or treating sexually transmitted diseases—the Pill and penicillin, as well as more reliable and available condoms. When unwanted pregnancies resulted nevertheless, abortion had also become safer—at least for the mother.

And as technology seemed to reduce the risks of casual sex, the general prosperity and technological progress of society made the sexual revolution appear economically feasible. Life changed to make sexual liberation seem not only attractive but also realistic and affordable in ways that it was not during a poorer, more agricultural era in which syphilis was untreatable and contraception was unreliable or nonexistent. For most of human history, regulating sexuality was a social imperative because it was a survival imperative. All those injunctions about caring for widows and orphans are in the Bible for a reason. The asymmetrical burdens of human reproduction made restricting sex to committed relationships a social norm that was in the best interests of a community's women and children.

That is why, even as the industrial revolution remodeled much of family life and relations between the sexes and improved the general standard of living, the sexual revolution did not succeed until after the Pill. Controlled (in)fertility, even more than general technological innovation and increased wealth, was the advance necessary to make the sexual revolution appear realistic and victimless and to encourage people to view sexual liberation as a genuine unshackling. Just as technology was liberating people from the brutal drudgery of preindustrial and early-industrial work and housekeeping, so, too, would it enable a movement toward more natural, honest, and enjoyable relations between men and women.

Stefan Zweig's memoir *The World of Yesterday* offers an early, albeit tragic, example of how many saw the old norms as oppressive, rather than protective. Zweig contrasted life in turn-of-the-century Vienna with the modern world he saw coming into being (and sadly despaired of seeing, committing suicide with his wife during World War II). He, and those of similar mind, viewed a more relaxed attitude toward sex as a release from repression and the inevitably unequal sexual standards and shaming it produced.

Some of his hopes are ludicrous in hindsight, such as his belief that sexual liberation was the key to ending what he saw as the nasty business of pornography.[18] Nonetheless, he showed why the sexual revolution had appeal beyond the simple promise of more self-indulgence. Many of his critiques of middle-class sexual mores were insightful. For example, he observed that, unlike more religious ages, which enforced sexual morals with genuine zeal, the world of his youth was "a tolerant epoch that long ago stopped believing in the Devil and hardly believed in God anymore"[19] and therefore resorted to hypocrisy on a grand and exploitative scale when it came to male sexual desire. He saw that much of this arose from a refusal (which is shared by too many middle-class Christians today) to reckon with the implications of delaying marriage long past the age of sexual maturity. Not all that pent-up sexual energy would quietly wait year after year until a respectable marriage was arranged, and the outlets it found in the meantime were often dangerous and exploitative.

The sexual landscape he grew up in thus seemed ridiculous and often cruel to Zweig. For example, he recalled "the army of thousands upon thousands of prostitutes whose bodies and humiliated souls were recruited to defend an ancient and long-since-eroded concept of morality against free, natural forms of love".[20] This "free, natural" love is what he set against the supposedly repressive and unnatural, and therefore hypocritical and unhealthy, sexual mores of middle-class nineteenth- and early twentieth-century respectability. Without the artificial constraints and customs society had established around eros, surely everything would be better as young men and women would pair off to satisfy their natural desires, both sexual and relational.

Everything is not better. The sexual revolution has produced a multitude of hypocrisies and cruelties of its own, and it has not ameliorated the ills of the old order nearly as well as its proponents hoped. The old norms were imperfect, and imperfectly practiced, but they existed to try to restrain the cruelty, selfishness, and shortsightedness of human nature—evils that have not been abolished by new technologies or more liberated norms. The old order needed reformation, not abolition.

Removing constraints is not enough to make people good or happy, especially with something as important and primal as sex, with all its relational and social implications. For instance, easy divorce was supposed to rectify the problem of miserable marriage. But there are still many miserable marriages, and no-fault divorce and cohabitation have added new cruelties, especially against children. The harms inflicted on children are well-known and have been for decades—per one 2005 study, "Young children who live in households with one or more unrelated adults are nearly 50 times as likely to die from an inflicted injury, usually being shaken or struck, as children living with two biologic parents."[21] Yet there is no serious movement to reimpose limits on divorce, let alone on the serial cohabitation that avoids divorce by not marrying—and that also puts children at great risk by cycling a string of men who are not related to them through their homes. Rather, Americans have decided that the suffering of the children is worth the freedom it gives the adults.

Nor have relaxed attitudes toward casual sex made relationships better or increased sexual pleasure. Even bastions of sexual liberalism such as *The New York Times* are struggling to pretend that the current dating and sexual landscape is healthy or even very pleasurable. Hope after hope held by sexual liberals has faded.

Nonetheless, the champions of the sexual revolution were correct that it was something new. Technological change, along with the inevitability of a revolution being shaped by the regime it revolts against, ensured that the sexual revolution was not just a return to pre-Christian pagan sexual norms, which were overwhelmingly patriarchal and hierarchical. Indeed, the sexual culture of the Roman Empire had elements that are repulsive to both Christians and post-Christian sexual liberals. In the Roman world, sexual rules were unapologetically unequal. There was no hypocrisy in this inequality; the Romans saw it as right and natural that sexual standards varied according to a person's status and role in society—of course there were different rules for men and women, and for slaves and free.

The men at the top of society were allowed to indulge in ways forbidden to their wives or to those lower in the social hierarchy. Male citizens had the sexual use of their slaves as well as prostitutes. Consent was essentially irrelevant in such cases, and the sexual abuse of low-status children was an accepted part of life. Even the famous Roman toleration of homosexuality, which might initially appeal to current sensibilities, was very different from today's ethos. For the Romans, the crucial concern was with playing the man's role; they saw it as manly to penetrate others, but effeminate, and therefore shameful, to be penetrated.

Part of the Christian overthrow of pagan religion was a revolution against pagan sexual culture. Christians upended the pagan world with a new set of sexual rules—as seen in the Christian insistence on chastity for men as well as women and in the worth and dignity Christians saw in those abused and discarded by pagan sexuality—that were grounded in a new vision of God, the cosmos, and man's relationship to them. As Kyle Harper observed in *First Things*, for the Apostle Paul, "sexual morality was part of the proclamation of a half-hidden story of God's restoration of the created cosmos." Indeed, "for the early Christians, sexual morality was woven inseparably into their whole effort to live rightly in the world. Sex, by its essence, is entangled in the most fundamental questions about the nature of the self and its relation to God."[22]

The Christian revolutionaries saw spiritual significance in sex far beyond what the pagan world ever saw. For Christians, the one-flesh union of sex in marriage is both a symbol of the union of Christ and the Church and the way in which human beings serve as cocreators with God in the begetting of new people who can know God and love Him forever. Likewise, a believer's identification with Christ gives a horror to sexual sin—it is not only a betrayal, but also a defilement, of Jesus.

The Christian view of sex displaced the pagan understanding not just because of this new spiritual vision but also because it comforted and protected those who were abused and neglected by the pagan order. Christianity shielded slaves and children from sexual exploitation. Christians rescued unwanted infants who were left to die on trash heaps. Christians insisted that husbands, as well as wives, be sexually faithful. Even imperfectly understood and followed, as all Christian teaching is, this new sexual morality was better than that of the pagan world, and it became the standard in the Western world until recent decades. It was overthrown, rather than just ignored or disobeyed, when perennial sexual temptations were made safer and more affordable through technological advances. And in the process, the modern sexual revolution, like the revolution the early Christians waged against pagan sexuality, radically changed human self-understanding.

This was not immediately clear; most people did not initially experience the sexual revolution in such dramatic terms. For many it began as a further falling away from the sexual morality preached by a Christianity they only half believed in, rather than a complete replacement for it. People preferred fun to the duties and limits of the old moral code and thought they could get that fun without doing much harm. A few ideologues dreamed of bringing down the entire system, but most people had no such grandiose schemes and presumed that the old moral, social, and spiritual order would largely continue, just with a bit more leeway where they wanted it.

But this time, aided by technology, theory followed practice, and a new sexual morality usurped the old Christian one. This new order has gone much further than promised. "Safe, legal, and rare" has morphed into enthusiastic support for unrestricted abortion and government proclamations praising abortionists. Tolerance for same-sex unions has been replaced by mandatory celebrations of same-sex relationships. Going along with Bruce when he decided to be Caitlyn has evolved into affirming "transgender toddlers" and sterilizing children.

This moral revolt could not remain confined to sexual matters. Christian sexual ethics were based on a Christian understanding of the human person. Even though both the religious belief and the ethics were always imperfectly realized, they were still intertwined. Discarding the sexual teachings of Christianity therefore led to rejecting the Christian anthropology and theology they were based on.

And so the modern sexual revolution has remade how we view ourselves.

In this new worldview, persons are not defined and fulfilled by obedience to God and conformity to the created order (including the moral order) but are instead self-creating, establishing their own meaning and identity. Desire—especially sexual desire, which is both intense and interpersonal—takes precedence in this attempt at autonomous self-definition. Indeed, sexual desire is perceived as perhaps the most authentic and essential expression of the self. This is why, for instance, Christians proclaiming their faith's traditional teaching on same-sex relationships are accused of denying the humanity, or even the existence, of those with same-sex attractions. For a Christian, controlling sexual desire to conform sexual behavior to God's will is an essential part of being fully human by living out one's faith. For the acolytes of the sexual revolution, demanding sexual self-restraint is a cruel, capricious suppression of the authentic self.

The Hope in Christian Resistance

Faithful Christians are therefore besieged spiritually, culturally, and legally by the triumph of sexual liberation. Previous generations of Christians were criticized for being too strict in upholding the rules of sexual conduct. Now Christians are also attacked as rule breakers in violation of the new moral code of sexual liberalism. We are denounced as hateful bigots, not just as killjoy scolds. Instead of being told to lighten up, we are ordered to shut up.

This pressure, along with the subtler process of cultural osmosis (and, too often, personal temptation), has induced many Christians to accept parts of the sexual revolution.

Even believers who hold true to traditional teachings often seem apologetic about it. The sexual revolution has carried all before it, and many Christians have internalized its victory even while nominally opposing it. For example, in his transition from conservative Christian litigator to *New York Times* columnist, David French endorsed same-sex marriage and argued for a parental right to chemically castrate boys experiencing gender dysphoria. Echoing many an old-school Catholic Democrat on abortion, French claimed to be personally opposed to the sexual revolution but declared that pluralism demanded that Christians not impose their values on society.

His argument, and many others like it, presumed an official state indifference to what is good—a government that is purely procedural, with no higher duty to encourage the good and punish evil. In practice, this means surrendering to the dominance of the sexual revolution in our culture and begging only to preserve small private spheres of Christian community. This capitulation is not only unsustainable—the sexual revolutionaries are eager to quash the rights of Christians and other nonconformists—but also an abrogation of our duty to love our neighbors as ourselves.

Christians should, of course, vigorously defend their legal rights to dissent from the reigning orthodoxies of the sexual revolution. The Apostle Paul asserted his right to appeal to the emperor, and we should assert our rights as well—onward Christian litigators! But it is wrong (and likely futile) to seek nothing more in policy than a right to be left alone in our families, churches, and Christian communities and institutions. We must reject a nihilistic pluralism that pretends that government cannot and should not distinguish between good and evil, God and Satan, truth and lies. The state cannot really be neutral between these things.

For Christians to claim that it can and should be so is to cede power and authority to those who hate the gospel.

Furthermore, the truths of Christian sexual teaching are not idiosyncratic religious rituals, nor are they merely exercises in spiritual discipline like fasting is. Rather, they are rooted in the realities of human nature, and they direct us toward our good and the good of others. Though Christianity is not devoted to well-being in this world, its moral and social teaching still support genuine human flourishing. God is the greatest good, but there are many other goods that can be realized or ruined in this life by following—or defying—the moral law that God has both revealed in Scripture and inscribed on our nature. Social justice requires pursuing righteousness, including sexual righteousness. This is why abandoning Christian sexual norms (imperfectly followed as they always were) has been disastrous for our culture and why our unprecedented prosperity and technological prowess are not saving our culture from the consequences, let alone providing happiness.

The hopes of the sexual revolution have been disappointed. And though its cruelty is not always as overt as that of pagan antiquity, it is still real. This misery is why there has recently been a spate of books critiquing the sexual revolution written by women who are not orthodox Christians. The leading examples are Christine Emba's *Rethinking Sex: A Provocation*, Louise Perry's *The Case Against the Sexual Revolution*, and Mary Harrington's *Feminism Against Progress*. There is much to applaud in these books, and they have reached readers who would never consider reading, say, Catholic writer Mary Eberstadt's book *Adam and Eve after the Pill, Revisited*. That there is secular debate over the sexual revolution (literally, in some cases, as seen by a 2023 clash sponsored by *The Free Press* in which Perry took part) is heartening.[23]

But these authors are not radical enough. They recognize that our sexual culture is broken and that there must be a better way of life than loneliness and porn punctuated by sexually disappointing and emotionally unfulfilling hookups. Unfortunately, their solutions are ungrounded, and they tend to neglect the living example of Christian marriage and family life.

Thus, as the victims of the sexual revolution pile up, the time seems ripe for a vigorous counterattack focused on the harms of sexual liberation and the benefits of Christian sexual ethics. We do not, for instance, have to live in a culture that views unrestricted abortion as essential and that has no answer when a podcast host asks what a woman is. The follies and failures of the sexual revolution provide an opening to evangelize those who have been injured and disillusioned by it.

Admissions of the sexual revolution's failures are often grudging, partial, and even inadvertent. Those who accept the framework of sexual liberation may apprehend that something is wrong, but they cannot offer a solution from within their own moral and philosophical tradition—except, that is, for yet more fervid indulgence and more vigorous self-assertion. A further obstacle to overcoming the sexual revolution is that it implicates much more than just sex; everything from our economy to our education system has been shaped by the demands of sexual liberation. Thus, critics of the sexual revolution must reckon not only with how it was enabled by material changes but also with how it has further molded material conditions around itself. Presenting a plausible alternative to sexual liberalism will require not only moral and spiritual persuasion but also material and political, as well as cultural, changes.

Despite these difficulties, the empty promises of the sexual revolution may be preparing the cultural soil for gospel truths about sex. Faithful Christians retain the intellectual, cultural, and spiritual resources not only to critique sexual liberalism but also to envision and model a superior alternative. Chastity, faithful marriage, and the successful raising of children are challenging tasks, but they offer joys and fulfillment that the regime of sexual liberalism is increasingly wanting. Indeed, many people who are ideologically committed to the sexual revolution still find their greatest happiness in the aspects of their lives that are furthest removed from sexual liberation.

The overwhelming triumph of the sexual revolution is creating the conditions in which Christian sexual morality will once again appear protective and merciful, rather than as a killjoy. Christian moral teaching may again be received as a liberation from both external exploitation and internal slavery to sin. In a sexual world (mis)ruled by the tyranny of desire, the Christian view of sex as a self-giving act of love looks pretty good, and the restraints around it appear as necessary protections for that love to flourish. Thus, Christians may see signs of hope and renewal even amid decline, as the failures of the world fertilize the fields of future evangelism.

From Liberation to Loneliness

The Party Is Ending

Like most revolutions, the sexual revolution has a propaganda arm. For decades, the beautiful and cool people told us by word and deed, on screen and through song, that sexual liberation is the key to the good, or at least fun, life. The entertainment industry's glamour has been deployed to sell the idea that everyone else, or at least everyone not yet old and boring enough to have settled down, is having great sex in a string of hookups and uncommitted relationships. If you aren't living this life, or if you aren't enjoying it, then there is something wrong with you.

But this story, and the glamour that sustains it, is wearing thin. There is an apparently endless series of former sex symbols sharing how they were abused, exploited, and sexually unfulfilled. Sometimes it is no surprise, as with Brooke Shields.[1] Sometimes it is unexpected—who knew that Paris Hilton spent her twenties treating sex as a chore and avoiding it when possible?[2] The people selling the party were often not enjoying it.

Of course, the publicity machine feeds on it all, from the ascent to fame to the crash, followed (for the lucky) by rehab and recovery. Even the eventual tell-all (or at least tell-some) documentary or ghostwritten memoir is fuel for the machine, along with every date and every breakup, every marriage and every divorce. Yet for all this attention, there is still a code of silence. Almost no one still in the game wants to reveal how dirty it is or to admit that the smiles are fake. And so abuse and unhappiness are covered up, often by victims who internalized the lesson that they were the problem for not enjoying what was done to them or not knowing how to protect themselves better.

Showbiz has always been rife with sexual abuse and exploitation, with some of the biggest stars among the predators and the victims. From Charlie Chaplin's lechery to the exploitation of Marilyn Monroe to Harvey Weinstein and all the other abusers revealed by the #MeToo movement, there has been a lot of evil beneath the glitter of Tinseltown. As for the denizens of the music industry, they have been, if anything, even worse—it is a meme among music fans that everything they love was made by terrible people.[3]

And just outside the spotlight are the discards: the women whose bodies kept the party going without ever getting their big break or even much of a chance at it. As the *Daily Mail* reported in 2022, "Teenage girls as young as 16 were trafficked, drugged, beaten, groomed for prostitution, and raped at 'mini mansions' owned by Hugh Hefner's friends and frequented by celebrities, a former president and state governor, Playboy insiders claim."[4] These girls were strung along with promises of opportunities they were never going to be given a shot at—at least, until they were hooked on drugs and could be controlled through them. This evil, along with those committed by the likes of Epstein and Weinstein, are just some of the high-profile examples of a culture of abuse. Behind the glittering curtains of high-end sexual liberation are a lot of wealthy and powerful men exploiting women, and at this point we all know it, even if we do not know the particulars.

The narrative of sexual liberation is also collapsing far away from the private playgrounds of the high and mighty. Despite sexual liberalism's cultural dominance, Americans are somehow having less (and often worse) sex. Men and women are finding it harder to form stable relationships with each other, or to beget, bear, and raise the children they want. Adult Americans are more likely to live alone than ever before, and a great many are lonely as a result. In short, sexual liberation has not delivered the general sexual delight it promised, and it has harmed our relationships and families, thereby creating an epidemic of loneliness.

The sexual and relational landscape leaves many people feeling far more victimized and exploited than liberated. In truth, many people are both victims and victimizers. As the ethos of sexual liberalism permeated the culture, it became simply the way things are. Thus, the narrative of the sexual revolution has been internalized to the point of fealty—people will stick with it even when it hurts. A lot of ordinary people, as well as celebrities, have tried to ignore their misgivings about sexual liberalism or repress and deny the hurt it has caused them, or the guilt they feel about what they have done, in order to fit in. And so, as the ethos of sexual liberalism became the norm, it was then reamplified even by those whom it wounded.

For example, *Washington Post* writer Christine Emba's 2022 book *Rethinking Sex* features many interviews with young men and (especially) women who discovered that casual sex was less pleasurable, and more painful (physically and emotionally), than promised. Yet they also had little hope of finding a spouse and settling down. They were stuck with neither enjoying happily-ever-after nor having lots of fun in the here and now. And yet the culture established by the sexual revolution is so pervasive that thinking about and longing for something outside it felt radical and unrealistic to them—love and commitment was a fairy-tale dream, not an achievable reality. Many of Emba's subjects seemed to doubt whether another way of life was possible; many wondered whether they were the problem, even as they realized that something was very wrong. As Emba put it in the introduction to her book:

> Things don't have to be criminal to be profoundly bad. And the fact that so many of the women around me relate so deeply to stories of harrowing dates and lackluster encounters shows that a lot of us are having a lot of *bad* sex. Unwanted, depressing, even traumatic; if this is ordinary, something is deeply wrong. The goal of this book is to reassure you that *you're not crazy*. That the thing you sense is wrong *is* wrong. That there is something unmistakably off in the way we have been going about sex and dating.[5]

This wretchedness is happening when conditions should be optimal for sexual liberalism. Fears of sexually transmitted disease have receded as HIV/AIDS is no longer a death sentence. Condoms are readily available, as are a variety of contraceptives that reduce the odds of unexpected pregnancy. And though the overturning of *Roe v. Wade* has allowed abortion restrictions in parts of the country, the urban liberal women Emba speaks to would still have no difficulty procuring an abortion. Socially, promiscuity is more acceptable than ever, especially in the circles that Emba and her subjects inhabit, where chastity is more stigmatized than fornication. If sexual liberalism can't make it here, it can't make it anywhere.

If sexual liberalism is not working for the wealthy and beautiful in showbiz, or for intelligent and ambitious young men and women in our cities, then it just isn't working. But the social pressure to soldier on is immense. When it comes to the pain inflicted by the sexual revolution, a lot of people keep a stiff upper lip as well as anyone in the days of the British Empire. They may find "lie back and think of England" ridiculous, but many have mastered lying back and thinking of something else because of how awkward and tedious it would be to have to say no, or how embarrassing it would be to admit (even to oneself) to being less than fully sex positive.

This points to a difficulty in addressing the problems of our sexual and relational culture, which is that many people lack the language to describe these problems adequately and the conceptual framework through which to propose alternatives. This intellectual incapacity is exemplified in the inability to evaluate sex in terms other than consent and pleasure, which by themselves are an inadequate moral vocabulary by which to judge sex and relationships. Something may be pleasurable yet bad for us, and though consent now provides almost the only moral standard for sex, it is insufficient to prevent exploitative and degrading sexual relations.

The idea that people will consent to only that which they desire and is good for them has proven farcical. Sex implicates much more than momentary pleasure or pain, and therefore it can be wrong and harmful despite being consensual and even enjoyable. But because the sexual revolution repressed all other standards by which to judge sexual behavior, consent remains the lodestar of discussions of sexual ethics, which is why there are constant efforts to shoehorn bad—but consensual—encounters into the consent paradigm or to condemn an exploitative sexual culture as "rape culture".

This inadequate perspective results from denying that sex has intrinsic meaning and instead assigning it only subjective value. From the viewpoint of sexual liberation, sex is seen as important only insofar as we have strong sexual desires or define ourselves by our sexuality; the meaning of sex is found in personal pleasure and authenticity. In this account the relational aspect of sex is optional, whereas the enjoyment and identity are essential. The physical "what" of sex thereby takes precedence over the personal "who".

Thus, though a woman's no is law, dividing fun from felony, there is an implicit pressure to give in to male sexual demands, almost out of a sense that no is somehow impolite or unkind. As Katherine Kersten put it in a 2019 essay, "Many women now believe they are *supposed* to—expected to—have casual sex with men who don't respect or care for them."[6] After all, if sex in itself is no big deal, why not dole it out to someone who really wants it? If it means nothing, it means nothing.

But, of course, sex does mean something. And so our sexual culture is less fulfilling and more hurtful, even when consent is nominally obtained, than the ethos of sexual liberalism promises. And it is not as easy as the glamour machine portrays it to be to transition from a life of hookups and "friends with benefits" to tying the knot with "the One". If the romantic comedy is dying, maybe it is because the entire premise, not just the Hollywood flourishes, feels unrealistic. We all know that the happily-ever-after rarely lasts in real-life Hollywood, and it seems increasingly unattainable to many outside showbiz as well.

It is also clear that although sex seems to be everywhere, in all sorts of novel varieties, Americans are having less of it than they used to. The 2022 data from the General Social Survey (GSS) showed that only around a third of Americans report having sex at least once a week, down from nearly half in 1989, when the survey began asking about sex.[7] Even under the most generous reading of the latest results,

Americans' sex lives are still much less active than they used to be, and they do not seem likely to recover anytime soon.

Sexual liberalism has been self-defeating because it discourages the long-term relationships that are the most reliable way to have sex, and satisfying sex in particular. It thereby fails on its own terms. For men, the promises of the sexually liberated life are plausible only for those who can attract a steady supply of women (and "supply" is the right word, as the point is sexual service, not relationship). But few men have the status or charisma to secure new sexual partners on demand. Thus, many men end up splitting the difference between commitment and playing the field, meandering through a string of hookups and short-to-medium-term relationships. But for most men, this pattern of intermittent sexual encounters results in extended sexual droughts that are likely to lengthen with age. The decline of marriage is a large part of why there has been a decline in sex. In 1980, 63 percent of American twenty-five-year-olds were married; in 2021, it was 22 percent.[8] Yes, some of those unmarried young men and women are in relationships or hooking up regularly, but on average, fewer marriages mean less sex. It takes a lot of hookups for an unattached man to have as much sex as the average married man of the same age. The sexual marketplace is ruthless, and it leaves more than a few men in want of a partner.

Unsatisfied

A result—and cause—of the decline in stable relationships is that sex itself is increasingly unreal. While mainstream entertainment tells Americans to hop into bed quickly with as many people as possible, its sleazier associates in the "adult entertainment" industry tell us what to do there. The ubiquity and acceptance of pornography in our culture demonstrate how the sexual revolution has triumphed—and failed.

Despite some hopes to the contrary, porn has always been included in the sexual revolution. Condemning porn depends on moral judgments about human sexuality that the sexual revolution has rejected. As long as porn is produced with consent and appropriate labor standards (perhaps including condoms as a mandatory part of workplace safety—yes, this has been legislated in some jurisdictions), the regime of sexual liberalism has no objections, and technology has now made it immediately available to anyone with a smartphone. Porn consumption is now seen as normal and inevitable.

Normalizing porn has been bad not only for relationships but also for sex. The porn industry sells fantasies and habits that keep many men, and therefore many women, from establishing fulfilling relationships and having satisfying sex. Porn explains the apparent paradox of declining sex during an age of unprecedented sexual permissiveness. For men in particular, porn offers a substitute for sex that may make pursuing and maintaining real romantic relationships seem both less urgent and more difficult.

Not only does the ready availability of porn make some men less likely to pursue real relationships with women, but it can also deform sex within the relationships that porn users do have. As the *Atlantic* article on the "sex recession" put it, "Women told me that learning about sex from porn seemed to have given some men dismaying sexual habits."[9] The piece cited Debby Herbenick, a sex researcher at Indiana University, who found herself explaining to her male students that the weird, degrading, or violent sexual habits porn has taught them are unlikely to go down well with real-world women. This obvious point is somehow not clear to some of the young men whose sexuality has been directed by porn since puberty.

A 2021 piece by Elizabeth Bruenig, also in *The Atlantic*, suggested that pornified sex is becoming normal among many young men and grudgingly accepted by young women. Ubiquitous porn is deforming sexuality, and it keeps upping the ante. Bruenig's interview subjects included one teenage girl who related that for many young men, "it's taken on a weird flavor, maybe, where it's like—who can have the most weird, violent sex?"[10] But weird, violent sex is harmful, even if pornography is grooming men to think it is normal.

Worse, both users and producers of pornography are incentivized to escalate. Though the internet offers an endless selection of "adult content" followed by immediate gratification, it is still constrained by the limits of the medium—it appeals to only some of the senses that are stimulated during actual intercourse. These limitations push porn to go to extremes in what it can convey, which in turn habituates regular users to these extremes and pushes them to seek still more.

And so the sexual revolution is strangling itself—literally. A 2024 *New York Times* piece by Peggy Orenstein reported that "twenty years ago, sexual asphyxiation appears to have been unusual among any demographic, let alone young people who were new to sex and iffy at communication. That's changed radically in a short time." Orenstein cited a large survey of college students that found that "nearly two-thirds of women ... said a partner had choked them during sex (one-third in their most recent encounter)"[11]— which is to say that most young women who are hooking up will be sexually strangled at some point.

Orenstein blamed online porn, in which choking women is now a "staple" that young men are emulating, sometimes encouraged by various internet guides purporting to explain how to do so safely. But as she bluntly put it, "There is no safe way to strangle someone." Nonetheless, she rushed to assure readers that "I'm not here to kink-shame (or anything-shame)."[12] She thereby showed how sexual liberalism is incapable of restraining itself. The truth is that people should be ashamed of doing bad things, such as seeking sexual pleasure by strangling women. For nearly all of human history, stigma and shame were effective means of regulating sexual behavior. They were, as with all things human, flawed, but they were rightly regarded as essential to restraining and guiding sexual behavior.

The sexual revolution's abolition of sexual shame has hamstrung our culture's ability to address problems such as the sudden proliferation of sexual strangulation. And so Orenstein had to deploy the jargon of health and safety, noting that "restricting blood flow to the brain, even briefly, can cause permanent injury, including stroke and cognitive impairment." She cited research studies in which MRI scans found that the brains of women who had been "repeatedly choked" were worse off than those of their nonstrangled peers. She also noted that women who have been sexually strangled were more likely to suffer from a litany of mental health problems.[13] But we should not need brain scans and mental health surveys to condemn men who choke women for sexual sport.

Such miserable consummations of sexual liberation are turning many people off sex entirely. Men's porn habits are making them less desirable to women and less capable of sustaining a good relationship. Some men become so enthralled with porn that they want it more than they want actual women. And even many of those who still pursue real-world relationships are bringing their porn habits with them. Given a choice between unsatisfying, perhaps brutal sex and no sex, many women will choose the latter, as they do not want to have sex in these painful and humiliating ways. And so omnipresent porn and kink, justified under the banner of sex positivity, are contributing to the sex recession. The result is that men and women are being driven apart.

This singleness suits the porn industry. Many—likely most—men will fill the gaps between intermittent hookups and relationships with porn, which in turn cultivates sexual habits that damage relationships, ensuring that the cycle continues.

But the porn industry also provides for lonely men who crave relationships as well as sexual stimulus, at least if they are willing to play pretend while handing over their money. Porn is no longer a one-way medium—customers can (usually for a price) send messages, make requests, and even have mutual webcam sessions with models.

But it's not always a model on the other end; flirting via direct message sells explicit photos and videos, but the person typing does not have to be the person pictured. Per a 2022 *New York Times* report, "When the product is intimacy—or at least a persuasive facsimile—scale can turn the seemingly simple exchange of dollars for sexts into a Rube Goldbergian transaction across layers of third-party intermediaries." As one of the e-pimp businesses profiled in the piece put it, "Our best customers come to us not so much to buy content as they come to us to just feel a connection."[14] And so men pretend to believe personal messages from a guy in Manilla who is pretending to be an Eastern European model who pretends to enjoy performing various sexual acts in front of a webcam for fans she pretends to like and be aroused by.

The illusion of intimacy is now an essential part of the porn industry's evolving business model. For instance, a 2020 story in *1843* magazine (an *Economist* spin-off) concluded,

> This illusion of proximity is critical to OnlyFans' appeal. "Hardcore porn is easy to come by, but a relationship with a girl is hard to get," explains Andrew, a 42-year-old engineer from Sheffield. "But with OnlyFans you get it." He's been following Brooks since September 2018 and estimates he spends around £300 a month on her page. He believes that Brooks does care for him. "If I go quiet and don't take part in things for a few days, she notices and will start messaging me and asking me how I am." I ask Andrew if it feels like he and Brooks are in a relationship. He pauses. "It's difficult to define," he says finally. "There are times when it feels like we almost are a couple."[15]

Meanwhile, this model was married and offering the fantasy of being almost in a relationship to as many men as possible. Of course she messages her customers if they go quiet, because she wants them to keep sending her money. As the reporter puts it, the model "knows she is in the business of digital intimacy. Through a constant stream of content and messages she indulges the fantasy that her customers could go out with a woman just like her. When asked, she sounds a lot like one of the men paying her to play pretend, concluding that, 'Porn is all over the internet. This isn't the same. My fans aren't paying for porn. They're paying to have a personal experience, one-on-one, with a girl.' "[16]

In this case, the messages sustaining the illusion for her clients may at least have actually been written by her, rather than a random guy in the Philippines with good English skills who has been hired by an e-pimp in Miami who is taking a cut from a model in Columbia or Russia. Or perhaps not. After all, for a successful model, it will become impossible to respond to all her customers herself.

What is clear is that the old line about reading *Playboy* for the articles has been updated to buying porn for the fake intimacy, and some men really mean it. This is a long way from the awesome sexual escapades that sexual liberation promised. The reality is that the sexual revolution has left a substantial proportion of men lonely and sexually frustrated, and they, in turn, create more victims. The "army of prostitutes" and piles of porn that Zweig denounced as sordid symptoms of repression are still around, and they are now augmented by hosts of camgirls and OnlyFans models. Though these websites are touted as entrepreneurial platforms that give sex workers more autonomy, they are still exploitative, especially for the many poor women overseas working for minimal returns in studios controlled by men. A slice of the take goes to the pimps running the studio, another to the hosting website, and another to the e-pimps managing customer service, with little left for the models themselves.

Even models with genuine independence often do not earn minimum wage, and though a few get rich, most don't. A 2021 piece in *The New York Times* reported that "there are wide discrepancies in pay." It explained that on OnlyFans,

> wealth is concentrated at the top. A spokeswoman for the site told me that "over 300" creators had been paid out "over $1 million," which suggests that the site has made millionaires of roughly 0.03 percent of its creators.... Downstream, a wider but still narrow band of creators take in thousands of dollars in a month, while a vast majority are lucky if they see a few hundred. If 10 percent of site creators earn $1,000 a month or more, 90 percent of creators take home less than $12,000 a year for what can amount to a full-time job.[17]

The paper's reporting on webcam models suggests a similar dynamic, with a small fraction of models dominating revenue and many others working extended shifts for meager earnings.[18] Models will often use multiple platforms to try to earn more, but while this can increase income (for example, live webcam shows can earn money directly and boost OnlyFans subscriptions), it also increases the amount of work required, as well as the need for the help of the e-pimps. The extravagant earnings of the top models help lure new girls into the industry, but many of the fresh recruits would earn more at almost any other job.

And even those who make it big are still harmed, though it often takes time for them to realize what they have given up for porn—and they have an incentive to keep quiet while the money is still coming in. As Louise Perry observes, "Women who have worked in porn will conform to the liberation narrative while they're still a part of the industry and share the dark side of their experiences only once they've left."[19] Or they'll acknowledge some problems but try to blame others. For example, in 2023 Riley Reid (to use her *nom de porn*) went viral with a video complaining that porn had ruined her life even though it had made her rich. She warned that "a lot of times when people ask me if they should do porn, I tell them no, I tell them that it makes life really hard, it makes dating really hard, it makes your family life really hard, it makes intimacy hard." She explained that her family either sought to dip into her wealth or told her to stay far away.[20] Reid's fans might reply that her sex work isn't the problem; the problem is that her family either shamed her or mooched off her porn profits. As the pro-porn and pro-prostitution activists say, sex work is work.

Yes, it is, and that is why it is wrong. Sex is not a commodity or service like any other, and it should not be for sale. Furthermore, the large demand for sex work proves the failure of the sexual revolution, which promised free love, not fake love for a monthly subscription fee plus add-ons and tips. The men most seduced by this industry are not always sympathetic ("creepy" and "pathetic" are likely more common adjectives), but they represent something gone very wrong in our culture. It is not good that a multitude of lonely men are forking over cash as much for the thrill of direct messages (supposedly) from an OnlyFans model as for the actual pornographic photos and videos.

The most reliable way for a man to have both companionship and regular sex is still to be in a long-term relationship, which marriage formalizes and secures. Thus, a social norm of lifelong monogamous marriage is the best way to provide most men and women with a stable relational and sexual partner. It is not that marriage is always a sexual paradise, or that men and women are never tempted to look outside it for sexual release and emotional intimacy. And marriage is much more than a means to provide people with sex and companionship. But we must recognize that the sexual revolution has failed to deliver the goods and that the benefits it promised were generally better provided by the institutions and norms it assailed and replaced.

The Cold War of the Sexes

Selfishness is often self-defeating. Humans are relational beings, and so looking out only for ourselves and our own pleasures tends to make us unhappy. Even if we get what we think we want, we often find that what we have selfishly desired is less fulfilling than we had hoped and that along the way we have lost, wounded, or never even formed the relationships that can provide real happiness. Thus, though the sexual revolution prioritized immediate pleasure over committed relationships, it has left many people with neither.

Fewer Americans are getting married. Those who do are getting married later in life. And while the divorce rate has dropped (in part because there are fewer marriages in the first place), it is still very high by historical standards. Thus, for many people, a happy (or even just OK) married life doesn't look boringly normal so much as unattainable. And yet many people still crave married domesticity, even if they are struggling to attain it. In a 2023 article in *Curbed* featuring interviews with young, childless New Yorkers, the authors professed themselves to be "surprised by how many people fantasize about a life with a partner and kids in brownstone Brooklyn—we expected more to plan lives as single artists or to build households of friends and throuples.... We heard a craving for high-end domesticity; so many people told us they wanted to be married with 'between one and two kids,' a shocking number said they wanted three or more, and nearly everyone said they wanted to own their homes."[21]

Visions of marriage, a home, and a kid or two (or even three or more) may be shocking to the sort of people who write at an offshoot of *New York* magazine, but it is still normal. Indeed, it is the American dream, which for most people consists not of becoming fabulously rich but of having family, friends, and enough money to enjoy a comfortable life with them. It's a picket fence, backyard barbecues, and a happy marriage, not mansion galas and orgies in exotic locales.

This dream has never been universally shared or attainable, but now even many who want it and have the financial means to achieve it are finding it relationally impossible.

The world, both online and off, seems full of complaints from men wondering where all the good women are and from women wondering the same about men. Of course, gripes about the difficulties of pairing off are perennial, but the declining marriage rates show that the problem is real. Some responses are easy to mock, such as that of the women profiled in a 2023 CNN report headlined "These Women Wanted a Symbolic Expression of Self-Love. So They Married Themselves",[22] but they are just a small manifestation of a civilizational malaise.

The relational habits our culture inculcates are not conducive to getting and staying married. The old models of how men and women were supposed to find a spouse had their flaws, but they did ensure a shared understanding of how men and women are to begin, advance, and sustain a relationship. Our culture has replaced this imperfect, but shared, understanding of how to pair off with no model whatsoever. And the apps designed to help us connect frequently seem to make things worse.[23] Indeed, it is often unclear what the state of a relationship is or where it is headed, even to those involved. That's how we get ever more imprecise neologisms such as "situationship", which one Urban Dictionary user defined this way: "Less than a relationship, but more than a booty call, a situationship refers to a romantic relationship that is, and will remain, undefined."[24] As the existence of this term illustrates, our relational and sexual culture encourages short-term gratification and keeping one's options open, while discouraging commitment and even definition. This culture does not make men fit to be good husbands, or women fit to be good wives. Men and women are being formed not for each other but away from each other. No wonder so many people who want picket-fence domesticity consider it unattainable, or at least unlikely.

Of course, forming men and women for each other presumes that men and women are different from, and yet meant for, each other, and our culture is uncomfortable with both these claims. Our embodiment as male and female is often treated as little more than a bit of plumbing, rather than an essential part of who we are. But we are different, and our flourishing as male and female depends on recognizing the differences, and wisely addressing the consequent asymmetries, between men and women.

In their critiques of our sexual culture, Emba, Perry, and Harrington each treated the argument that men and women are different as if it is provocative, which, in the circles these women work, socialize, and were educated in, it probably is. Emba and Perry even had chapters with almost identical titles: "Men and Women Are Not the Same" (Emba) and "Men and Women Are Different" (Perry)—a trifecta was avoided only because Harrington chose more colorful chapter titles such as "Meat Lego Gnosticism" and "Abolish Big Romance". Despite the prejudices of the educated professional class, men and women are different, and this is far more than just a matter of how our erogenous bits are shaped. Rather, human sexual dimorphism includes fundamental physical and sexual asymmetries.

One consequence of these differences is, as Emba points out, "when sex is bad for women, it tends to be really, *really* bad.... For men, bad sex might look like not orgasming, or maybe being a little bit bored or anxious on the way there. For women, bad sex looks like blood, tearing, actual tooth-gritting pain."[25] Men, especially in the age of endless internet porn, are far more likely to pressure women for sex acts that are uncomfortable, degrading, or painful than the other way around. And that is during consensual sex. Men are also far more physically dangerous to women than the other way around, yet the hookup culture encourages women to put themselves at the mercy of men they do not even know. And when women are hurt, their vulnerability and suffering are often ignored because they conflict with the narrative of sexual empowerment—Perry noted with rightful horror the increasing success of "rough sex" defenses when men have seriously injured or even killed women during violent but supposedly consensual sex.

Violence is intrinsic to sexual liberation in other ways as well. Despite the contraceptive revolution, casual sex can still create an unwanted pregnancy. When that happens, the woman has to choose whether to resort to the lethality of abortion, to place her baby for adoption, or to care for her child without a committed father. Even when fathers are present and supportive, there is still enormous asymmetry between men and women when it comes to pregnancy, childbirth, and caring for an infant; a lack of paternal commitment makes mothers even more vulnerable.

These disparities persist even though they are ideologically inconvenient. And the physical differences between men and women go beyond sex organs and strength; adult human brains are highly sexed. Our bodies and minds, and therefore our needs and desires, have been shaped by generations of necessity. As Harrington put it, "A few short decades of sexuality unmoored from reproduction via technology are no match, it seems, for millennia of evolution."[26]

Thus, we should not be surprised that men and women tend to view sex and relationships differently. As Perry observed, we know that on average, men "prefer to have more sex and with a larger number of partners, that sex buyers are almost exclusively male, that men watch a lot more porn than women do, and that the vast majority of women, if given the option, prefer a committed relationship to casual sex."[27] In short, the conventional wisdom is right: Men are more sexually driven and more interested in hooking up. And it is easy to see why women would want commitment as a prerequisite for sex, given the vulnerability that reproduction imposes on them. For all of human history, natural selection has favored women who are supported by their mates during pregnancy, childbirth, and child-rearing.

Of course, as we are constantly reminded, women have libidos too. But our culture emphasizes this to the point of ignoring important distinctions in how men and women experience sexual desire. Rather than accounting for the differences between male and female sexuality and reproductive roles, our culture tries to efface them, largely by treating women as defective men whose fertility is a problem to be solved. Women's equality has come to mean that women should suppress their fecundity to fit into a world—from sex to the workplace—shaped for men and their preferences.

Our culture has especially put women in a bind when it comes to realizing their hopes of having children. Human fertility is a high point of asymmetry between the sexes. Men can try for a quantity-over-quality approach to passing on their genes; women cannot. For a man, begetting a child takes little time, and male fertility declines only gradually. In contrast, bearing children takes far more time and effort for women, and female fertility falls off sooner and more sharply than male fertility. We routinely hear of some fossilized rocker or actor fathering a child with a young-enough-to-be-his-granddaughter girlfriend, but no one contemplates an aged female pop star like Madonna having a baby.

But our culture relentlessly tells women, especially high-achieving ones, to delay marriage and children. This is sold as sexually and relationally empowering, and it is reinforced by the demands of education and the marketplace. This is why Elizabeth Bruenig's 2021 Mother's Day column in

The New York Times, declaring that she did not regret becoming a mother at twenty-five,[28] sparked meltdowns.[29] Her piece was amusing, observant, and reflective, but it is taboo for an educated, professional woman to proclaim her joy at having children during her prime childbearing years—this is blasphemy against the doctrine that women should suppress their fertility to emulate male careerism and promiscuity. As another *New York Times* piece put it in 2024, "Liberal conventional wisdom encourages people to spend their 20s on journeys of personal and professional self-discovery and self-fulfillment. Children are treated as a bonus round, something to get to only after completing a long list of achievements: getting a degree, forging a satisfying and well-established career, buying a house, cultivating the ideal romantic partnership."[30]

Yet even setting aside other critiques, there are obvious practical reasons for women to have children before their fertility is waning. Female fertility begins declining around age thirty, which is a problem for women who follow the culture's advice to wait until around then, if not later, to marry and have children.[31] Furthermore, letting the biological clock tick close to midnight not only increases the likelihood of fertility problems but also narrows the window in which they can be diagnosed and treated. Relatedly, putting off children makes it more difficult to have more than one or two. And advanced maternal age also poses risks to a mother and her baby, so much so that pregnancy at thirty-five and older is sometimes bluntly described as "geriatric".[32]

There is something cruel about the expectation that, as *Washington Post* columnist Megan McArdle once put it, educated professionals "must time pregnancies exquisitely to optimize a career".[33] The measures that some corporations offer to rectify this hardship (which, again, disproportionately falls on women), such as paying for egg freezing, merely highlight the exploitative, even dystopian, nature of their corporate culture. Surrogacy, for example, treats pregnancy as a boutique service job, with the well-off renting wombs from poor and working-class women both here and abroad.

This system has worked, insofar as young women are surpassing their male counterparts according to many educational and economic measures. It has failed, insofar as it has not made women happier. Indeed, the young liberal women most committed to this model report the highest rates of mental distress.[34] Pretending that men and women are essentially interchangeable was a prerequisite for the sexual revolution, and it has also served the interests of corporate overlords. It is just not good for people.

Genuine justice for women must account for them as women—especially their more intensive and time-limited role in human reproduction.[35] This does not mean excluding women from education or achievement outside the home—complementarity does not mean adherence to the model of family life featured in 1950s magazine illustrations—but rather ensuring that their womanhood is respected. Right relations between the sexes must reckon with the asymmetries between them. No matter how much women are encouraged to speak up and lean in, they will always be disadvantaged in a society that denies the importance of womanhood and takes male individualism as its model.

Nature can be suppressed only so far. And so, as Harrington observes, we are seeing the return of masculinity and femininity in grotesque, caricatured forms, such as the young women who simply accept being physically hurt by porn-addled men as part of dating today. Reinforcement for such distorted relations between the sexes is readily available in mainstream culture, not just odd corners of the internet. It is easy to denounce crude men such as the kick-boxer turned pimp turned influencer Andrew Tate. And yet *Cosmopolitan* magazine, which is omnipresent at checkout counters and is meant for liberated young women, bills itself as an endless series of sex tips to please men. Somehow, liberation keeps returning to crude stereotypes and roles. No wonder that for an increasing number of people, this dating and sexual culture is producing neither liberated sexual ecstasy nor domestic bliss. Rather, both men and women are increasingly alienated and embittered.

Always Connected, Forever Alone

In the biblical story of creation, being alone is the first thing God declares to be "not good". More Americans are alone than ever before, and it is indeed not good. In 2023 surgeon general Vivek Murthy warned of an "epidemic of loneliness and isolation". He declared that loneliness kills and that the "increased risk of premature death associated with social disconnection is comparable to smoking daily—and may be even greater than the risk associated with obesity".[36] And he touched on a deeper truth: Loneliness is not terrible because it is unhealthy; rather, it is unhealthy because it is terrible—a failure of human well-being that goes far beyond ill health, an affliction of the soul. We are social beings, and to be lonely is to be deprived of the communion with others that we need.

Yet Dr. Murthy's social diagnosis ignored the sexual revolution, which, by dissolving family and community bonds, may be the chief culprit behind our increased loneliness. For instance, the sexual revolution changed the definition of success in the romantic landscape. Previously, with sex closely tied to lifelong marriage and the begetting of children, success meant leaving the relational marketplace with a permanent partner. Decoupling sex from commitment and procreation has enabled and encouraged people to keep their options open and explore what's out there in a sort of sexual and relational tourism that has intensified in the age of the dating app. As this becomes the norm, it is more difficult even for those who want to settle down to find willing and suitable partners. Somehow, instantaneous communication and a culture that thoroughly approves of casual sex are leaving more of us lonely, as there are fewer marriages, fewer children, and more Americans living alone.[37] And yet there are still many who actively cheer the decline of marriage. For example, in 2021, *New York Times* columnist Charles Blow's response to the news that those who are married would soon be a minority of American adults was to argue that we need to eliminate any "government policy that rewards the married".[38] In his view, marriage is just another lifestyle choice, and policies encouraging it are unjust privileges for the married and therefore unfair punishments for the single.

This anti-marriage attitude is just a particularly blunt expression of a culture that is making adults lonely and miserable by discouraging stable relationships between men and women—and discouraging the begetting of children, who are best raised in such relationships. And when it comes to children, another disappointment of sexual liberation is that Americans are having fewer children than we would like. In 2023, *The Wall Street Journal* reported that the "U.S. birthrate is down sharply from 15 years ago, as women report that economic and social obstacles are causing them to have fewer children than they want."[39] The article explained that "the gap between women's intended number of children and their actual family size has widened considerably" to an average of "about one child less than they planned". As is normal for this sort of piece, the subjects cited a mix of factors, from trouble finding the right spouse to financial concerns and even worries about the environment and the general state of the world.

Though some of these reasons are more compelling than others, it is clear that our culture is not delivering what people want and need in the way of family formation. And yet, little is done to rectify this. Even to raise these issues in normative terms is to risk denunciation. We are told to view marriage and children as optional objects of subjective desire, rather than a norm that culture is built around. It is socially acceptable to say that it is unfortunate when people who want to get married and have children do not; it is unacceptable to say that marriage and parenthood are vocations that most of us are called to and that society should be organized around them.

Our culture does not want to admit that men and women have a natural need to come together to form families and that this is the best way of life for most of us. Though lip service is given to the idea that there is nothing more important than family, in practice we are taught that all sorts of ambitions and acquisitions are more important. For the successful strivers, family is what you do after achieving all the other things, if you still want it. And though some people succeed in forming a family later in life, many are left behind, even among the professional-managerial class. Our culture is built for pleasure seeking and ambition, not family and community. This is a large part of why neither men nor women can really be said to be thriving. Men are falling behind on measures such as education and employment, with many stupefied by porn, pot, and video games. Meanwhile, our culture has premised female empowerment on effacing female embodiment. The result is that both men and women are increasingly alone.

Addressing this loneliness requires enabling and encouraging marriage and family formation through both public policy changes and a positive cultural vision. This in turn demands consideration of how material conditions influence family life and childbearing. For instance, an education system that pushes as many people as possible into college for as long as possible (often incurring significant debt) is in practice anti-family. Housing policies that make working-class family homes unaffordable in many areas are anti-family. Even policies meant to protect children can have anti-natal effects—for example, increasingly stringent car seat mandates have been shown to discourage having children because families can't afford the bigger car necessary to fit that third or fourth car seat.[40] These and many other factors need to be considered by pro-family politicians, pundits, and policy wonks.

But policy changes alone cannot correct an anti-marriage and anti-baby culture. Thus, we need to provide an alternative to the dominant narrative among the educated professionals who direct our economy, politics, and culture. They are told to define themselves through accomplishments and indulgences—youth is for achievement and enjoyment while finding oneself, and children are an optional capstone when the party is winding down. The message is clear: Build up your career and don't get trapped by depending on anyone else or having anyone permanently depend on you, at least not while you're young. This ethos depends on, and reinforces, sexual liberalism. For instance, delaying marriage until close to thirty makes Christian chastity increasingly implausible. Likewise, a culture that emphasizes choice and freedom tends to view the commitment of lifelong marriage as stifling as well as risky—after all, it forecloses so many options.

This message is pushed throughout the culture, with particularly devastating results for poor and working-class people, who are especially vulnerable when deprived of the support of stable family life. However, a social norm of monogamous marriage benefits everyone. Monogamous marriage acts as a sort of relational and even sexual distributism by pairing off as many people as possible, thereby ensuring that most men and women can secure a partner with whom to form a family. It is the relational counterpart to a wide distribution of property. Historically, limiting the number of men who are isolated and sexually frustrated is good for civilizational stability and prosperity, even if it crimps the style of powerful men who would otherwise be patriarchs or rulers fathering prodigious numbers of children via a well-stocked harem.

And children, of course, are better off being raised in a stable home by their biological parents. Children are not expendable, nor are they luxury goods and lifestyle choices. They are persons, and adults should sacrifice for them, not the other way around. We all know the terrible truth, which is that adult sexual and relational chaos hurts children, often very badly.[41] Protecting children should not end where adult sexual and relational choices begin. And yet a man will catch more legal trouble for driving his young children around without car seats than for abandoning their mother.

Children need parents whose relationship is durable, not disposable, but sexual liberalism encourages adults to focus on their own selfish desires, rather than prioritizing the needs of their children. Our culture will spend money to protect children, but it is reluctant to limit adult autonomy, especially sexual autonomy, for that purpose. From the internet (where there is often no real age verification required to access porn) to family structure and stability (where expecting parents to be married is a relic of the past), adult freedom is prioritized over children's well-being. Predictably, this harms children, especially poor children, in many ways. But the importance of intact natural families cuts against the grain of liberal and sexual individualism.

In addition to the benefits for society in general and children in particular, monogamy is good for us because it develops our higher nature and fulfills many of our deepest longings. Men and women are meant for each other, and marriage enables our flourishing in ways that flitting from partner to partner cannot. The ideological assertion that, except for our plumbing, men and women are basically interchangeable sets us at war with each other and distorts our relationships, creating conflict instead of complementarity and cooperation. Unlike the life of self-indulgence, marriage demands that we give of ourselves—it begins by binding ourselves with oaths regardless of what the future brings. Marriage and parenting are sacrificial. Yet this self-giving is more likely to lead to genuine flourishing because as relational beings, we do not thrive without love. Thus, marriage is both the basis for civilization and the fulfillment of many of our deepest needs and desires. As the union of the two halves of the human race, it is both foundational and the source of much of what is highest and best in this life. Marriage can both give joy and sanctify sorrow.

The sexual revolution offers us autonomous pleasure seeking, but it is by giving up our autonomous selves that we gain our lives as persons in communion with others. Autonomy means keeping our options open and keeping our hearts free by keeping them closed, always having an out from our obligations and relationships. Autonomy holds us back from full commitment, and it therefore limits love, which requires vulnerability. In this sense, autonomy imposes limits that restrict essential aspects of human flourishing—the autonomous individual sacrifices love in exchange for a sort of freedom.

Yet this freedom stunts us, while the constraints of family life cause us to grow and develop. They teach us to subordinate our personal desires for creature comforts and pleasures to the good of other people. The self-sacrifice of loving parenting is one of the great examples in this world of Christ's teaching that we must lose our life to gain it. Life as Daddy or Mommy is possible only through interruptions and effacements great and small. It is a more difficult but better life than one devoted to personal ambition and indulgence. Getting married and having children help us build and establish more substantial identities than those sought through professional advancement, personal pleasures, or relationships that always come with an exit option. In particular, the permanence of marriage and parenthood establishes them as deep aspects of our identities, while also reflecting the truth that we are ordered toward giving and receiving love.

Christianity teaches that marriage mirrors the relationship between Christ and His Church and that children are a gift from God. Yet even as Scripture commands that "marriage be held in honor among all" (Heb 13:4), it also instructs us that those who are unmarried and childless have a special place in the community of believers. And this is not just for those who are members of the Roman Catholic clergy and religious orders vowed to celibacy but for all believers who are free from the responsibilities of marriage and children and are therefore able to devote themselves more fully to the work of God and the Church, making them spiritual fathers and mothers. This is because love is the heart of the Christian life, whether one is married with children or single. In all cases, Christians are to find their lives by losing them in loving relationship with, and service to, others.

Singleness is not an excuse for selfishness, and the responsibilities of family life cannot become a barricade against reaching out to others. Christian families must make a point of including those who are otherwise alone, enabling them to become entwined with the families of their church and community. This inclusion is, of course, easier when living alone is rarer, which is why the decline of marriage is isolating even for those who have a vocation of singleness. Roles such as the fun single aunt, the teaching Brother or Sister, or the doting childless godparent depend on other people having children.

In this age of loneliness, Christian communities need to share the benefits and burdens of both family and single life. This is because Christianity knows that it is not good for man to be alone and that the deepest fulfillment and joys of this life are found in human relationships. Most of us are called to the vocations of marriage and raising children; all of us are meant to love and be loved.

Abortion Hardens the Hearts
It Doesn't Stop

Death in the Age of Ultrasound

America is broken because it is haunted.

To understand what has gone so wrong with family, romance, relationships, and sex in America, we must see what haunts us—the things that we don't like to speak or even think about. We must look at the specters we don't want to see, but who are tormenting us. And so we must look at the ghost in the cradle.

When *Roe v. Wade* was decided, it might have been said, "Forgive them, for they know not what they do." For most people in 1973, the womb was a black box; few knew much about fetal development.[1] But now we know. When announcing a welcome pregnancy, we share ultrasound photos via text and social media. We stick the printouts on our fridges and display them in picture frames with Sneak Peak emblazoned on the border. Pregnancy-tracking apps tell expectant mothers and fathers how their baby is developing each week; there are even options to customize how developments are reported so we can better visualize them—for example, this week, Baby is the size of a Lego figure.

We know what abortion does; the humanity of the unborn has never been clearer. We have seen the moving limbs and the tiny fingers and heard the beating of unborn hearts. And the details of fetal development stick in our minds—such as fingernails developing by the end of the first trimester. Even abortion advocates know, which is why they so often hide behind euphemisms—preferring to speak of reproductive freedom and choice, without mentioning the a-word. Few consciences are as seared as those of the zealots of Shout Your Abortion and similar campaigns, and so many abortion supporters prefer to cover abortion in a rhetorical haze, viewing it as a necessary evil and preferring not to think about its violent reality.

The perceived necessity of abortion is dictated, above all, by the sexual revolution, which encourages our sexual appetites to exceed our willingness to care for the children who are the natural result of sex. And a culture committed to sexual liberalism cannot contracept its way out of this moral failing. It is not just that contraceptives sometimes fail or are neglected but that sexual liberalism encourages sex in situations where a pregnancy is not only unplanned but unwanted, and the baby, if born, would be unsupported by one or both parents. A culture of hookups and casual relationships may have less sex overall than one that promotes committed marriage, but the sex it does have is more likely to result in pregnancies that end by abortion. As Ryan Anderson explained in *First Things*, "Four percent of babies conceived in marriage will be aborted, compared to 40 percent of children conceived outside of marriage. Meanwhile, 13 percent of women who have abortions are married, and 87 percent are unmarried. Nonmarital sex is the main cause of abortion. Marriage is the best protector of unborn human life."[2]

Abortion eliminates the perceived problems of an unwanted pregnancy, but it encourages the sexual and relational dynamics that produce more unwanted pregnancies. Thus, for those for whom rolling back the sexual revolution is unthinkable, abortion is indispensable. But what abortion does is more evident than ever. This is why it is abortion supporters, not opponents, who indulge in metaphysical arguments about when a human being becomes a human person. These defenses of abortion require concocting a distinction between the humans killed by abortion and everyone else. Though abortion advocates rarely put it in terms of "ensoulment", such metaphysical, even mystical, assumptions are at the core of their argument, which is that at some gestational point (perhaps birth, perhaps sometime earlier), the developing human being becomes a human person, with a right not to be killed. But before that point, the unborn have no rights that the born are bound to respect.

This position is obviously morally dubious—the idea that some human beings are not human persons, and are therefore disposable, has an abominable record. And abortion advocates insist on elective abortion long past the point at which the full humanity of the unborn is undeniable. As one abortion clinic tweeted, "Abortion is good in all trimesters. Your reason is the right reason, don't let anyone tell you differently."[3] Planned Parenthood, the nation's largest abortion provider, has echoed this sentiment, tweeting that when it comes to abortion, "Every reason is the right reason."[4]

These abortionists, along with their media apologists and political champions, blow past all the qualms that most people have about late-term abortions and the restrictions they would prefer to impose on them. Under the influence of these activists, some states have no restrictions on abortion, and others have restrictions in name only due to exceptions that essentially allow abortionists to do whatever they want. Some abortionists will indeed commit abortions up to birth for any reason whatsoever, including sex selection. One such abortionist, Warren Hern of Colorado, was the subject of a long 2023 *Atlantic* profile in which he admitted that half or more of the late-term abortions he commits are elective.[5] Likewise, a 2024 *New Yorker* puff piece on a Maryland clinic that specializes in late-term abortions closed with a profile of "Amanda", who did not realize she was pregnant until she was about thirty weeks along. Several weeks later she got an abortion because neither she nor the father wanted a child.[6]

The truth of this reporting is confirmed by the data we have on late-term abortions, which suggests that they are generally done for the same reasons as other abortions.[7] As this shows, these abortionists and their enablers do not care whether the human being *in utero* is a person or not, because they believe that the mother's right to bodily autonomy gives her an absolute right to dispose of the person developing in her womb. The classic illustration of this argument is Judith Jarvis Thomson's famous violinist hypothetical: If you were kidnapped and used as a life-support system for an ailing virtuoso, would you have the right to disconnect him?[8]

The image is striking, and moral philosophers have been arguing over the scenario for decades. The assertion of bodily autonomy has become even more central to the case for abortion as more ultrasound pictures are posted on our fridges and social media feeds. It is difficult to dismiss human lives *in utero* as worthless clumps of cells when you can count their fingers and look at their faces. Abortion supporters increasingly echo Thomson's claim that no one should be compelled to sustain another person's life, whether violinist or fetus. Thus, a woman has a right to have the human being developing in her womb killed, just as she would (presumably) have the right to disconnect the imaginary violinist. An unwanted embryo or fetus is a trespasser on a woman's bodily autonomy, and trespassers will be dismembered.

But though Thomson's hypothetical is ingenious as an attempt to make the ordinary, natural process of human reproduction appear alien and horrifying, that is also why it fails. It is a ridiculous scenario that tells us nothing about the morality of abortion. Human reproduction is not a bizarre medical experiment, and to evaluate it as such is an error of moral philosophy. The violinist hypothetical is science fiction, with no more moral authority than *Ender's Game*, *The Empire Strikes Back*, or any other sci-fi classic.

The real value of Thomson's strange comparison is not that it is morally insightful but that it provides a memorable illustration of the radical inequality of human reproduction. Though pregnancy, childbirth, and breastfeeding are natural, rather than experimental, they do place significant burdens on women, and on women alone. Fathers can and should provide support, but they cannot take these tasks upon themselves. Thus, because women bear the brunt of reproductive burdens and risks, abortion advocates have long cast abortion as essential to women's equality. The asymmetry of human reproduction is perceived as unjust, and abortion is seen as a means to rectify it. Abortion supposedly allows women to stand on an equal footing with men romantically, economically, socially, and politically.

This argument is ill-suited to stand alone—trying to achieve equality through the deliberate killing of innocent humans is obviously not morally justified—but in practice the various arguments for abortion are blended together to provide mutual reinforcement: Human life *in utero* isn't fully human, and abortion is necessary for women's bodily autonomy, which in turn is necessary for women's equality.

This rhetorical mélange is often spiced with appeals to the wrenching cases of pregnancies resulting from rape and incest or those that endanger the mother, but the fight over abortion is never really about these rare instances. Abortion advocates don't want exceptions for these difficult situations; they want to defend the ordinary elective procedures that constitute nearly all abortions. There is no dodging the issue by pointing to the edge cases.

The fight is over abortion on demand, and that debate can be very loud indeed. But when the yelling is over, we can still hear the rhythm of tiny human hearts, some of which are suddenly, violently stilled.

The Violence Inherent in the Revolution

These sudden silences scream out the violence inherent in the sexual revolution. The pleasures promised by sexual liberation require the death of those who are inconveniently conceived in their pursuit. Joseph Bottum poignantly realized this as a young man one day, while he looked at a mother and her child:

> It all started with the sudden, absolute conviction that babies are good. No thought exists in isolation. One conviction leads to another, too fast sometimes to follow, and I stood there remembering in a mad rush all the college girls I knew who had abortions. I stood there in the library window, on that green April day, remembering all my complicity in joining the great sexual revolution that was supposed to empower women but mostly ended up empowering college boys to enjoy free and apparently consequenceless sex. And I knew that, fun as the pleasure dome had been, I must leave—for it was kept bright and warm with the bodies of aborted babies, burned in the basement furnace for fuel.[9]

The violence of abortion was baked into the sexual revolution's pursuit of sex separated from constraints and consequences. The elevation of recreational sex required it to be depersonalized and stripped of any intrinsic meaning—people may assign value and significance to it, but any meaning is purely subjective preference. Furthermore, if sex does not matter, except subjectively, then it follows that whom we have sex with does not matter, except also in terms of individual preference and subjective value. The relational aspect of sex may, of course, have tremendous personal significance, but then again, it may not, and it is a central dogma of sexual liberation that no one ought to tell others how to perceive and value sexual relations and partners. Thus, the interpersonal reality of sex is subordinated to personal whims.

But sex cannot be depersonalized so easily. This is not just because of the physical vulnerability and intimacy that is intrinsic to sex but also because of its capacity to bring a new person into being. The natural result of sex is the gametes of a man and a woman combining to form a new human being. And like all of us, these nascent humans begin their lives in a state of absolute vulnerability and dependence. To avoid the demands of this dependence, which tend to crimp the mirth of sexual liberation, the sexual revolution declared war on fertility. The depersonalization of sex recast sexual responsibility as the diligent and effective suppression of fertility, rather than the bounding and channeling of sexuality for the sake of stable relationships and the new human beings sex naturally brings into existence.

The consummation of the sexual revolution requires repressing the natural consummation of human sexuality—the conception of new people. Consequently, sexual liberation is constantly at war against the nature of human embodiment and existence. A right to sexual autonomy is presumed to include a right to be free, by any means necessary, from the natural consequences of sex. Thus, sexual liberalism often regards conceiving and bearing a child as some sort of malevolent, alien imposition. The writer Thomas Chatterton Williams exemplified this attitude in a tweet, declaring that it is "hard to imagine anything more dystopian than being forced to give birth".[10]

The nonsensical language of "forced birth" has become commonplace among supporters of abortion. The real complaint, of course, is not that birth is forced in any meaningful sense but that restrictions on abortion limit the ability to end a pregnancy legally by killing the human growing in a mother's womb. Birth is the natural, healthy conclusion of a pregnancy, which is itself a natural, healthy result of sexual intercourse. Describing giving birth as "forced" reveals hostility toward the reality of human embodiment and the natural process of human reproduction. Birth is forced only as much as any other normal bodily process is forced; one might as well complain of "forced digestion" or "forced breathing".

That abortion advocates are depicting natural and healthy bodies as somehow alien and horrifying reveals how sexual liberation leads to viewing the normal order of human existence, and the realities of physical embodiment, as dystopian, even evil. This might seem odd, given sexual liberalism's glorification of the physical pleasure of sex. But it is precisely this unbalanced elevation of sexual desire and pleasure that leads to rejecting the constraints of our embodiment when they interfere with the fulfillment of sexual desire. Sexual liberalism seeks to free us from obligations related to our sex lives, including those intrinsic to our bodies.

Not even the bond between mother and child is safe from the sexual revolution's prioritization of the pleasure-seeking selfishness of autonomous adults. That conception, gestation, and childbirth are the natural results of sex is seen as beside the point—the ideology of sexual liberation presumes that there is a right to sterile sex, and so the reproductive consequences of sex are seen as "forced" upon us unless they have been deliberately chosen. Thus, the sexual revolution's liberation of the body for sexual pleasure ends up being a revolt against the very nature of our bodies, and therefore a revolt against existence itself.

We are finite beings with natural limits and bodily constraints that we do not choose. Indeed, existence itself is given to us on terms we do not agree to; we cannot consent to existence until we are already well into it, with all the contingencies of life, body and soul. As the great religious philosopher Søren Kierkegaard sarcastically wrote, "How did I come into the world; why was I not asked, why was I not informed of the rules and regulations.... Am I not free to decide? Am I to be forced to be part of it? Where is the manager, I would like to make a complaint!"[11]

In this existential sense, every birth is a forced birth, insofar as it brings a person into the broader world without his consent. Existence is given to us: We do not choose to exist, nor do we choose the conditions under which we will be born and raised. And the unchosen givenness of life often seems unfair; we often feel that the world has been poorly arranged. For instance, why should the intense but brief pleasure of sex come with the possibility of the lifelong commitment of begetting a child?

Well, because that is how the world is. More specifically, because that is how we humans are. And so the goals of sexual liberation are incompatible with the natural realities of human reproduction. The sexual revolution presumes that the natural fertility of our bodies is the enemy of our happiness, which is found in sexual gratification. This is why the Pill was essential to the sexual revolution, which required rebelling against our natural fertility, and especially female fecundity. But birth control sometimes fails or is not used, and so the fullness of sexual liberalism requires abortion to ensure complete freedom from the unchosen constraints and duties of having children. Sexual liberalism thereby culminates in asserting an absolute right to take the lives of the weak and dependent—precisely because they are weak and dependent, and therefore inconvenient. Human lives in the womb can offer nothing but need; to respond to that need with violence is to assail human dependence in its purest form.

The bloodshed of abortion thus lays bare how sexual liberalism revolts against our humanity, and therefore why its vision of human flourishing is a mirage. Abortion is a violent severing of the primal human bond of mother, father, and child. The intrinsic obligations of family are treated as contingent upon whether they are wanted, and so the duties of these relationships are rejected if they impede the sexual freedom of ostensibly autonomous adults. This view, exemplified in complaints about "forced births", is an anti-human ideology that poisons the self-giving of love. It is not just that, try as we may, we cannot escape dependence and contingency but that accepting our mutual human dependence and obligation is necessary both for individual well-being and general human flourishing.

Abortion Makes Everything Worse

The attraction of abortion is the promise that good may come from doing evil, that eliminating unwanted children in the womb will allow the rest of us to live better lives. But the evil of abortion is not so easily instrumentalized and contained. Rather, it infects our culture and spoils even the goods that it supposedly supports. Abortion deforms everything from law and politics to relationships and families as it brings selfish violence into the fundamental human relationships of mother, father, and child. Instead of solidarity, there is a violent assertion of primacy. Instead of care for the dependent and vulnerable, there is the bloody exercise of power against them. Abortion hardens the hearts it doesn't stop.

America's national abortion regime began with an illegitimate exercise of judicial power when the Supreme Court declared a constitutional right to abortion. Neither the text nor the history of the Constitution gives any warrant for this; indeed, there is a much stronger case that the Constitution forbids elective abortion than that it requires it.[12] But the political and legal elite's support for abortion ensured that a half century passed before the egregious error of *Roe* was corrected by the *Dobbs* decision, which returned abortion regulation to the democratic process.

The Supreme Court's attempts to settle the debate over abortion damaged our laws and our politics. In particular, leaving a womb-shaped hole in legal protections for human life precluded a culture and politics of solidarity. The American Left and the Democratic Party traded solidarity for sexual liberation, with a wholehearted embrace of the sexual revolution. This is why when abortion comes up, avowed socialists suddenly argue like radical individualists. How the political parties would develop on abortion was not predictable in 1973, but it is now undeniable that the heart of the Democratic Party is no longer the (often socially moderate, even conservative) blue-collar union hall but urban white-collar workers who are uncompromisingly pro-abortion.

Thus, instead of Right and Left arguing and compromising over how best to help and protect the most vulnerable, the Left simply denies that unborn human lives have any value. And so abortion opponents have had to default to the GOP, which has at least nominally opposed abortion, though it often advertises itself as merely the lesser evil. Many pro-life voters would happily compromise on other issues in order to restrict elective abortion, but few Democratic leaders have been willing to cut a deal or to do anything to restrain abortions in states they control. Indeed, Democratic politicians have done everything possible to enable, encourage, and fund abortion. And so, despite claims that welfare-state liberalism is the key to reducing abortion,[13] the highest abortion rates in the United States, both under *Roe* and after it was overturned, have been in deep-blue states such as New York and Illinois. A polity that disdains human life *in utero* can never spend enough money on social services to eliminate the demand for abortion.

Furthermore, there has been a shift by many abortion supporters to being pro-abortion rather than just "pro-choice". The famous "safe, legal, and rare" formulation from the charismatic half of the Clintons was mendacious (Bill Clinton supported even the most gruesome of late-term abortions), but at the time it was politically effective. This line appealed to voters who regarded elective abortion with the sort of attitude their ancestors held toward the man in the black hood and his work—as an unsavory but sometimes necessary evil, professionally executed. Although such attitudes are not particularly consistent, these voters were genuinely discomfited by abortion, and they recoiled at the suggestion that they were pro-abortion.

But now Democratic politicians are increasingly likely to praise abortion as a positive good, rather than defend it as a necessary evil. For example, in 2023, Illinois governor J. B. Pritzker declared an Abortion Provider Appreciation

Day.[14] Pritzker was fulsome in his praise for abortionists' "courage, compassion, and dedication to their work".[15] He expounded upon how essential abortion is and how wonderful it is that Illinois has become an abortion tourism destination.

This enthusiasm for abortion arises from its indispensability to the sexual revolution and the way of life that has been established upon it. Because of the asymmetry of reproduction, the sexual revolution is palatable to women only if something is done to reassure them that they won't be stuck cleaning up the mess when the party stops. That is why the sexual revolution promotes abortion as necessary for women's equality. As Erika Bachiochi has noted, abortion is perceived as a fix for the particular risks and burdens human reproduction places on women—a technological solution to the perceived injustice of nature.[16] Without abortion to back up contraception, sex has more significant consequences for women than for men. As one female writer put it, "Without safe, legal access to abortion, women will always be slaves to their fertility."[17] This is why, in a world of casual sex, the sexual revolution tells women that without abortion, they cannot be sexually and economically—and therefore socially and politically—equal to men.[18]

The sense among the sexually liberated that abortion is needed for women to compete fairly with men also explains the apparent paradox of high-achieving women being, on average, more supportive of permissive abortion laws than poor women, even though the latter are more likely to have abortions. Ambition justifies as good what desperation recognizes as bad even while committing. The pressure on high-achieving women to optimize the timing of children for education and career purposes pushes them to support abortion strongly as an indispensable backup to contraception. They therefore view opposition to abortion as antithetical to female achievement and status.

But pursuing equality through abortion sets men and women against each other. Even the justification of abortion as a private matter of female freedom implicitly relieves men of their responsibilities: Why should a woman's choice be a man's problem? He signed up for a good time, not diapers and a minivan. In hookups and uncommitted relationships, it is understood that if intercourse fulfills its biologic purpose, it is the woman's responsibility to deal with it by having the child growing within her womb killed. It may be the last resort, but the prospect of deliberately ending a human life is there, lurking—if the condom breaks, if the Pill fails, then there will be violent death.

Women know what is expected of them by the men they hook up with or by the boyfriends who are just not "ready to have a baby". This was, according to pop star Britney Spears, the reason given by her then-boyfriend Justin Timberlake when he pressured her into aborting the child they had conceived together. Spears said it was "one of the most agonizing things I have ever experienced in my life" and something that she "never would have done" were it just her decision.[19] There was no financial need; both Spears and Timberlake were rich and famous. The decision to abort was made, as it so often is, because a man did not want to take responsibility for his child. And so sexual pleasure became intertwined with violence because abortion—the intentional, targeted killing of a unique human being—is a necessary backstop to a culture of sex without consequence or obligation.

Thus, a sexual ethic theoretically based on consent is in practice reliant on violence; abortion makes force, domination, and the subjugation of women's bodies central to our sexual culture. If we really want to address "toxic masculinity", we must reject a culture in which violence is intrinsic to male sexual satisfaction. If men are encouraged to let nothing except the bare legal boundary of consent come between them and sexual gratification and are told that they incur no duties or obligations in the process, it should surprise no one that they are especially selfish in their pursuit of pleasure without relationships, obligations, or commitment. Not only are sexual partners disposable, but so are the lives created through intercourse. And men who view their progeny as disposable are unlikely to honor and respect the women with whom they conceive these unwanted children.

Abortion's vitiation of political and social solidarity is rooted in the damage it does to the fundamental relationships of our humanity. Abortion shatters the unity of mother, father, and child. Instead of the family solidarity foundational to human society and well-being, the begetting and bearing of new human life become a battleground of competing interests. Abortion cannot help women thrive as women, let alone establish stable families and ensure that every child is loved and cared for. Even as a possibility, abortion creates a chasm between the interests of mothers, fathers, and their children. A regime of abortion on demand affirms a view of human sexuality as essentially selfish and of relations among men, women, and children as fundamentally contentious. It replaces love and responsibility with self-interest and violence. No wonder the dating and sexual landscape seems so bleak to so many.

Casual hookups and cheap sex are not a recipe for lasting human happiness; they are a poor bet even for short-term pleasure. Thus, from outside the framework of the sexual revolution, abortion looks less like liberation and more like a devil's bargain in which we do not get even what we think we were promised. The widespread sexual and relational misery of our culture suggests it is not worth it, especially for women. Tales of our miserable sexual landscape call to mind Screwtape, C. S. Lewis' fictitious devil, who gloated over a damned soul who had spent his life doing neither what he ought nor what he liked.[20] The sexual revolution is not worth the price. Selling one's soul is not worth it even to gain the whole world—but for bad sex and ruined relationships?

We Are All the Violinist

Abortion reveals the intrinsic violence of the sexual revolution, which is rooted in a false understanding of who we are and how we ought to live. Sexual liberalism, like much of the liberal philosophical tradition, presumes that we are rational, autonomous individuals who thrive by pursuing our desires, bounded only by the constraint that we not impinge on the rights of other individuals. But this is wrong. We are social beings who flourish through living in communion with others. Living well requires acknowledging our dependence and interconnectedness, rather than striving for atomistic pleasure.

This is why the common framing of the debate over abortion as the weighing of a woman's right to bodily autonomy against an unborn human's right to life misstates the issue. Accepting this opposition as the heart of the matter concedes the validity of viewing the relationship between mother and child as fundamentally antagonistic. But motherhood should not be understood, either morally or legally, as a source of conflicting rights claims in a deadly zero-sum game. To treat a mother and her child as essentially in conflict is already to accept the substitution of selfishness in the place of love.

Returning to Judith Jarvis Thomson's violinist, the problem is that her creativity in trying to make pregnancy seem alien was self-defeating. The scenario is an imagined freak of medicine, whereas pregnancy is the normal reality of human reproduction. This normalcy, in turn, reminds us that we were all once utterly dependent *in utero* and that most of us will be dependent again, whether from illness, injury, or old age. In short, we are all the violinist.

Human solidarity recognizes this shared dependence. As Leah Libresco Sargeant put it, "Dependence is our default state, and self-sufficiency the aberration. Our lives begin and (frequently) end in states of near total dependence, and much of the middle is marked by periods of need."[21] Ignoring dependence, or trying to avoid it, has been a great failure of the liberal political tradition, which prioritizes independent, rational adults (or at least adults who imagine themselves to be so). After all, independent, rational adults do not need solidarity; they need a nonaggression pact, a free market, and mechanisms for conflict resolution—which is what classical liberal theorists such as John Locke sought to provide.

Sexual liberalism takes much of this framework for granted. It is posited on a world of rational, autonomous adults who can look after their own interests, whether in the sexual or economic marketplace. It therefore presumes that an emphasis on the free choices of consenting adults is the correct way to regulate sexual behavior. But a politics and culture based on the rights of autonomous adults cannot account for the fullness of human vulnerability and dependence.

In contrast, solidarity begins with the truth that our shared humanity is suffused with dependence and weakness. Instead of boasting that we are born free and rational, solidarity knows that we are born vulnerable and attain limited freedom and rationality only through the assistance and instruction of others. An ethos of solidarity knows not only that we are always at risk of a relapse into physical dependence but also that our mental, emotional, and relational needs make us dependent on others for fulfillment and happiness. Regardless of our consent, we often have obligations not only to refrain from harming others but also affirmatively to help them, communally or individually. By making the false ideal of independence the basis of our political and social order, we end up denigrating actual, dependent human lives.

Children in particular unsettle the ideal of liberal individualism. A system based on the free consent of independent persons overlooks the dependence of childhood. This is why Locke struggled to fit children into his system, which was based on the idea that "all men are naturally in ... a state of perfect freedom" and "equality". This natural liberty of man, in which he is subject only to the "law of nature" but not to any person, is surrendered only by his consent.[22] But children do not, and cannot, consent to the parental, social, and political authorities that care for and govern them and that are essential to their survival and well-being. Locke dealt with this difficulty by arguing that children will eventually grow to be adults who can freely opt out and leave family, community, and nation.

This approach sidesteps the problem of dependence while also ignoring our contingency—how much our ostensibly free and rational adulthood is governed by our unchosen childhood. But the gravest misstep of liberal theorizing is making the supposed natural freedom of independent adults normative—justice is defined by the ideal of the free and rational adult. This ideal is ungrounded, for autonomous adults are not self-creating, and we must account for how they come into being and are sustained.

Not attending to this reality leads to further distortions: Dependence, which is equated with subjection, becomes viewed as a temporary burden to be put up with, rather than an essential aspect of humanity that must be incorporated throughout our political and social understandings and systems.

In practice as in theory, children, pregnant women, and other dependents are inconvenient to a culture and politics of autonomous individualism. Parents in particular cannot be autonomous, for parental choices are circumscribed by the needs and well-being of their children. And these limits necessarily include sex—our sex lives ought to account for the good of children, both those already existing and those whom we might conceive. To the extent that sexual liberalism admits this truth, it is by treating children as an optional lifestyle choice, preferably undertaken as a capstone to success in other areas of life. Technology and an unregulated fertility industry even ensure that children can now be ordered like high-end consumer goods, while genetic screening and abortion ensure that defective or unwanted products are culled.

This commodification of children is another example of how, by making free and rational independence the standard for personhood, liberal individualism suggests that those who lack this autonomy might be less than fully human and therefore not entitled to the rights liberalism promises. Thus, the most dependent are sometimes entirely excluded from liberalism's legal protections. Human lives *in utero* are particularly vulnerable to this ideological unpersoning because they doubly infringe on the ideal of autonomy. Not only are the unborn completely dependent themselves, but they also decrease the independence of others, especially their mothers. Pregnancy makes women more dependent on the aid of others, as do the rigors of childbirth and caring for infants. Thus, as Erika Bachiochi explained,

> There is a deep male normativity in this autonomous body-as-property right account, and not only because the state of nature theorists from whence it came conceived of rights as limited to unencumbered and duly autonomous male citizens. After all, when a woman is pregnant, she is not physically autonomous in the way the man who sired the child is. This is the great, defining, asymmetry between men and women: women reproduce inside themselves, men outside (as Aristotle observed long ago). A man can choose then with full physical autonomy from the child he has sired whether affirmatively to enter into paternal care. Or he can just (autonomously) walk away. But a pregnant woman's body has already begun sustaining the life of the new human being before she is even aware. So to approach the kind of autonomy of a child-abandoning man, a pregnant woman must engage in a life-destroying act.[23]

In contrast to the liberal ideal of independence, babies are dependence personified, and so they are the ultimate rebuttal to attempts to root politics and culture in the ideal of autonomous individualism. Babies remind us that life is given to us, with all its particularities and inequalities. As ancient wisdom handed down from generation to generation reminds us, life isn't fair. Existence is not fair and cannot be consented to ahead of time. We are born into a world of dependence, contingency, and obligations for which we have not signed a contract. Thus, real human equality must be based not on individual autonomy but on our common dependence, finitude, and mortality. Understanding this provides the necessary foundation for human flourishing in this life, which is found through relationship

with others, rather than through an abundance of possessions, achievements, or even pleasures.

Thus, the obligations by which we are bound to others
are not without blessings of their own. Society's true beginning is not, as various liberal theorists have imagined,
a distant state of nature; rather, it is the primordial human
relations of mother, father, and child, which require us to
embrace dependence with love. It is impossible to know
when getting married or having a child just what will be
required of us, which is why wedding vows are unconditional and very different from the social contracts of liberal
political theory. Likewise, because not all the obligations
of parenting can be foreseen and agreed to in advance,
contract theory cannot encompass the unconditional obligation parenthood demands.

Liberalism postulates a world of independent, indifferent strangers negotiating with one another out of self-
interest. But the rules established to govern relations among
strangers—the liberal framework of personal autonomy,
rights claims, and market decisions—are insufficient for
the dependencies and obligations of family life. Family is
not a contract. Family requires solidarity, which abortion
destroys, both directly by violently ending unborn lives
and indirectly through the culture this enables and encourages. And when solidarity decays within family life, it will
not endure socially or politically.

This is why the sexual revolution's promises regarding
abortion have proven false. Thomson's weird hypothetical invites us to disconnect the violinist, but abortion dis-
connects all of us from the love and solidarity that enable
genuine human flourishing. The partial independence we
attain in life is reached only through the unearned aid of
others, beginning with our mothers while we were still in
the womb. Recognizing this truth about ourselves points

us toward the moral truth that the dependence of others confers moral obligations upon us, obligations that are strengthened by the proximity of need and the exclusivity of our ability to meet it. A mother must care for the child in her womb precisely because only she, and no one else, can do so.

From the perspective of undifferentiated, autonomous individualism, this is unfair. But to reject it is to reject the nature of our existence, with all its givenness and contingency, blessings and burdens, rejoicing and curses. The claim of some abortion supporters that not allowing for the bloody ending of an undesired pregnancy is slavery implies that our very existence is a form of slavery or imprisonment. The activists who equate the demands of motherhood with slavery reveal the hardness of their hearts; someone who regards life as a prison cannot be happy. Motherhood has its unique pains and labors, but it also has unique joys and delights that cannot be had otherwise.

The sources of real happiness are based in love. Abortion rejects this by denying the call to care for the other. As the political philosopher David Walsh has written, of "all the epiphanies of the person we might say that the vulnerability of the fetus is the one in which otherness is most deeply invoked". We know that the child in the womb is human, with a need and vulnerability that we understand but can see only in glimpses. These nascent human lives present us with the call to care for others in its purest form, needing everything, able to give nothing. Thus, "to the extent that we turn our back on the other in his or her most elemental state, at the very beginning, we have not simply failed in our responsibility for the other. We have undermined that very possibility of responsibility.... The fetus evokes responsibility in its most primordial form."[24] This is why abortion is, in an existential sense, a choice for hell, a closing of the self in the face of the needs of the other. Abortion's violent rejection of the responsibility to care for the other when the other is most vulnerable and needy is precisely the sort of self-imprisonment of the soul that constitutes hell.

Circumstance may mitigate the subjective guilt of an abortion, but abortion's intellectual defenders have less excuse. Attempts to define the unborn as outside the family of human persons only compound the guilt of turning away from our essential responsibility to the needs of the other. These justifications for abortion invert the injunction that ethics are prior to ontology. Our responsibility to act rightly precedes our attempted philosophical definitions of the world, but the abortion advocates arguing that the unborn are not fully human reverse this moral wisdom as they try to redefine the world in ways that eliminate our responsibility to care for human life from its beginning.

It should not surprise us that after decades of abortion on demand, which is only now being checked in some states, we live in a nation with cratering marriage and birth rates and an epidemic of deadly loneliness. Much of this is due to the ghosts in the empty cradles that haunt us. Many want to look away. It is hard for individuals and societies to admit guilt, and some will double down rather than repent. But to understand the evils that beset us, we must face the sins of abortion and of the sexual revolution it sustains. Confronting the wrongs of this way of life is essential to finding a better way to live.

The faithful Christians who have led the fight against abortion have much to offer here. Though Christian beliefs are not necessary to recognize and oppose the evil of abortion, they have provided essential moral backbone for many. And Christianity's general rejection of the sexual revolution has made it easier for Christians to see abortion for the unmitigated evil it is, rather than excusing it as a necessary evil, let alone a means of liberation.

Christianity also urges us to look at the ghosts in the cradle now, lest we confront a more dreadful possibility: looking at them later. If the dead rise again for a judgment in which all secrets are revealed, then the aborted children of this age will be waiting for us to face them. And when we look at them, what excuse could we offer? That (often-mediocre) sex lives were more important than their lives?

Lord, have mercy. Christ, have mercy.

The Abolition of Man and Woman: From Self-Creation to Castration

Casualties of the Gender Revolution

Chloe was fifteen years old when they cut off her breasts.[1] Layla Jane was only thirteen.[2] Neither girl had a physical ailment requiring such drastic surgery. Rather, they were upset by their developing female bodies and wanted to be boys instead. They have both now sued the doctors who responded to their teenage psychological distress by amputating healthy body parts. Such "treatments" have become routine as doctors operate according to the dictates of gender ideology, which teaches that children can be born into the wrong bodies—that everyone has an innate gender identity and that this interior sense of self may conflict with bodily sex. Activists insist that even very young children can know their gender identity and that if it is at odds with their bodies, children should immediately begin to "transition" (the younger the better), living according to their subjective gender identity, taking drugs to delay puberty, and eventually taking cross-sex hormones and undergoing "gender-affirming" surgeries.

The sexual revolution sought liberation from the reproductive and relational realities of our embodiment as male and female; the gender revolution that followed demands that we be freed from being male and female. The gender revolution is both a fulfillment and a negation of the sexual revolution. Treating the body as clay to be remade at will is the consummation of the sexual revolution's stripping the body of all intrinsic significance, leaving only that which is subjectively asserted. But while the sexual revolution gloried in the pleasures of the body, the gender revolution promotes disdain for one's natural body—and undergoing medical transition can impair or even eliminate sexual function.

Both revolutions regard our bodies as material with no meaning beyond our desires. Thus, we may do as we please with our bodies, with no regard for any essential nature or purpose inherent in them. If we dislike our bodies, then, as Carl Trueman pithily put it, "biology becomes a nightmare from which we have a right to be delivered."[3] And increased demands for such deliverance have moved transgenderism from a niche issue on the periphery of American consciousness to the contentious center of our politics and culture.

The controversy has intensified because of the obvious bait and switch of gender activists. The trans agenda was initially presented as, for example, being nice to Bruce when he decided to become Caitlyn, not amputating healthy body parts from children. There is a natural revulsion at the needless chemical and surgical alteration of children's bodies. Transgender activists have sought to overcome this by deploying the threat of dead kids. They insist that preventing or delaying transition, or even questioning a child's self-declared gender identity, will inflict serious psychological harm. Medical transition is defended as "life-saving" on the grounds that it prevents suicide—transition the kids before they kill themselves.[4] This was the line given to Chloe's parents, who were reluctant about her transition. As Chloe recounts, "They were told that if I wasn't allowed to transition as I pleased I would have been at risk of suicide."[5] Her concerned parents were right, and the supposed experts were wrong. Chloe's transgender identity was not the product of an innate, immutable gender identity but the result of being an awkward young girl who was too online. As she has explained,

> I didn't really get along with the other girls, and I started to wonder what exactly was setting me apart from them. I started to become a little bit insecure about this, and I also started developing some body issues.... I started using social media after I got my first phone at eleven; the first platforms I used were primarily Instagram and Snapchat. Both of those are very image-oriented, and I would see a lot of very, you could say, idealized or sexualized images of adult women and young women on there ... that I didn't really match up to.... Compared to other girls I felt like I looked like a boy, and it just felt like I couldn't really match up to other women.[6]

But there was a way out of the unrealistic expectations that our toxic culture pushes on girls: Stop being one. The social media algorithms helped deliver this message to Chloe, sending a torrent of pro-trans content at her. This dynamic, in which a poisonous environment for young women makes transition more appealing, was also present offline, exemplified by a bully groping her. Though Chloe tried to ignore this assault, the trauma pushed her further toward having her breasts removed.

Chloe's experience illuminates the sources of the surge in adolescent girls claiming trans or nonbinary gender identities. Gender ideology offers unhappy girls an explanation for, and a way out of, the awkwardness and discomfort of female adolescence—difficult times that are being made much worse by the internet. Social media ensures constant comparison to, and judgment by, what seems like the entire world. And there are also the sexual abuses and assaults that many young women suffer and the porn-fueled sexual culture many of them find repulsive.[7] No wonder these girls don't want to be female anymore. In Chloe's case, though she didn't realize it at the time, "it was actually my transition that was worsening issues that were going unaddressed, or even creating new issues." For instance, though she could now pass as male, she was still attracted to boys, which meant that "my dating pool was pretty restricted, and this was a major point of distress for me over the years.... I was really insecure about this since I had a lot of shame and I felt lonely."[8]

Transitioning had not solved Chloe's social or emotional problems, and she began to realize that it had been a mistake. She started to experiment privately with living as a young woman again: "I didn't live as a girl and I didn't have breasts anymore, but in the comfort of my room or whenever nobody was home I would ... you know I had bought some skirts and dresses and wore some of my old girl clothes in secret and my feelings about this just got worse over time, and I never really talked to anybody about it."[9] But she found the courage to speak up, first to tell her family and then to tell the world. And not only has she shared her story, but she has also amplified the voices of others hurt by gender ideology.

These stories are the ultimate rebuke to the arrogant claims of transgender activists and the medical groups they have captured. It is not just that "gender-affirming" surgery and chemicals have left Chloe with complications "years after the fact", though the high rate of complications and side effects from medical transition is a scandal. Rather, it is also that transitioning took things from her that she, as a child, could not give informed consent to. She has related how painful it was to learn that "breastfeeding is a major part of building the bond between mother and child and that that bond will later affect a child's social and emotional and cognitive development.... I realized that when I got my breasts taken away there was so much more that was taken away.... I felt like a monster."[10] But Chloe is not the monster. The monsters are those who are encouraging children to sterilize themselves chemically; the monsters are those who are profiting from amputating the healthy breasts of confused adolescent girls.

Much of Chloe's story is echoed by other female detransitioners. Kayla Lovdahl, who often uses the pseudonym Layla Jane in public, was chemically and surgically transitioned at thirteen, even younger than Chloe, and with even less screening—she claims that the process began after a mere seventy-five-minute consultation that affirmed her self-diagnosed transgender identity while ignoring her real mental health problems.[11] Her parents, like Chloe's, were told that she would be suicidal without transition. The promise of transition as a cure-all, and the threat of suicide if it were to be withheld, are routine in these cases. This focus on transition not only irreversibly harms children's bodies but also ignores the real problems they face.

In an eloquent column, Soren Aldaco, another young woman suing the doctors who medically transitioned her, explained that "social media usage, early exposure to pornography, insistent bullying, rapid-onset puberty and a history of abuse and neglect (among other things) made girlhood painful and traumatic." Encouraged by online acquaintances, she adopted a trans identity as a way of escape: "By age 18, I received a written referral for double mastectomy. By age 19, I went under the knife." Transitioning seemed to offer the affirmation and affection she craved. She wrote that the positive attention she received while transitioning "felt like night and day compared to the awkward 'othering' I was made to endure when I was perceived as an autistic, gender-nonconforming weird girl." She concluded, "I needed community. I needed love. I needed affirmation and acceptance. Trans identity was the framework through which I achieved those things." She wasn't a boy trapped in a girl's body but an awkward young woman struggling with trauma in addition to the difficulties of adolescence.[12]

Her social problems were medicalized, rather than treated on their own terms, and so they eventually caught up with her. She explained that "after a series of complications, including a botched double mastectomy, I began to question the legitimacy of my experience with gender affirming care. I had essentially traded mental anguish for physical anguish—and the mental anguish had not even subsided. Soon, I stopped taking hormones." She is now "able to accept the truth of my distress, as well as the truth of my sex and body."[13] This self-acceptance did not magically cure her problems, such as autism and social awkwardness, but it allowed her to see them more clearly and confront them in reality.

Chloe, Layla, Soren, and others like them are flesh-and-blood refutations of the medical authority and scientific expertise claimed by the transgender movement. The injured psyches of detransitioners rebut the gender ideology's assertion of compassion. Their bodily scars are marks of its fallibility, and their existence shows that the science is not settled. They are living proof that the affirmation-only approach to transgender claims is hurting people.

The courage of their testimonies is evident in the vulnerability it requires to share intimate details about their bodies, mental health, and social and even family life. The cost of telling the truth about transition includes surrendering a lot of privacy. For example, Chloe related that "after about a year or so being on testosterone I started experiencing some urinary tract side effects. I was more prone to getting UTIs [urinary tract infections] and sometimes I would even get blood clots in my urine."[14] Few adults would want to talk about this on a national stage, especially as part of a heated culture-war debate. Yet she began talking about this while still a teenage girl, barely out of high school, which in turn highlights how very young she was when the medical profession endorsed her internet-induced trans identity and began altering her healthy body through puberty blockers, testosterone, and surgery.

This radical course of childhood body modification is derived from a treatment plan known as the Dutch protocol, made famous by the medical transition of Jazz Jennings, the trans-identified reality TV child star who was born a boy but has very publicly tried to become a girl. The Dutch protocol repudiates the watchful waiting that characterized earlier approaches to treating childhood distress over being male or female. Instead, it encourages immediate affirmation of a transgender identity via social transition—name changes, wardrobe changes, using the bathrooms of the other sex at school, and so on.

The first chemical step is the off-label use of drugs to suppress puberty as soon as, or even before, it begins. Though often touted as a harmless "pause button", these drugs have side effects and risks, which even doctors pushing gender ideology will sometimes admit.[15] Inhibiting normal puberty may harm cognitive development along with the development of bone mass.[16] Furthermore, by shutting down the hypothalamus, these drugs do more than just stop puberty; they inhibit the normal capacity to feel emotions.[17] Additional dangers will likely become apparent as more children are given these drugs.[18]

The second step in the process is cross-sex hormones. For patients who have not yet gone through natural puberty, cross-sex hormones will be sterilizing—for boys, the Dutch protocol is literal chemical castration, using the drugs that are administered to sex offenders for that purpose. Older children, such as Chloe, who have already begun or completed natural puberty may skip puberty blockers or be given them only briefly before taking cross-sex hormones. In either case, there are many side effects and risks, as well as irreversible changes, such as lowering the voices of females taking testosterone or causing them to grow facial hair. And while these masculinizing effects may be welcome by trans-identifying girls, other effects of testosterone on the female body, such as vaginal atrophy, are just painful. A 2024 study found that those taking cross-sex hormones were significantly more likely to suffer from chronic pain.[19] The risks also include potentially deadly heart problems.[20] One large Danish study found that cross-sex hormones correlated with significant increases in the risks of heart disease and stroke.[21]

Surgeries are the next step in medical transition. For females, this means mastectomies and perhaps even hysterectomies, both of which are irreversible. Likewise, phalloplasty procedures, which create a pseudo-penis using tissue from elsewhere (often the forearm), and other genital surgeries cannot be fully reversed. These procedures are all medically unnecessary and carry significant risks of complications.

For males, surgical transition means castration and penile inversion, which creates an artificial "neovagina". These fake vaginas must be regularly dilated because the body will respond to them by trying to close them, as it would heal a wound—one episode of *I Am Jazz* featured Jennings' mother discussing how she once forced him to dilate. Furthermore, in cases such as Jazz's, in which the patient did not go through male puberty, the underdeveloped penis will likely not have enough tissue for the creation of a fake vagina, so material may be taken from elsewhere, such as the colon, to complete the surgical construct, which increases the already-high danger of complications.[22] In Jazz's case, "four days after the operation, Jazz experienced 'crazy pain.' It seems what surgeons call [Jazz's] 'neovagina' had split apart." Two surgeries were needed to fix this.[23] These surgeries can even be deadly; at least one young man in the Netherlands died from infection resulting from penile inversion surgery.[24]

All these surgeries are being done on children.[25] Mastectomies are the most common major surgical procedure minors receive in the cause of "gender-affirmation", but genital surgeries are also being done on minors.[26] Children who are medically transitioned without undergoing their natural puberty will never develop sexually and will remain anorgasmic for life.[27] Somehow, the sexual revolution's promise of pleasure has led to castrating children.

Surgeries are not the end of the process. The final stage is a lifetime of medical interventions and complications. Patients are subject to perpetual doses of cross-sex hormones, with all their compounding health risks. And genital surgeries in particular have high rates of complications and requisite follow-ups, which even the surgeons who do them will admit.[28] Incontinence is a common, if merely embarrassing, complication. The grim reality of how bad the sum of complications resulting from genital surgery can get was demonstrated by a Canadian man's request to be euthanized because of the pain and regret arising from his surgical transition.[29] The Canadian health care system, which has aggressively expanded its MAID (medical assistance in dying) program, denied the request, perhaps out of fear of bad publicity.

These radical physical interventions to treat psychological distress are abnormal medicine. As Jay Richards of the Heritage Foundation has pointed out, the course of medical transition, even for minors, is far more aggressive and less nuanced than the way doctors respond even to grave physical ailments such as prostate cancer, which kills tens of thousands of American men each year.[30] Despite the dangers of this disease, doctors are nonetheless careful to treat patients proportionately and not always to rush to the most extreme measures, reserving those for severe cases. Medical journals even host dueling perspectives on how aggressively to treat cases.[31]

Such caution is absent when it comes to "gender-affirming care". Its unrestrained approach is premised on the theory that transgender self-identification, including by children, arises from a stable and innate gender identity. This is the justification for gender clinics expediting the prescription of cross-sex hormones, even prescribing them on the first visit.[32] But trans identity is self-diagnosed and often unstable. Researchers who used a watchful waiting approach to children with gender dysphoria (previously labeled "gender identity disorder") reported that a majority, even a supermajority, of such cases resolved without transition if given time.[33] And that was with stringent diagnostic criteria for what constituted gender dysphoria, compared to the current explosion of influencer-induced trans self-identification.

Even many who believe that some people are truly transgender nonetheless acknowledge that false positives are a concern, particularly given the exponential increase in cases of gender dysphoria.[34] Especially among young women, this rise appears to be socially driven—aided and abetted by organizations such as Planned Parenthood, which has added gender transition to its abortion business.[35] Planned Parenthood has even prescribed cross-sex hormones to autistic patients after only a half-hour consultation with a nurse practitioner.[36]

According to a 2022 *Reuters* report, "In 2021, about 42,000 children and teens across the United States received a diagnosis of gender dysphoria, nearly triple the number in 2017."[37] Medicalized transition for children also dramatically increased, with a 2022 study suggesting that "gender reassignment surgeries being carried out on American children" had "risen 13-fold in the last decade".[38] Americans have begun to realize that children are being rushed into "gender-affirming care". Even *The New York Times* had to admit as much in a 2023 report on Jamie Reed, a whistleblower[39] from Washington University Transgender Center at St. Louis Children's Hospital.[40] As the paper acknowledged, Reed's allegations about children being rushed to transition were true.

The warning signs were there even for those who believe that some children are truly transgender. Theories about innate, immutable gender identity do not explain why entire cliques of teenage girls are suddenly declaring themselves to be transgender.[41] A more likely explanation for the increase in trans identification is suggested by a 2023 study from Finland that found that

> reporting transgender identity was associated with mother's low level of education, accumulating family life events, lack of family cohesion, perceived lack of family economic resources and female sex.... Transgender identity in adolescence is associated with socioeconomic and psychosocial family factors that are known correlates of negative outcomes in mental health and psychosocial well-being. However, transgender identification is also associated with emotional disorders independent of these family factors.[42]

In short, youth transgender identification correlates with teenagers, especially teenaged girls, having family problems and mental health struggles. Trauma and social contagion are far more plausible explanations for the transgender phenomenon than superstitious ideas about children being born into the wrong bodies.

The unstable nature of transgender identities has been illustrated even by celebrity "trans children". For example, in 2023, "Milo" of the 2016 MTV show *Transformation* suddenly released social media videos saying that she regretted her transition.[43] Similarly, buried deep in a 2023 *New York Times* story was the news that Avery Jackson, the 2017 *National Geographic* cover child for a special issue on the "gender revolution",[44] no longer identifies as a girl and now identifies as nonbinary. But Jackson has reportedly already been put through the Dutch protocol regime of puberty blockers and cross-sex hormones, presumably chemically castrating him permanently.[45] His unstable sense of gender, and the irreversible consequences of medicalizing it, demonstrate the perils of medically transitioning children.

Nonetheless, activists, especially Jackson's mother, are still using him as an example of the need for transitioning children. This stubbornness shows the personal investment the champions of "gender-affirming care", especially for children, have in the cause. Some doctors and researchers cannot admit error without discrediting themselves and destroying their careers. Parents cannot acknowledge that transitioning their children was a mistake without admitting that they catastrophically failed them.

But the youth gender revolution is not a natural development among children expressing innate identities. Rather, it is an artificial social contagion encouraged by adult ideologues indoctrinating kids—a six-year-old does not conclude on his own that a boy can have a vagina and a girl can have a penis.[46] And more than anyone else, it is detransitioners whose wounds prove the lies and folly of transgender ideology and whose courageous voices will lead the way in defeating it.

The Other Victims

Detransitioners rebut the supposed urgency of affirmation and thereby create space for other victims of gender ideology to be heard, such as the women and girls who have suffered as trans-identified men have shoved their way into female spaces.

The mantra "Trans women are women" means that female athletes have to compete against men; female prisoners have to share cells with men, including rapists and murderers; and girls and women across America are no longer able to assume that their locker rooms, bathrooms, and changing rooms are occupied only by other females. Furthermore, many of these men are sexually intact; gender ideology does not require medical transition before a man can claim to be a woman. Medical transition is somehow both essential "life-saving care" and optional. This may seem nonsensical, but it follows from divesting our bodies of all meaning and purpose: We now are whatever we identify as. In this view, it is subjective self-identity that is real and true, not our physical being. People are allowed to claim the gender identity they want, regardless of their natural bodies or how they have been modified. If someone desires bodily alterations to affirm an interior identity, then these changes are essential; but if not, they are unnecessary.

Thus, being a woman means nothing more than claiming to be a woman. The case of Lia (formerly Will) Thomas provided a high-profile example of how this results in "trans women" displacing real women. Thomas, a middling male swimmer at the University of Pennsylvania, claimed a transgender identity, began to compete against women, and started winning championships and trophies. The subsequent outcry was not just about swimming. That is to say, the reason so many people suddenly cared about collegiate women's swimming was that it was no longer women's swimming. The triumph of a male swimmer in the women's pool was national news because it showed that there are no limits to the absurdities transgender ideology will push.[47]

And the victims started to speak out, led by Kentucky swimmer Riley Gaines and Thomas' female teammates. They, along with everyone else, had been told to pretend that a hulking man was actually a woman[48] and that it was a sign of moral progress when he beat female athletes in the pool and exposed his penis to them in the locker room.[49] As one of Thomas' teammates put it, "It's definitely awkward because Lia still has male body parts and is still attracted to women."[50] When they complained, they were told to get "reeducated". As teammate Paula Scanlan told Congress, "We were expected to conform, to move over and shut up. Our feelings didn't matter. The university was gaslighting and fearmongering women to validate the feelings and identity of a male."[51] Scanlan said that she had nightmares for weeks over this invasion of her privacy.[52]

Though the trans agenda was presented as a polite fiction—playing along with a small number of distressed people who wanted to be the other sex—the supposed white lies were becoming much darker. And in this case the trans movement quickly pivoted from assuring us that such things would never happen to telling us that they are good and that we need to get used to them. One NBC writer argued that Thomas should be celebrated alongside

the likes of Jackie Robinson: "Thomas, as the first transgender athlete to win a Division I NCAA championship,
deserves to be placed among the other firsts. She should be
embraced in the history of progress that sports represent
and recognized as the trailblazer that she is."[53] According
to gender ideology, men are the best women.

The transgender invasion of women's sports takes something joyous and excellent from women. In Connecticut,
two boys competing as girls won fifteen high school track
championship titles between 2017 and 2019—titles once
held by nine different girls.[54] As displaced high school
female athlete Selina Soule, who sued over this injustice,
explained, "It's very frustrating and heartbreaking when
us girls are at the start of the race and we already know
that these [male] athletes are going to come out and win
no matter how hard you try. They took away the spots of
deserving girls, athletes ... me being included."[55]

These examples are only the tip of the iceberg of men in
women's sports. There are many more; the online feminist
magazine *Reduxx* has diligently chronicled the steady stream
of stories of men entering and often dominating women's
athletics.[56] Men pretending to be women have even com-
peted in the Olympics.[57] Meanwhile, women who protest
a male takeover of their sport have been punished.[58]

But though these athletic injustices are especially obvious, they are not the worst of what gender ideology is
doing to women and girls. When being a woman is merely
a matter of subjective identity untethered from biology,
it becomes impossible to establish safe havens for women
and girls. Every female locker room, bathroom, shelter,
prison cell, and even fifth-grade science camp cabin goes
from being presumed female-only to permitting men as
well.[59] Women's shelters such as the Downtown Hope
Center in Anchorage, Alaska, have had to go to court to

try to keep men away from the vulnerable women who have taken refuge in them.[60]

The Biden administration, along with many liberal states, adopted a policy of putting men who identify as women into women's prisons, even if these men are still physically intact and sexually functional. The old-guard corporate media has largely ignored this, but conservative outlets, alongside gender-critical feminist sites such as *Reduxx*, have reported on the influx of male criminals, including murderers and rapists, into women's facilities. Alarmingly, as Mary Harrington has observed, there is "consistent data from prisons across the Anglosphere showing around 50% of trans-identified male prisoners are sex offenders."[61]

Sexual predators disproportionately want to be housed in women's prisons—and are being granted their wishes. And transgender activists are pushing for them to be transferred to women's prisons regardless of medical transition. To be sure, trans activists believe that medical transition should be available to male prisoners. For example, the ACLU successfully sued Indiana to force the state to pay for the surgical transition of a man who had murdered a baby girl.[62] But they also believe that physical alteration is optional; it was an ACLU lawsuit that forced New Jersey to allow men to self-identify into women's prisons. The same activists who encourage children to be chemically and surgically sterilized do not insist on any such requirements before a violent, predatory man can self-identify into a women's prison.

The results have been predictably horrible. In 2021, Caroline Downey of *National Review Online* reported on alleged rapes and sexual assaults within the Washington state prison system, which houses men in female prisons.[63] The story suggested that these incidents were being covered up, presumably by prison officials eager to placate their pro-trans political overlords. And so allegations of sexual abuse by male prisoners housed with women continue,[64] which is no surprise, given that the men being transferred to Washington state women's prisons have included murderers, rapists, and pedophiles.[65] Examples include Brett David Sonia, who was found guilty of multiple rape, child abuse, and child pornography charges[66] and Jolene Charisma Starr, born Joel Thomas Nichols, who violently raped an eleven-year-old girl and tried to kidnap a nine-year-old.[67] Nonetheless, and despite at least one trans-identified man (serving a life sentence for murdering his parents) being moved back to a men's prison due to "safety concerns", Washington continues to place men in women's prisons.[68]

The same evils have unfolded in California, which also puts male prisoners who claim a female "gender identity" into women's prisons. One such man, Tremaine Carroll, was moved back to a men's prison—after he had been accused of raping two female prisoners.[69] The feminist Women's Liberation Front has filed a federal lawsuit against the state on behalf of female prisoners. As Brittany Bernstein reported, "Plaintiff Krystal Gonzalez says she was sexually assaulted by a biological male who was transferred to Central California Women's Facility under the law. According to the suit, when Gonzalez filed a complaint and requested to be housed away from men, the prison's response called her alleged attacker a 'transgender woman with a penis'."[70] Perhaps no phrase sums up gender ideology so well as "woman with a penis".

Sexual predators are using gender ideology to be housed in women's prisons from coast to coast. A New Jersey inmate, speaking to *Reduxx*, said that female inmates are "scared to death" of the males and that "we feel like we are part of some sick joke. This is a nightmare that we can't wake up from."[71] These fears are well-founded. In 2023, a female prisoner in New Jersey was reportedly badly beaten after she refused the sexual advances of a trans-identifying male prisoner.[72] This followed the 2021 rape of a female prisoner at New York's Riker's Island jail by a man who identified as transgender.[73] Despite these horrific results of gender ideology in action, activists keep pushing for men to be housed with female inmates.

Though athletics and prisons are especially acute examples, all women and girls have lost their expectation of privacy and the safety that comes with not allowing males into women's spaces. In a case that made national news, a teen girl in Virginia's Loudoun County was raped in a school bathroom by a skirt-wearing male student.[74] The rape was covered up by administrators, and the assailant was transferred to another school, where he committed another sexual assault. Letting males self-identify into girls' spaces is dangerous, especially when transgender ideologues are committed to covering up the crimes committed by sexual predators.

This was illustrated by another viral incident, this one from 2021 at Wi Spa in Los Angeles. Female patrons complained when a man exposed himself to women and girls in the women's section.[75] Yet many people denounced their complaints as transphobic or a hoax until the man was revealed as a serial sex criminal.[76] Other examples come from the American heartland, where a man was allowed to use the women's locker room at various suburban YMCAs, with one mother describing him as naked and leering at her and her teenaged daughters as they showered and changed.[77] In a Wisconsin high school in 2023, an eighteen-year-old male student allegedly showered naked next to a group of shocked freshman girls.[78] These incidents can turn violent. In Oklahoma in 2022, a male student who identified as transgender allegedly assaulted and injured two female students in a high school girls' bathroom.[79] Women and girls are being hurt as gender ideology tears down the literal barriers civilization puts in place to protect them from predatory men.

Perhaps the most overlooked victims of gender ideology are those whose lives are upended and whose hearts are broken by the transition of someone they love. There is the wife whose husband tells her that he is actually, in some mystical way, a woman and that he is now going to try to live as one. There are the children whose father is no longer willing to be their father but wants to pretend to be another mother. And there are the parents whose hearts are crushed, and whose rights are violated, by the contagion of gender ideology claiming their children.[80]

The film *Dead Name* includes the story of Bill, whose son Sean persevered through many hardships, including cancer, only to adopt a trans identity in college. Because of his medical history, physical transition would have been especially dangerous for Sean, but Bill suspects that he may have taken cross-sex hormones anyway, leading to his sudden death. And even Sean's death did not stop the wrangling over his identity. His new friends complained bitterly about the memorial service using his "dead name" rather than his new trans moniker: They considered it an insult for a father to mourn his dead son by the name he had given to him.

Parents such as Bill love their children and oppose transition because they want the best for their kids. Consider the agony of a father whose daughter suddenly, during a difficult adolescence, announces that she is actually his son; demands harmful, mutilating chemicals and surgeries; and is encouraged by her peers, the internet, and even her school to treat any disagreement as a threat.[81] This is the story of

Jay Keck, a distraught father whose autistic daughter suddenly began identifying as transgender after making a new friend with a trans identity. Her school did everything it could to affirm this new identity, keeping her parents in the dark and undermining their efforts to intervene.[82]

The trans movement's aggressive antipathy toward parents has produced horrifying results, as documented in a 2023 lawsuit filed by the parents of a young girl named Sage. The troubled young Virginia teen had adopted a transgender identity, which her school encouraged while keeping it hidden from her parents. Bullied and mentally distressed, Sage ran away and was sexually trafficked and abused. She was found and rescued in Maryland by the FBI, only for the local authorities to collude to keep her from her parents, who were seen as insufficiently affirming of her trans identity. She was instead placed in a male juvenile home, where she was sexually victimized again before running away and being trafficked again, finally being rescued in Texas.[83]

There are many other cases of government officials working to hide children's transitions from parents. In 2022, the *Daily Mail* summarized a parental-rights case brought by Florida father Wendell Perez this way: "Catholic father sues elementary school after his daughter, 12, tried to kill herself following 'months of secret meetings about her gender identity with teachers who encouraged others to call her a boy and gave her a new name behind her parents' backs.'"[84] In a similar case, Yaeli, a young woman in California, killed herself after her school secretly pushed her into a trans identity while failing to address her mental health problems.[85]

Treating parents as enemies was the inevitable result of the transgender movement's premises, which declare that children are being born into the wrong bodies and are destined for lives of misery, likely ending in suicide, if their trans identities are not socially affirmed and medically aided by radical body modification. If this were true, then parents who resist "life-saving gender-affirming care" for their children really would be ignorant at best and abusive at worst and would deserve to be treated as dangers to their children. Thus, there are intense efforts by transgender activists, especially in education and medicine, to identify "trans kids" and to push them to transition, even if this means keeping parents in the dark, lying to them, and perhaps taking their children away from them.

Not only have curricula been rewritten to teach children that they may have been born into the wrong bodies,[86] but also schools across the nation have been socially transitioning children without telling parents. In the words of one Wisconsin district's training on the matter, "Parents are not entitled to know their kids' identities. That knowledge must be earned."[87] Even worse, states such as Washington have implemented laws allowing minors to transition medically without parental approval.[88]

The assumption that teachers and school officials are experts and authorities, and are therefore due deference in such matters, was stated clearly in 2023 by Miguel Cardona, the Biden Administration's Secretary of Education. He tweeted, "Teachers know what is best for their kids because they are with them every day."[89] This is, of course, not true. Teachers are, at most, with a roomful of other people's kids for about half the days of the year, for one year of a child's life in lower grades, or for a class or two a year in the upper grades. But the narrative of teacher expertise and devotion is essential to elevating teachers over parents and to transitioning children without parental consent or even knowledge.

There is more than just arrogance and ideology at work here; transgenderism is also financially lucrative—every troubled teenage girl who identifies as trans is worth a fortune to the medical and pharmaceutical industries.[90] In 2022, right-wing commentator Matt Walsh dug into Vanderbilt's gender clinic and found a video in which Dr. Shayne Taylor "explained how she convinced Nashville to get into the gender transition game. She emphasized that it's a 'big money maker,' especially because the surgeries require a lot of 'follow ups.'"[91] Dr. Taylor was right. The U.S. market for "gender-affirming" surgeries alone was reportedly valued at 1.9 billion dollars in 2021 and was expected to grow to an estimated 5 billion by 2030.[92] The number of surgeries on children has increased dramatically, with one study focused on California suggesting a thirteen-fold increase in amputation of girls' breasts, with patients as young as twelve years old.[93] Another study, with a shorter timeframe, found that "gender-affirming surgeries" nearly tripled from 2016 to 2019, with the age range for patients again beginning at just twelve years old.[94]

Greed and gender ideology are a potent combination, and the LGBT lobby and Big Pharma have joined forces to expand "gender-affirming care".[95] Safeguards are being discarded, as demonstrated by another investigation by Walsh's team, in which his producer secured a letter approving him for surgical castration in just twenty-two minutes.[96] This illustrated that "gender-affirming care" is consumer-driven, not evidence-driven, medicine. And many doctors are happy to play along and even to try to ban alternatives—helping a troubled teenage girl feel comfortable with her body is not nearly as lucrative as turning her into a lifelong pharmaceutical client.

As *City Journal* reported in 2023 regarding Oregon Health and Science University's genital surgery practice, run by Dr. Blair Peters, "Business is booming. According to Peters, OHSU's gender surgery clinic has 'the highest volume on the West Coast,' and his robot-assisted vaginoplasty program can accommodate two patients per day. His colleague Jens Berli, who specializes in phalloplasty, boasts a 12- to 18-month waiting list for a consultation and an additional three- to six-month waiting list for a surgical appointment."[97] Minors appear to be among those receiving these irreversible procedures, which carry grave risks and do not heal any physical ailments. The corporate media has little interest in reporting on this medical scandal. Thus, though in 2023 *The New Yorker* ran a long exposé on the perils of penis-enlargement surgery, it is laughable to imagine it doing the same on the much larger transgender industry.[98]

Despite this indifference to their suffering, those harmed by gender ideology have found their voices. There are unexpected alliances, including between conservative Christians and radical feminists, as seen in the conservative Heritage Foundation hosting gender-critical feminists.[99] Female athletes are speaking out about the transgender destruction of their sports. In a 2024 echo of the Lia Thomas saga, women's collegiate volleyball was upended by controversy over a male playing for San Jose State University. Instead of women keeping quiet, there were forfeits, lawsuits, and a mass exodus of female players from the team after the season.[100] And brave reporters and writers have aggressively covered the stories that the corporate media hesitates to report on—such as male rapists and murderers in women's prisons.

Lawmakers are also standing up to the trans lobby and its profiteering medical allies, and lawyers are helping its victims demand justice in the courts—and winning. In 2023, a California school district agreed to pay a six-figure settlement to a mother whose daughter was transitioned behind her back,[101] and a judge ruled against a Wisconsin school district's policy of transitioning children without informing parents.[102] And the number of cases filed by detransitioners continues to increase, with more victims coming forward to sue the doctors who injured them, often while they were still children.[103]

Lies, Damned Lies, and Statistics

As the costs of gender ideology have become clear, trans activists and their allies have ratcheted up their fearmongering about suicide risk. They tell the public in general, and hesitant parents in particular, that the only alternative to transition is misery and suicide. Yet their own propaganda reveals the shaky basis for supposed transgender identities, especially for young children. Consider another story from Virginia's Loudoun County, which has been at the fore of conflicts over gender ideology and children. In 2021, *Loudoun Now*, a local weekly newspaper, reported on a seven-year-old girl named Sophia who had adopted a new identity as a boy named Max.[104] The narrative relied on the girl's mother, Emily—the unnamed father was almost entirely absent from the report.

The article revealed how sex-based stereotypes are often the basis for transitioning little children. We are told that as a toddler, "Sophia showed a preference for 'boy toys' and sports", though Emily "continued to offer dresses and dolls, thinking Sophia would eventually show interest". But when Sophia was only five, Emily gave up on her efforts to interest her tomboy daughter in girly-girl stuff and decided that what she really had was a transgender son. In this, Emily followed fashionable opinion, which has shifted from insisting that it is fine—even good—for girls to like sports, trucks, and other stereotypical boy stuff to declaring that such girls must really be boys. Goodbye tomboys, hello trans-boys.

The reporter provided no examples of Sophia saying that she was, or wanted to be, a boy, even though this should have been the heart of the story. Instead, the article told how Sophia, then age five, admired Max from *Stranger Things* to the point of wanting to be called Max. This was presented as a major milestone in revealing Sophia's trans identity. But that character is a girl. This was nothing more than one tomboyish little girl admiring and wanting to be like an older tomboyish girl on TV. This is a weak basis for the lifelong medicalization of a child, and Emily admitted to concerns about the future medical transition of her daughter. But she dismissed these fears by repeating word for word the mantra, "I'd rather have a trans son than a dead daughter", even though this story presented no evidence that little Sophia had ever contemplated, let alone attempted, suicide.

The specter of suicide is indispensable to the trans movement. Because there is no objective diagnosis for being transgender, nor any physical need for transition, transgenderism has to be self-authenticating, proving itself by whatever mental health benefits can be attributed to transition. This is especially so for children, who are otherwise considered unable to consent to procedures such as sterilization. This is why trans activists constantly tell parents that the alternative to transition is suicide—it is the only argument they have.

In most contexts, threatening suicide in order to get one's way is recognized as manipulative and even abusive. But it has become the go-to argument for trans activists and their allies. Parental love is turned against parental judgment so that they will approve chemically and surgically mutilating their children's healthy bodies. This pressure is necessary because "gender-affirming care" is obviously abnormal medicine. It hugely disrupts healthy bodily functions for dubious mental benefits; it is like using intense chemotherapy to treat anxiety. Responding to psychological distress over one's body with major, irreversible body modification in an attempt to mimic the opposite sex would need, at the very least, to meet an extremely high standard of evidence, especially when it comes to children.

It does not. Research in this area, especially regarding children, is often of low quality and beset by a multitude of difficulties. It is instructive to contrast the rigor, focus on measurable health improvements, and concern for patient safety seen in studies of testosterone-replacement therapy for men with the casual prescription of cross-sex hormones to minors and the sloppiness of studies on the effects. Nothing in "gender medicine" can be accurately described as "a rigorously conducted, randomized, placebo-controlled trial" the way research on testosterone-replacement therapy for men can be.[105] And yet trans activists and their allies relentlessly hype medicalized transition, including for children, as "life-saving", "evidence-based" medicine.

An example of this mendacity was provided by a study published in *The New England Journal of Medicine* in 2023. The study, blandly titled "Psychosocial Functioning in Transgender Youth after 2 Years of Hormones", reported that two subjects out of 315 committed suicide, which is a poor result for a treatment that is supposed to prevent self-harm.[106] This research should have been devastating for the transgender narrative—dead patients are not usually considered a medical success story. Nevertheless, trans activists and their allies tried to spin the results as vindication.[107] Furthermore, males in the study showed no improvements in depression and anxiety scores or "scores for life satisfaction". If giving female hormones to young men who identify as transgender does not improve their mental health, then there is no reason to keep giving female hormones to young men.

The researchers claimed to find minor mental health improvements among young women taking testosterone. But as critics pointed out, the lack of a control group made it impossible to assess whether these slight improvements resulted from other causes, such as ongoing talk therapy.[108] Additionally, the research team reported on only some of the variables they had proposed to cover, which raised suspicions that they were cherry-picking the best possible results.[109] Finally, even if these improvements in mental health were real and due to cross-sex hormones, small, possibly temporary, psychological boosts from the initial rush testosterone gives are not worth the physical toll high doses of testosterone inflict on young women.

Despite the suicides, null results for males, and marginal (at best) mental health benefits for female subjects, the researchers reported their findings as though they were positive results. And the corporate media bought it. NBC's coverage led by touting this study as proving the benefits of adolescent transition and noted the suicides and the lack of improvement among male participants only deep into the story.[110] ABC's write-up ignored the bad outcomes entirely.[111] This deliberate obscuring of bad methodology and poor outcomes exemplifies how weak studies are presented as solid scientific evidence for the benefits of transitioning children.

Systematic reviews of the research show that there is no good evidence that transition helps children. In particular, the Cass Report, commissioned by the British government and released in 2024, has put gender ideologues on the defensive.[112] The report's careful examination of the evidence destroyed the narrative that transitioning children has been proven to be a safe and effective treatment.

Rather, transitioning children is, at best, an unproven, experimental treatment with many risks and harmful side effects. There are, Dr. Cass and her team concluded, no proven benefits to transitioning children, whether socially or medically.

It is not just that the studies purporting to demonstrate the benefits of transition are often riddled with methodological flaws but that they are also beset by disqualifying conflicts of interest. The clinicians providing these procedures are also the ones writing the research papers purporting to show that they are effective. Yet people whose livelihoods and reputations depend on proving the efficacy of these procedures are the last ones who should be evaluating them. This is demonstrated by a 2024 *New York Times* report on the refusal by Dr. Johanna Olson-Kennedy, who "runs the country's largest youth gender clinic at the Children's Hospital of Los Angeles", to publish the results of a study (begun in 2015 and funded by millions of taxpayer dollars) on puberty blockers. She explained, "I do not want our work to be weaponized" and said she was "concerned the study's results could be used in court to argue that 'we shouldn't use blockers'".[113] Instead of following the evidence, Olson-Kennedy, who is being sued by a former patient who transitioned as a child, is hiding it.[114]

However, such problems are ignored when there is a narrative to sell, and a common sales technique is to bundle weak studies together to try to establish a supposed scientific consensus proving the efficacy of medical gender transition. But a pile of weak studies does not combine to provide a strong conclusion. A notable example of this tactic is seen in a 2018 *New York Times* op-ed by Nathaniel Frank, director of the What We Know Project at Cornell University, who declared, "Our findings make it indisputable that gender transition has a positive effect on transgender well-being."[115]

The basis for this assertion was a review of fifty-six studies of adults that, per Frank, "directly assessed the effect of gender transition on the mental well-being of transgender individuals". Frank asserted that the "vast majority of the studies, 93 percent, found that gender transition improved the overall well-being of transgender subjects", while the rest showed null or mixed results. He insisted that regret after transition is rare and downplayed the limitations of the research, claiming that "the quality and quantity of research on gender transition are robust, showing unmistakably that it's highly effective."[116]

That would seem to settle the matter—except that examining these studies, which I did in 2019 for *Public Discourse*, revealed a more complex picture that challenges the transgender narrative. To borrow an analogy from the classic film *My Cousin Vinny*, Frank claimed to present us with a brick wall of evidence—solid scientific study stacked on solid scientific study. But a closer look revealed a lot of cardboard painted to look like brick.

The most obvious problem was that most of these studies were small, and some were very small. Of the fifty relevant papers identified by the project, only five studies had more than three hundred subjects, while twenty-six studies had fewer than one hundred. Seventeen studies had fifty or fewer subjects, and five of those had a sample size of twenty-five or less. Smaller studies can be useful, but when a paper's findings are presented as authoritative, it matters whether it had a sample size of 2,800, 280, or 28. And yet the What We Know Project made no effort to distinguish among study types and sizes. Thus, among the studies touted as providing overwhelming scientific evidence for the efficacy of transition were a qualitative study based on interviews with eighteen subjects[117] and a study of twenty-two "transwomen" that examined the utility of occupational therapy in transition.[118] The "mounds of scholarly studies" that Frank cited included a lot of molehills.

Worse still, the five largest studies were methodologically weak. A "2014 British study" that Frank cited in his *New York Times* piece was actually "a narrative analysis of qualitative sections of a survey" from 2012 that was hosted online by SurveyMonkey and promoted throughout the UK by LGBT groups and support organizations.[119] A "narrative analysis" of parts of a self-selecting online survey disseminated by LGBT advocates is not scientifically dispositive, even if *The New York Times* permitted it to be presented as such. Another large study recruited subjects for its online survey by advertising "on online groups and discussion forums that were dedicated to FTM [female-to-male] members.... Upon survey completion, participants were entered into a lottery drawing for cash prizes."[120] A survey was also used by a study that recruited subjects online and via flyers and postcards in the San Francisco area, though in that case participants only "received a discount coupon redeemable at an Internet store".[121] Yet another study consisted of a "1-time self-report survey" completed by a "community sample of 573 transgender women with a history of sex work" who "received financial compensation for their time".[122] Paying prostitutes to take a survey does not provide results reliable enough to declare that the science is settled with regard to transgenderism.

The most rigorous of the five largest studies cited by the What We Know Project was a Swedish review of fifty years of applications for sex reassignment surgery. It found that the "regret rate defined as application for reversal of the legal gender status among those who were sex reassigned was 2.2 percent for the whole period 1960–2010".[123] Transgender activists often cite regret-rate results of this sort, but they ignore several essential points. This study's methodology probably undercounted the regret rate, as its definition of regret overlooks those who were unhappy with their transition but did not apply to reverse it. It also excludes those who succumbed to depression or addiction or who lived unhappily after transition. And this data was drawn from a population with strict pretransition screening; it is reckless to assume that the regret rate of rigorously screened Swedish adults will apply to self-diagnosed American adolescents. Worst of all, the What We Know Project did not note that a related study by some of the same researchers showed a horrifyingly high rate of suicide among its post-surgery subjects—nineteen times that of the general population.[124]

Many of the smaller studies aggregated in the What We Know project had similar problems. But whether large or small, self-selecting, self-reported, one-time surveys are more anecdotal than authoritative. They lack the reliability of representative, controlled scientific studies, and the What We Know Project seems to have intentionally elided the difference. Evaluating the effects of transition on well-being requires rigorous long-term longitudinal studies, but many of the longitudinal studies touted by the What We Know Project were crippled by low response rates as well as self-reported data. For instance, a European study of patients who had undergone surgical transition had only 62 of 107 patients participate, while 30 could not be reached and 15 refused.[125] Another European study had 201 out of 546 respond—just 37 percent.[126] In addition to these poor response rates, some follow-up studies were also extremely small, such as a sample of 12 women (out of 17) who completed a survey after breast reduction surgery.[127]

These follow-up losses make it hard to draw reliable conclusions from this research, especially given the possibility that the pool of nonparticipants is where bad outcomes are most likely to be found—not just those with regrets, but also the depressed, the addicted, the homeless, and the dead. It is reasonable to suppose (and some research suggests) that those with worse outcomes would be unreachable or uncooperative,[128] and it is reckless to ignore the low response rate of these studies when promoting them. The What We Know Project sought to overwhelm with numbers—dozens of scientific studies! But many of these studies have serious methodological flaws, and looking into them shatters the illusion of overwhelming scientific evidence in favor of transition.

These studies do not prove that transition is the best treatment for gender dysphoria, let alone that it should be the only treatment permitted. But this has not stopped activists from referring to the What We Know Project as proof that transition is safe and beneficial. A 2023 *New York Times* essay by leading transgender surgeon Marci Bowers cited it as providing overwhelming evidence for the efficacy of medical transition.[129] Similarly, in 2022 the paper published an essay arguing against screening before medical transition—if someone wants hormones or surgery, doctors should immediately break out the syringes and prep the operating room. Alex Marzano-Lesnevich of Bowdoin College asserted, "That gender-affirming health care saves lives is clear: A 2018 literature review by Cornell University concluded that 93 percent of studies found that transition improved transgender people's heath [sic] outcomes, while the remaining 7 percent found mixed or null results. Not a single study in the review concluded negative impact."[130]

These pieces are written to evoke images of careful statisticians sifting through data collected by diligent doctors. But the reality consists more of self-selected online surveys with cash prizes, studies with tiny samples, and studies missing many, sometimes most, of their subjects. Stacking these weak studies on top of one another doesn't provide a strong result, but *The New York Times* presumed readers won't check the details—the editors do not seem to have bothered to. Nor did they check Marzano-Lesnevich's claim that "gender-affirming health care has some of the lowest rates of regret in medicine."[131] Had they done so, they might have noticed not only that the 2021 review cited to support this claim had significant weaknesses but also that its authors argued against Marzano-Lesnevich's anti-gatekeeping conclusions.

Looking at the actual research papers reveals that of the twenty-seven studies used in that 2021 analysis, the review authors ranked only five as "good" and only four as having a low risk of bias.[132] Many studies had the same flaws as those examined in the What We Know Project (indeed, some studies were cited in both). Furthermore, most of the data in the 2021 review came from a single study conducted by a Dutch group retrospectively examining the records of their own gender clinic.[133] Even setting aside other limits of the data set, a retrospective review of medical files will identify regrets only from patients who shared them with the same gender clinic that performed their surgeries.

To their credit, the authors of the 2021 review discussed some of the limits and difficulties of their work, including poor evaluative tools, patients' reluctance to admit regret, and the lack of a set definition of "regret" being used across various studies. But none of these qualifications were even hinted at in the *New York Times* piece citing this review as reason to abolish all safeguards surrounding medical transition. Furthermore, even if we uncritically accepted that regret rates from transition are low, that does not support the argument that gatekeeping before medical transition is unnecessary and harmful. To the contrary, the review's authors argued that medical gatekeeping reduces regret rates.

And yet *The New York Times* allowed the review to be cited as evidence against medical gatekeeping.

Additionally, even if there were reliable research showing consistently low regret rates, that would still not justify medical transitions. In other areas of life, we recognize that someone's subjective assertion of regretting nothing does not prove that he has lived wisely and well. Many people hurtling down the road of self-destruction claim to have no regrets. Self-assessments are a weak metric by which to judge the efficacy of "gender-affirming care", especially when so many former patients do not participate.

The research does not back up the confident rhetoric of the providers of "gender-affirming care". Far from being proven, these procedures are experimental at best, and while adults might nominally be able to give informed consent to them, children cannot. This is why, after reviewing the research, more and more European nations have restricted medical transition for children. Even before the Cass Report, Britain's infamous Tavistock pediatric gender clinic had been shut down[134] and a massive medical malpractice action begun against those responsible for rushing children into transition.[135]

The push to transition children was misbegotten from the start. There were major flaws in the study that was used to establish the Dutch protocol in which children are subject to a regime of puberty blockers, followed by cross-sex hormones and surgery.[136] As a recent evaluation noted, "Three methodological biases undermine the research: (1) subject selection assured that only the most successful cases were included in the results; (2) the finding that 'resolution of gender dysphoria' was due to the reversal of the questionnaire employed; (3) concomitant psychotherapy made it impossible to separate the effects of this intervention from those of hormones and surgery."[137]

In short, everything from subject selection to data collection to untangling factors from one another was hopelessly compromised. Worse still, American gender clinics tend to ignore even the modest limits established by the Dutch researchers, such as resolving other mental health problems before beginning medical transition.

An emphasis on transition, rather than mental health treatment, may harm those struggling with gender dysphoria, who tend to self-report high rates of mental health problems. One study of American college students found that almost 80 percent of such students reported at least one mental health issue, a percentage far greater than their peers.[138] The transgender lobby's explanation for this is that people who identify as transgender are stressed because they're oppressed. A more likely cause is that gender ideology offers people with trauma and mental health problems an attractive alternative identity. Transgenderism gives them a reason for their suffering, a path to healing, and, in many cases, social and cultural affirmation.

This explains both the increase in transgender identification and its correlation with other mental health problems. This explanation also tracks much better with the data on suicide. Trans activists claim that without affirmation and transition, people who identify as trans will kill themselves in despair. These activists also claim that current rates of transgender identification are naturally occurring and are not the result of social contagion—increased rates of trans ID are due to trans people, including kids, being more aware of who they are and more comfortable coming out about it.

But if we accept these claims, then where were all the dead trans kids throughout history before current transition procedures and affirmation? As Leor Sapir noted in a 2023 piece for *City Journal*, if the transgender narrative were true, "we would expect to have seen an epidemic of suicides among gender-distressed teenagers before 'gender affirming' drugs and surgeries first became available 15 years ago. Yet no evidence of such an epidemic exists. Indeed, rates of suicidal behavior among youth have increased since 2011."[139] The obvious truth is that either trans activists are wrong about the naturalness of current rates of trans identification or they are wrong about the inevitability of self-harm without transition.

Indeed, because there is a well-known contagion effect to youth suicides, promoting the transgender suicide narrative may actually increase the likelihood of children killing themselves. The case of Isabelle Ayala, another young woman suing those who medically transitioned her, provides an example. As the *New York Post* reported, "She learned from trans activists that fabricating suicidal ideation is a surefire way to get a testosterone prescription quickly. So, at age 14 she did just that: 'I learned that from the internet that ... I had to convince [my doctors and family] that if they don't affirm me, I'm gonna kill myself.' "[140]

At least one psychologist has encouraged such threats of suicide. In 2019, Canadian doctor Wallace Wong told an audience, "So what you need is, you know what? Pull a stunt. Suicide, every time, [then] they will give you what you need." Wong added that kids with gender dysphoria "learn that. They learn it very fast."[141] Another doctor was caught on video at a medical conference in 2022 glorifying a trans-identified teen's suicide. Dr. Morissa Ladinsky, of the University of Alabama at Birmingham, praised an Ohio seventeen-year-old who "stepped boldly in front of a tractor trailer", leaving a suicide note that "went viral, literally around the world".[142]

The claim that medical transition is "life-saving, evidence-based medicine" is not true. The more one digs through the research on transition, the weaker the evidence for it appears, especially when compared to actual rigorous medical studies. This is why systematic reviews such as the Cass Report are concluding that there is no good evidence that transitioning children, in particular, is beneficial to them. But the activists who have dedicated their lives to gender ideology, along with the medical profiteers who make their livings from it, are clearly willing to encourage troubled children to take themselves hostage in order to keep advancing the trans agenda.

Of Intimidation and Castration

The transgender suicide narrative exemplifies gender ideology's reliance on intimidation and emotional blackmail. It has to use these tactics because it demands that we believe the ridiculous and impossible. Pretending that a man can become a woman (or, in some mystical internal sense, already is a woman) requires ignoring the lived reality we all experience. Yet this is what we are told to do as our culture continues to follow the logic of the sexual revolution into the gender revolution. For example, we are instructed to believe not only that the actress Ellen Page is now the actor Elliot Page but also that this has always been so in some metaphysical sense.[143] The Wikipedia and IMDb pages must be rewritten, along with credits on past films—what of the Oscar nomination for Best Actress?—and even the once-proud lesbianism of Ellen Page must be erased or converted into a generic "queerness" to serve the new narrative of Elliot Page.[144]

This might be dismissed as one more bit of celebrity lunacy, but it has powerful corporate and media interests behind it. From the Oscars to ESPN, from Wall Street to Silicon Valley, the transgender movement has sought to silence all opposition. Sometimes this is overt, as when Amazon banned Ryan Anderson's book *When Harry Became Sally*,[145] when Target pulled Abigail Shrier's *Irreversible Damage* from its shelves,[146] and when Vimeo took down the documentary *Dead Name*.[147] Likewise, there are a multitude of speech restrictions enforcing transgender dogmas on most social media platforms. Furthermore, from teachers to coaches to transit workers, many people have been punished[148] and had their livelihoods threatened[149] for questioning[150] gender ideology. Dr. Allan Josephson, a child psychology professor pushed out of his position at the University of Louisville for questioning gender ideology, is just one example.[151] People have gotten the message, and many from the academy to the C-suite to the union hall have been intimidated into silence.

Similarly, research that does not reach pro-transition conclusions is ignored, if it is published at all. For example, a 2022 study using records from the U.S. military health care system found that about 30 percent of patients who went on cross-sex hormones stopped taking them within four years.[152] A 2021 study, also using data from the military health care system, found that there were no mental health improvements after beginning cross-sex hormones and that there was actually an increase in prescriptions of psychotropic medications.[153] These studies were not trumpeted by corporate media.

On the rare instances that legacy media outlets such as *The New York Times* have published pieces questioning transgender orthodoxy, there has been immediate pushback, led by the heavy hitters of the LGBT movement, such as the Human Rights Campaign. The pattern was established in 2018, when liberal writer Jesse Singal was assailed for raising the problem of false positives in *The Atlantic*.[154] Singal's mild suggestion that not all children

who claim to be transgender are actually transgender pro-
voked ferocious backlash that cowed the magazine into
running a series of responses.[155]

The goal of this intimidation is to keep critical views
and information from breaking through into public awareness. And so insightful and moving first-person accounts of
transition and detransition tend to be confined to conservative or nontraditional outlets.[156] Likewise, worries from
doctors (such as Canadian doctor Susan Bradley, an early
leader in treating childhood gender dysphoria) that child
transition has gotten out of control are largely relegated
to conservative media.[157] Even cautions from people with
impeccable pro-trans credentials struggle to get traction in
national corporate media outlets. For example, the concerns of trans-identified gender-medicine psychologist
Erica Anderson were published in the opinion section of
a San Francisco paper.[158] Likewise, an interview in which
Anderson and Marci Bowers expressed worries about rushing children into transition was published on Substack.[159]

Trans activists are vicious to researchers who do not toe
the latest party line. For example, Canadian psychologist
Kenneth Zucker, the leader of a gender identity clinic,
was fired when trans activists smeared him.[160] Zucker supported transitioning children in some cases, but he was more
cautious about it than activists wanted. He was eventually
vindicated in court and received a large settlement, but
attacking him still sent a warning to any researchers who
are seen as insufficiently pro-trans.[161] Similarly, Lisa Littman, whose qualitative research identified the phenomenon
of rapid-onset gender dysphoria,[162] was vilified[163] and lost a
consulting position.[164] Yet for all the fury, her observation
that some children are suddenly, and without prior signs,
falling into gender dysphoria is obviously correct, and the
efforts to rebut it have been junk science.[165]

Trans activists are also eager to use the coercive power of civil rights laws to enforce their ideology. They want to hijack the state power used to break segregation and deploy it to force Americans to pretend that men are women. Some states, such as Washington, have even banned using talk therapy to help reconcile people to their natural bodies, preventing counselors like Brian Tingley, who sued the state in response, from helping clients become comfortable with their natural bodies or talking through the process of detransitioning.[166]

Yet these schemes to shut down alternatives to transitioning and to intimidate and smear critics—even when they are very pro-trans writers and doctors offering very mild critiques—cannot conceal the truth that gender ideology is medically fraudulent and that it draws from dark and perverse places.

This is evident in a string of revelations about WPATH, the World Professional Association for Transgender Health. This group billed itself as the leading medical authority on transgender issues—and many regarded it as such. In particular, WPATH's standards of care were treated as authoritative by many major medical groups that did not bother with any real study or debate of their own. But WPATH has been exposed as an activist fraud rather than a serious medical organization. The publication of the so-called WPATH Files[167] showed WPATH doctors privately admitting (among other things) that they could not get informed consent from children and that transition procedures come with a host of potentially severe, even deadly, side effects, such as cancer.[168]

Worse still was the 2024 revelation that Biden administration officials, led by Rachel Levine (a man pretending to be a woman), successfully pressured WPATH to eliminate any recommended age restrictions for medical transition procedures. The reasons for this were explicitly political and legal, rather than medical.[169] If WPATH recommended age limits, it would support the many state legislatures enacting laws restricting transition procedures on minors, and it would undermine WPATH-supported lawsuits against these laws.[170]

It was also discovered that WPATH tried to censor and suppress[171] a report it commissioned from outside experts when they did not find any good evidence for the benefits of transitioning children.[172] Not only did WPATH squelch this finding, but it also made a point of claiming that transition is "medically necessary" so that these procedures would be covered by insurance.[173]

Most grotesque was WPATH's declaration that "eunuch" is a valid gender identity,[174] a decision reached, in part, by relying[175] on online forums filled with violent fantasies of child sexual abuse.[176] Not only did WPATH add "eunuch" as a new type of gender identity potentially requiring surgical "affirmation", but it did so in collaboration with people who fantasize about raping and castrating children. As *Reduxx* reported when the draft guidelines were released, the section on eunuchs "refers extensively to research collected from a hardcore fetish site called the Eunuch Archives—a site that features child sexual exploitation fantasies centered around stopping little boys from going through puberty".[177] Many men with a eunuch fetish are aroused at the idea of others, including children, being castrated. As *Reduxx* discovered in examining this website, many of the site's stories

> focus on the eroticization of child castration.... Children may be forcibly castrated under extreme duress. Some narratives contain violent sexualized depictions of children with stunted puberty being raped by doctors, written in

sickening detail.... Within the protected fiction archives, there were over 3,000 stories involving minors, including the explicit sexual abuse of children, and "minor" was a specially-curated tag that users could select to easily access stories specifically featuring children.

The fictional pornography includes themes such as Nazi doctors castrating children, baby boys being fed milk with estrogen in order to be violently sex trafficked as adolescents, and pedophilic fantasies of children who have been castrated to halt their puberty, "freezing" them in a childlike state.[178]

Reduxx also learned that prominent members of this site are academics with connections to WPATH and that they have published "research" based on the site.[179] Their work includes "academic research justifying the pedophilic fantasies amongst castration fetishists. In a 2015 paper titled 'The Sexual Side of Castration Narratives,' fictional child sexual abuse material was called 'therapeutic' and helpful for those with eunuch ideations."[180] *Reduxx*'s reporting was released while the 2022 WPATH guidelines were in draft form, yet the organization went ahead with its addition of "eunuch identity" anyway.[181] All this should have induced reconsideration of WPATH's prominent place as a supposed medical authority, but the corporate media, academia, major medical organizations, and government officials continued to treat WPATH as the respectable arbiter of issues of gender identity and transition, even though parts of WPATH's standards of care were written by someone who also wrote child sex-abuse fantasies.[182]

These revelations about WPATH demonstrate the hollowness of the claim that there is an evidence-based medical consensus in favor of transition. The doctors of America (let alone of the world) did not get together, carefully study the matter, and conclude that gender ideology—now with eunuchs!—was good medicine. Rather, they and their institutions have proven unable to resist their most radical activist members, who were, naturally, the most outspoken and the most eager to sit on the relevant committees. Bureaucracy belongs to those who show up, and everyone from the medical establishment to the legacy media refused to challenge WPATH, even after the group decided that "eunuch" was a valid gender identity that required a surgeon, rather than a psychiatrist.

At least one surgeon was eager to cash in on this market. Sidhbh Gallagher, a Miami doctor[183] who had aggressively[184] used social media to promote[185] the hundreds of "gender-affirming" surgeries she performs each year (including on children),[186] posted a video about her eagerness to castrate men who identify as eunuchs. As she explained, eunuchs are just "a group of gender-diverse individuals", albeit one that has not "been very visible". She appealed to the new WPATH guidelines, pointing out that "there is an entire chapter devoted to these folks in the most recent version of the WPATH standards of care."[187]

As gender ideology sinks to bizarre new depths, of which the lady who wants to get into the eunuch business is just a particularly vivid example, its evils become harder to overlook. Thankfully, there are signs that the wall of intimidation and censorship may be cracking. For example, in a 2022 piece in *The New York Times*, columnist Pamela Paul denounced the crude stereotypes that inform transgender ideology (for example, a girl who likes short haircuts and playing with trucks is really a boy).[188] If this example is taken alongside the paper's reporting that same year on the risks of puberty blockers[189] and the problems of men in women's sports,[190] we can see that there may be a permission structure developing that allows challenges to transgender orthodoxy, especially regarding children. In 2023 the paper even published a story about schools that hide children's gender transitions from their parents.[191] Despite scrupulously observing the pronoun pieties of gender ideology, the piece was surprisingly evenhanded and even sympathetic toward the parents it featured.

Similarly, in 2023 *The Atlantic* published a piece headlined "Take Detransitioners Seriously".[192] Despite extensive pro-transition throat clearing, the article not only conceded that detransitioners are real but also confessed that many of the studies cited to dismiss them are weak or inapplicable to current debates. As the authors admitted, "Data are relatively scarce, and anyway the cultural context for trans people has since evolved so much and so quickly that older studies may not adequately predict outcomes for today's ... population." That is to say, studies of carefully screened European adults do not apply to essentially unscreened American adolescents. The authors of the *Atlantic* piece added that the "existing research has major gaps" and concluded that "ultimately, nothing is certain from these data except that more information is necessary." By the end of 2024, *The Atlantic* was even willing to run a piece with the headline "The Push for Puberty Blockers Got Ahead of the Research".[193] Now they tell us.

Such pieces offer hope that the information bubble might be popping, but, as noted earlier, they have faced aggressive pushback as the LGBT movement seeks to maintain the transgender narrative. These activists are aided by many people who are in too deep to back down, a situation that may be personal as well as political. Accepting the reality and importance of our embodiment as male and female would challenge more than gender ideology; it would threaten the entire sexual revolution and the culture it has created. The connection between gender ideology and the various strands of sexual and cultural radicalism was conceded by Lydia Polgreen, who, in the middle of a pro-trans rant in *The New York Times*, wrote, "Trans rights, much like abortion, present a profound challenge to the gender binary, which upholds the world's oldest and most persistent hierarchy. People who don't want to or cannot fit within their traditionally prescribed roles—mother, father, woman, man, boy, girl—increasingly have the freedom to live their lives beyond those circumscribed identities."[194]

As this shows, at the heart of gender ideology is a hatred of our embodied existence as male and female, husband and wife, son and daughter. The difference between the sexes, which is how we all came into being, is viewed as hierarchical and oppressive and therefore as something that must be overcome. The natural, healthy functioning of our bodies is perceived as an enemy to be conquered, whether through the violence of abortion or the chemical and surgical alterations of medical transition. The sexual revolution's freedom to enjoy bodily pleasure has become a freedom to alter our bodies at our pleasure—human desire is to be unimpeded, regardless of how disordered or bizarre it may be. Instead of the discipline of self-control, there is technological control to remake ourselves. This worldview regards the body as, in Mary Harrington's evocative phrase, a "Meat Lego" to be not only used but also deconstructed and reassembled at will.[195] It is a revolt against human nature, and rolling it back will require more than just rejecting new aberrations such as "eunuch identity".

Heresies of the Body

The gender revolution regards the givenness of our bodies as imprisoning and longs for them to be as malleable as digital avatars. This is what unifies the otherwise-incompatible claims of gender ideology. It is intellectually incoherent:

Gender is socially constructed, but gender identity is so intrinsic and immutable that bodies must be remade to better match it—but sometimes gender identities are fluid. Yet there is a consistency to these otherwise conflicting ideas, insofar as they are rooted in the belief that our desires are the essence of our most authentic self. Thus, if this undefined self wants a different body, it is the responsibility of medicine to oblige as best as it can and the duty of the rest of us to affirm this subjective sense of self as real.

A 2022 *Vox* article demonstrated this belief that the natural, healthy body may be a prison of the true self. Written by transgender activist Emily St. James, the piece aggressively defended transitioning children by imploring readers to "stop worrying about what happens if we let kids transition. Worry about what happens if we don't." St. James claimed that when it comes to puberty, "for a trans person, the changes dictated by the body they were born into might prove incredibly painful, destabilizing, or even life-threatening."[196] The presumption is that our authentic self is a gendered but immaterial entity that can somehow end up in the wrong body and that in such cases the natural and healthy processes of physically maturing are the enemy of this true self.

This belief is rarely explained but routinely presumed. This implicit body/soul dualism of transgender doctrine is far beyond the bounds of what science can determine. It is a spiritual claim, though it is rarely acknowledged as such. Rather, its adherents ignore the massive theological and philosophical work needed to support their claims about a disembodied self that is at war with the body. Theirs is a faith that dare not admit itself as such.

For instance, the *Vox* article opened with an anecdote about a young man distressed by puberty: "When Mae Sallean was a teenager, her body and mind began to slip away from each other. Her body and face began to sprout thick hair, her voice dropped, and she felt dissociated from her physical form." This framing of mind versus body persists through the piece, but the nature of this division is left mysterious, never addressed beyond a complaint about a world that "cannot conceive of a self that doesn't begin from the body".[197] We are told just to accept that such an incorporeal self exists with a gender identity that can diverge from bodily sex, that this mismatch is knowable early in life, and that it should be resolved by drastic and irreversible bodily modification. These are not scientific assertions; rather, they are mystical claims that must be taken on faith. The author did not even attempt to make the argument that transgender identities arise from having a "girl brain in a boy body" or vice versa—a claim that is made by some trans activists, such as Jazz Jennings, but that is medically unsupported. This is why, instead of transgender identities being objectively detected by CT scans or MRIs, they are subjective and self-diagnosed.

Gender ideology's metaphysical incoherence was also evident in a 2024 *New York Times* piece by Jack Turban, a California psychiatrist who has made a career of promoting and participating in the medical transition of children. Turban wrote that "the most basic part of gender identity is what I call our transcendent sense of gender. In a way that goes beyond language, people often just *feel* male or female." He added, "As is the case with many emotions, it's hard to describe this transcendent feeling in words. But it is the foundation of our gender identity, the scaffolding we're born with." This belief in an insubstantial gender identity is mystical, not medical. Turban tried to argue that research "suggests these transcendent gender feelings have a strong innate biological basis", but the closest the research he cited came to demonstrating such a "biological basis" for a "transcendent feeling" was mere speculation about possible genetic sources for transgender identities.[198]

Turban further undermined his theory of transcendent (but somehow also biologically based) innate gender identities when he turned to social life. He claimed that "as we move through life, we build on the biology of gender identity with language and social experience, influenced by everything from the TV shows we watch to how we interact with classmates and our families." Apparently it is now permissible to say that "gender identity" can be socially influenced. Indeed, Turban admitted that "these feelings can evolve over time—the way an 18-year-old college student thinks about her womanhood is likely different from how she thinks about it when she becomes a 40-year-old mother of three."[199] Well, yes. The unstable nature of childhood feelings and identities is part of why Turban's career of medically transitioning children is wicked.

There is no sound basis for transgender identities, for either children or adults. To plead a metaphysical cause (i.e., gendered souls stuck in the wrong body) turns the discussion into a religious debate that trans activists are ill-equipped for. To plead a physiological cause (i.e., gendered brains stuck in the wrong body) or psychological cause invites solutions focused on reconciling minds to bodies, rather than modifying bodies into a facsimile of the other sex. Nor, despite the claims of transgender activists, do the various "differences of sexual development" that are grouped together as "intersex" explain transgenderism. They are unfortunate disorders that do not constitute a genuine third sex, let alone justify modifying healthy bodies into a (often poor) semblance of the other sex.

Rather than defining and defending their mystical claims about the true nature of the self, trans activists and their allies have attempted to support their beliefs by demonstrating that transition leads to human happiness. This is why so much effort is devoted to manufacturing evidence showing that transition reduces suicide and generally improves patients' well-being—science can, in principle, show that transition helps, regardless of the metaphysical details. But examining the evidence shows that it does not justify transition, especially for children who are incapable of informed consent.

Indeed, the *Vox* piece reveals that the push to transition children is driven in large part by unhappy adults. The author references the "many trans people, who despair that they were kept from transitioning as youths" and later cites a survey of "trans women at all stages of life who did not transition as young people. The picture ... of these women in middle and old age is deeply sad."[200] Yes, it is, but the problem is not that these men transitioned too late but that they are living a lie by pretending to be women. Transitioning earlier would not have made the lie true, even if it made the physical pretense more believable.

There is no simple, uniform reason for why some people feel acute distress regarding their bodies and desire to be the other sex. Rather, the causes appear to be varied and sometimes complex.[201] This variance makes sense; we should not expect the reasons a young boy wants to be a girl to be the same as those of a middle-aged man who wants to be a woman, or for either to have the same basis as an adolescent girl's desire to be a boy.

Despite its diversity of sources and expressions, transgenderism has coalesced into an aggressive ideology that insists on a right to define ourselves even against our own natural bodies. Transgenderism admits the reality of sex— otherwise, there would be nothing to *transition* from or toward—even as it works to efface it. Embodiment is seen as imprisoning, and healthy bodies are declared to be "wrong" and treated as mere material to be mastered and reshaped. In this, the gender revolution adheres to the core of the sexual revolution, which is hatred for the limitations of our embodied existence, whether limits on our sexual appetites that are necessary for relational flourishing and social justice or the realities of male and female embodiment.

The absurdities that transgender ideology foists upon its adherents (such as saying "birthing parent" instead of "mother") are meant to repress the reality of embodiment in favor of a spurious sense of self-creation. This results in all manner of absurdities. For example, Gender Spectrum, a major gender identity educational group, has promoted the notion of endless varieties of gender identity, including identification with animals and even with inanimate objects such as rocks or the moon.[202] And these increasingly bizarre ideas are making their way into medicine, as some clinicians rush to affirm all manner of strange gender claims, such as the idea that children can be "gender hybrids"—examples of which include changing gender by season, or being a boy on top and a girl on bottom.[203]

These fantasies are distinct from anything so mundane (even if wrong) as the idea of a boy's brain in a girl's body, but they were always latent in the claims of transgenderism. No amount of social transition, hormones, or even surgical amputation and alteration will change the physical reality of one's sex. Trans-identified persons must therefore define themselves by something they can never be. For a man to claim to become a woman is an annihilation of the reality of womanhood. Given this, it was not such a leap from transgenderism to an endless variety of gender identities expressed in ever-more esoteric pronouns, pursued through ever-more experimental surgeries.

But to try to create a gender identity at odds with one's physical sex is to have civil war always raging within oneself as a dominant passion tyrannizes over one's body and soul. It is also to be at war with the world, if one attempts to force others to affirm one's subjective identity as objective fact. This culminates in a self-worshiping ideal of self-creation—we are whatever we decide to be. This principle was illustrated by a 2024 cover story for *New York Magazine* in which the trans-identified writer Andrea Long Chu declared that "the belief that we have a moral duty to accept reality just because it is real is, I think, a fine definition of nihilism."[204]

This may seem mad, but madness often has a perverse inner logic. Chu sought to skip all the debate over the medical harms or benefits of transition and instead establish a right to physical self-determination and modification, even for children. He feared that subjecting the transgender movement to evidence-based scrutiny would restrict and ultimately destroy it. Instead, he suggested that transgender activists and their allies "stop relying on the increasingly metaphysical concept of gender identity to justify sex-changing care, as if such care were only permissible when one's biological sex does not match the serial number engraved on one's soul. . . . We must rid ourselves of the idea that any necessary relationship exists between sex and gender; this prepares us to claim that the freedom to bring sex and gender into whatever relation one chooses is a basic human right."[205]

He thereby made explicit what has always been the position of gender ideologues, which is that there should be medical transition on demand for everyone. He insisted that "we must be prepared to defend the idea that, in principle, everyone should have access to sex-changing medical care, regardless of age, gender identity, social environment, or psychiatric history."[206] This is not about medical need but about a subjective desire to flee from the reality of one's embodied self. Chu argued not that children are being born into the wrong bodies but that there is no such thing as a right or wrong body outside of human desire.

In response to the inconsistencies of gender ideology and the lack of evidence showing that transition improves well-being, Chu insisted on the primacy of unfettered human will as the basis for a right to bodily modification for whatever reason—and without regard for the results. This view does not deny the biology of sex but regards it as an enemy to be subdued and made subject to our whims. Chu even admitted that this approach "does not promise happiness. Nor should it.... If we are to recognize the rights of trans kids, we will also have to accept that, like us, they have a right to the hazards of their own free will."[207] This might seem reasonable to Chu, but it is madness to anyone who cares about children and their well-being. Good parenting requires a great deal of limiting children's free will and the hazards it exposes them to.

Chu was extending to children an argument he had already made about himself. In a 2018 *New York Times* piece shortly before he underwent genital surgery, he wrote, "This is what I want, but there is no guarantee it will make me happier. In fact, I don't expect it to. That shouldn't disqualify me from getting it."[208] This despair was perhaps to be expected, given that Chu's desire to transition was, by his own account, driven by fetishes induced by a porn addiction.[209] For all his appeals to free will, his own will was enslaved to a tyrannical desire. No wonder he claimed that the "surgery's only prerequisite should be a simple demonstration of want" and that "no amount of pain, anticipated or continuing, justifies its withholding." But as Ryan Anderson observed, this is not only bad for Chu; it also perverts medicine by treating doctors as mere technicians, paid to deliver the services the customer demands, regardless of whether the procedures help the patient.[210]

Thus, Chu reveals the real heart of gender ideology, which is not medicine but revolt. Chu insisted that "trans kids ... do not owe us an explanation. They are busy taking charge of their own creation. They may not change the world, but they will certainly change *themselves*."[211] Gender ideology despises the givenness of our existence and longs for the godlike but unattainable power of self-creation.

It is difficult to reason with a revolt against reality itself. What can be shown is that it is immiserating. A way of life that rejects happiness, health, and well-being in pursuit of an impossible rebellion against the very nature of our existence is self-refuting. The despair of gender ideology is due not to insufficient affirmation but to the fact that no amount of affirmation and bodily modification can change the reality of our embodiment as men and women.

To be at peace with ourselves and the world, we must recognize that we are finite, dependent creatures who cannot change our nature as male and female. And Christians have a particular responsibility to provide a true account of our nature to a culture that has lost its sense of what it means to be a man or a woman. Christianity insists that our bodies matter and resists the rebellion of gender ideology because it is incompatible with the essential doctrines of creation, incarnation, and resurrection.

Our embodiment is part of the natural, good order created by God, who made us male and female to fulfill His purposes for His glory. Scripture is insistent, consistent, and persistent on the essential distinction between male and female. Indeed, the sexual dimorphism of humanity is indispensable to fulfilling the first commandment given in Genesis, to "be fruitful and multiply, and fill the earth and subdue it" (1:28). The male or female nature of healthy human bodies is part of the created order, and it is integral to the Christian understanding of everything from family and sexuality to Church leadership.

What is more, Christians worship a God who became incarnate, with a fully human male body. John's Gospel opens with the astounding doctrine of the Incarnation, declaring that the Word (*logos*) became flesh (*sarx*), a shocking idea to ancient philosophy. The physical reality of Jesus' body is central to the Christian faith. After all, if our bodies are not essential to who we really are, then why was it necessary for Jesus to become incarnate and physically die? The Incarnation is the basis for the assurance in Colossians that "you, who once were estranged and hostile in mind, doing evil deeds, he has now reconciled in his body of flesh by his death, in order to present you holy and blameless and irreproachable" (1:21–22). Without the Incarnation, there is no salvation. In the words of the Nicene Creed, we believe of Jesus that "for us men and for our salvation he came down from heaven, and by the Holy Spirit was incarnate of the Virgin Mary, and became man. For our sake he was crucified under Pontius Pilate, he suffered death and was buried, and rose again on the third day." Physical bodies matter because it is the physical suffering and death of Jesus that frees us from suffering and death.

Of course, the suffering and death of Jesus was followed by the Resurrection, and the doctrine of the Resurrection is also critical to how we understand the body. The Gospels emphasize the physical Resurrection of Jesus. For example, Luke records that when Jesus appeared to the disciples, "they were startled and frightened, and supposed that they saw a spirit." Jesus replied by saying, "See my hands and my feet, that it is I myself; handle me, and see; for a spirit has not flesh and bones as you see that I have" (Lk 24:37, 39). He then pointedly ate in front of them.

Christianity preaches the physical resurrection of the dead to a glorified life everlasting, not just an ethereal heaven for souls. As the Apostle Paul explained to the Corinthians, without the physical Resurrection of the incarnate Christ, our hope is in vain.

If Christ is preached as raised from the dead, how can some of you say that there is no resurrection of the dead? But if there is no resurrection of the dead, then Christ has not been raised; if Christ has not been raised, then our preaching is in vain and your faith is in vain. We are even found to be misrepresenting God, because we testified of God that he raised Christ, whom he did not raise if it is true that the dead are not raised. For if the dead are not raised, then Christ has not been raised. If Christ has not been raised, your faith is futile and you are still in your sins. Then those also who have fallen asleep in Christ have perished. If for this life only we have hoped in Christ, we are of all men most to be pitied.

But in fact Christ has been raised from the dead, the first fruits of those who have fallen asleep ...

The dead will be raised imperishable, and we shall be changed. For this perishable nature must put on the imperishable, and this mortal nature must put on immortality. (1 Cor 15:12–20, 52–53)

The ancient creeds conclude by attesting to this hope. The Nicene Creed declares, "I look forward to the resurrection of the dead and the life of the world to come", and the Apostles' Creed proclaims belief in "the resurrection of the body, and the life everlasting".

But if we can be born in the "wrong" body (a body that is not just damaged or diseased but "wrong", even if fully healthy), then what does that mean for the resurrection of the body? Denying that the body is essential to what it is to be human suggests that there is no physical resurrection or that instead of our bodies, healed and glorified, this resurrection might be to someone else's body. But Christians do not believe that our bodies are meat puppets driven around by souls that are our true selves; rather, our bodies are intrinsic to our full humanity. We are body and soul.

To deny this is to repudiate the goodness of God's order of creation, the indispensability of the Incarnation, and the hope of the resurrection. And so the doctrines of gender ideology, which treat the body as accidental material in which we are imprisoned and that ought to be reshaped on a whim, are intrinsically opposed to Christian orthodoxy.

However, rejecting gender ideology does not obviate the need to reckon with gender. Gender, as Ryan Anderson has observed, is "how we give social expression" to the "bodily, biological reality" of sex. Thus, gender "properly understood is a social manifestation of human nature.... Human beings are creatures of nature and of culture, but a healthy culture does not attempt to erase our nature as male or female embodied beings."[212] We are stuck with gender because we are our bodies. Masculinity and femininity derive from the reality of male and female, and so we must learn how to live together as men and women in marriage, family, and community. A right understanding of gender cannot be unduly rigid, but neither can it be separated from our physical embodiment.

Thus, the issue is not whether to have gender but whether it will be rightly ordered based on a true understanding of our nature as male and female, or whether it is to be abstracted away into an identity disassociated from the physical reality from which it develops. Getting gender right is difficult, and, as with everything human, some failure is inevitable. But we cannot avoid the responsibility to help men and women grow and flourish as men and women, which cannot be reduced to mere performative social roles and identities. There is no getting away from our embodiment. Attempting to do so results in a war against ourselves, for try as we might, we cannot abolish man and woman.

4

The Wrongs of Gay Rights

The Slope Was Slippery

In 2001 *The Onion* ran the article "Gay-Pride Parade Sets Mainstream Acceptance of Gays Back 50 Years." The satirical piece gleefully imagined lewd displays and the horrified reactions of onlookers: "After this terrifying spectacle, I don't want them teaching my kids or living in my neighborhood."[1] Twenty years later, a *Washington Post* headline declared, "Yes, Kink Belongs at Pride. And I Want My Kids to See It."

The slope really was slippery.

There was public indecency at Pride events in 2001, of course, but it was not praised in national newspapers as important childhood viewing. But by 2021, *The Washington Post* was willing to run a piece arguing that "children who witness kink culture are reassured that alternative experiences of sexuality and expression are valid.... We don't talk to our children enough about pursuing sex to fulfill carnal needs that delight and captivate us in the moment."[2] Pushing kink and hedonism on children was not part of the gay-rights PR pitch, but it was implicit in its radical premises.

The sudden dominance of gender ideology is another example of the steep incline and low friction of the cultural slope. For years, the T was the quiet hanger-on as the LGB movement ascended to victory, but after the *Obergefell* decision in which the Supreme Court invented a constitutional right to same-sex marriage, trans became the next big thing. The momentum of the gay-rights movement, and the commitments many people had to it, made it hard to say no to the dogmas of gender ideology, even though they were absurd. For example, Elizabeth Spiers, a writer for *Slate* and *The New York Times*, tweeted, "I've never boxed in my life but if I did I'd be fine with boxing a trans woman in my weight class."[3] It is easy to believe that she has never boxed, but there is more than ignorance at work here. People such as Spiers will say and believe anything as they scramble to keep up with the supposed right side of history.

As LGBT activists keep pushing the envelope, they undermine the narrative that carried their movement to victory. The gay-rights agenda succeeded by downplaying its liberationist side in favor of a nonthreatening normalcy. How, its advocates asked, would your neighbor's same-sex marriage harm you and your family? Furthermore, why should those with same-sex attractions be excluded from all the goods of marriage and family life that conservatives otherwise praise? After all, love is love, and gay people just want to be normal—or at least almost so.

This was a tremendously successful PR strategy, pushed by almost every powerful institution in the country. This messaging was essential to the gay-rights movement's decisive wins. If those triumphs are at all precarious, it is because the LGBT movement is now routinely vindicating its critics and breaking its promises. And as it does so, it calls the entire sexual revolution into question, including the sources of identity it encourages us to cultivate.

In particular, the onslaught of gender ideology has alarmed many who had supported same-sex marriage. There are tensions between the LGB and the coattail-riding

T, exemplified by lesbians complaining about trans women (that is, men pretending to be women) pressuring them for sex.[4] Likewise, the explicitness with which the radical side of the gay-rights movement has reemerged, and its targeting of children, has shocked many. It is now routine for naked men to parade[5] in front of children or to flash them[6] at various Pride festivities.[7] A group of New York City Pride marchers went viral for chanting, "We're coming for your children."[8] And they are. Parents who don't take their kids to the local Pride festival need not worry about them missing out. Pride, capitalized like any other high holiday, is coming to their school, library, grocery store, and, well, everywhere.

The live-and-let-live promises of the LGBT movement have also been shattered by its vindictiveness. This was not part of the movement's messaging, but it was inherent in its legal strategy, which routinely analogized opposition to same-sex marriage as the moral and legal equivalent of supporting racial segregation. And so civil rights laws are being contorted to make endorsing LGBT relationships and identities mandatory. There has been no magnanimity from the LGBT movement in victory, only a determination to punish dissenters, such as artists and small-business owners who do not want to participate in promoting or celebrating same-sex marriage ceremonies.

For example, one might think that Jack Phillips of Masterpiece Cakeshop is the only baker in the state of Colorado, given how activists and officials have spent years hounding him to create custom work to celebrate same-sex wedding ceremonies and gender transitions.[9] After winning once at the U.S. Supreme Court, he was immediately harassed and dragged back into court by a transgender activist who demanded he create custom work celebrating transgenderism, along with other obscene requests. Neither his case nor similar high-profile examples have been about businesses denying people ordinary services—anyone can walk into Phillips' shop and buy all the pastries he wants. Rather, these fights have been about a right to decline special events and custom work.

LGBT activists' determination to punish dissent even extends to targeting children. For example, in 2023, a Catholic couple in Massachusetts sued after the state banned them from fostering children because of their Christian beliefs. According to their lawyers, "The couple's home study said, 'Their faith is not supportive.' DCF [Department of Children and Families] officials said that while they had strengths, their answers about sexuality and gender barred them from being licensed."[10] They are not the only ones; other foster parents across the county have been prevented from giving kids a loving home, simply because they are Christian.[11]

Likewise, LGBT activists have sought to eliminate non-conformist education options. For example, the Biden administration, with an attitude of "Let them eat rainbows", tried to take food programs away from poor children to pressure schools (especially Christian schools) to conform to the new rainbow orthodoxy.[12] More radical still, the Human Rights Campaign demanded that the Biden administration strip accreditation from Christian colleges and schools.[13]

Not even a global pandemic stopped the spite. In the early, overwhelming days of the COVID-19 pandemic, New York City officials denounced a field hospital and ran it out of town because it was set up by conservative evangelicals. Samaritan's Purse wanted to care for all patients, but they were pushed out because of their beliefs on LGBT issues.[14] NYC politicians preferred to risk their constituents suffering and dying rather than have them be helped by dissenters from the city's sexual and gender orthodoxies.

Additional examples—of public obscenity, of targeting children, and of viciously punishing dissent—abound, and a few homosexual writers and activists are beginning to worry that things have gone too far. For instance, Andrew Sullivan, an early and ardent advocate for same-sex marriage, has written that he is repulsed and now worried about a backlash. Nonetheless, he still denies any responsibility for the fruits of his labor, insisting that his ideas are not responsible for the illiberalism and radicalism of his side. He is adamant that we could have, however uneasily, agreed to live and let live if only the gay-rights movement had taken his advice and closed up shop after its legal victories. He argues, "There is no slope in the case I made. There is a clear line: formal legal equality alongside cultural and social freedom on all sides."[15]

He is wrong. Both the tactics and the ideology of the movement he championed ensured that it would not end where it promised or where he wanted it to. And same-sex marriage specifically was always a radical project with implications for all of society. What Sullivan deplores as unnecessary excesses were always implicit in the arguments used to establish same-sex marriage. In particular, the claim that people are "born this way"—that LGBT identities are intrinsic and immutable—enabled the hijacking of civil rights law to serve the LGBT agenda. This ensured not only that opponents of the LGBT movement were defamed as the equivalent of racists but also that the enormous state power used to break racial segregation would be deployed against them. That is why government officials have sought to make every artist and creator in the wedding industry bow before the doctrine that sex is irrelevant to the nature and meaning of marriage. Likewise, the dogmas of gender identity demand that women and even little girls must get comfortable with males ogling and flashing them in what used to be female-only spaces.

President Biden declared that this is the civil rights issue of our time.[16]

This vindictive extremism is the result of the LGBT movement going beyond breaking with Christian moral teaching on human sexuality to stage an anthropological revolution. That is, the LGBT movement did not just argue that Christianity was wrong about the ethics of homosexual actions or that the government ought to stay out of policing them regardless of their morality; rather, it effaced the difference between men and women. Male and female are treated as essential only in matters of personal preference and as interchangeable for all other aspects of marriage and society, such as raising children.

Thus, the seemingly tradition-oriented, respectable demand for same-sex marriage was in fact the most radical portion of the gay-rights agenda. It did not just liberate sexual desire from any teleological orientation toward the other sex but also sought to erase the significance of male and female in family and culture altogether. And it made this radical reimagining of what it means to be human the basis for cultural norms and government policy.

Many cultures have, in various ways and to various degrees, tolerated or even celebrated some manifestations of homosexuality. But they did not regard such relationships as marriages or view men and women as interchangeable. The modern invention of same-sex marriage reduces the differences between men and women to a matter of idiosyncratic self-identification and individual sexual preference, rather than a fundamental division on which civilization is based. If the sex binary doesn't matter in marriage, it doesn't matter anywhere.

The collapse of the older understanding of marriage began before the LGBT movement, but the triumph of same-sex marriage sealed it. Instead of a lifelong covenant that unites the two halves of the human race in a relationship that provides for its continuation, marriage was redefined as the mere legal recognition of an indefinite, androgynous pairing, dissolvable at will and disconnected from begetting and raising children.

As the Lutheran pastor Hans Fiene once put it, expecting that same-sex marriage would have no significant social effects is like blowing up Hoover Dam and expecting Lake Mead to move only a few inches.[17] The entire landscape of family and society is being remade, as seen in a 2023 *New York Times* puff piece (and not the first) pushing legal recognition for polygamy, which has been rebranded as polyamory.[18] The difference is that while polygamy traditionally consisted of a man having more than one wife, polyamory consists of a group of men and/or women all having one another in various permutations. The subject of the *Times* piece was Somerville, a city in Massachusetts that had spent the past few years creating new legal rights for polyamorous partner groups. The motive for this is that, as the *Times* notes, "interest in nonmonogamy seems to be on the rise across the country."[19]

During the same-sex marriage debate, the suggestion that polygamy would be next was treated as a monstrous slur. Yet less than a decade later, the leading newspaper of upscale liberal opinion was favorably reporting on legal recognition of *de facto* polygamy. The conservative Christians were right. And they were right for the reasons they gave at the time. The poly movement's champions see their cause as a natural extension of the LGBT movement. Thus, *The New York Times* describes how "Somerville is alive with events like Indecent, a fetish- and kink-positive party, and Boudoir, a queer underground dance party. There are polyamorous speed-dating evenings, drag shows at the venue Crystal Ballroom and a gender-neutral CrossFit gym." If that is not clear enough, the *Times* reports, "There is a significant crossover between those who identify as lesbian, gay, bisexual, trans and pansexual and those who practice nonmonogamy, according to multiple studies."[20]

Apparently the math is more complicated than those equal-sign bumper stickers made it seem. On the one hand, there is marriage as one man and one woman. On the other hand, there are relational webs such as that of "Mr. Malone, who ... currently has a nesting partner, a long-term partner, two long-distance partners and a kink-based relationship with another person."[21] Love is love is love is a kink-based relationship.

The article mournfully reported that "people in nonmonogamous relationships are still often perceived and represented negatively."[22] Good. But that may soon change. There is an extensive campaign to normalize polyamory. *The New York Times* has led the way, with articles such as "How a Polyamorous Mom Had 'a Big Sexual Adventure' and Found Herself",[23] "I Was Content with Monogamy. I Shouldn't Have Been",[24] and "Lessons from a 20-Person Polycule".[25] Not to be outdone, *The New Yorker* had a long 2023 piece asking, "How Did Polyamory Become So Popular?"[26] And in 2024, *New York Magazine* introduced a cover story titled "A Practical Guide to Modern Polyamory: How to Open Things Up, for the Curious Couple"[27] by tweeting, "It's not just you; everyone is talking about being open."[28] Well, at least everyone working for publications with New York in their name.

The campaign for polyamory is also underway in the entertainment industry and media. For example, NBC subsidiary Peacock created a show called *Couple to Throuple*,[29] while *People* ran a story headlined "What Is a Throuple—and How to Know When the Relationship Type Is Right for You".[30] This gush of favorable media coverage may supercharge already-increasing public support. According to 2023 polling, almost a quarter of Americans believe that polygamy is morally acceptable. Approval had been stuck in single digits for the first decade of the century, but it has been steadily climbing since, with a trajectory similar to that of approval for same-sex marriage.[31]

As this illustrates, the more moderate partisans of sexual liberation always insist that the obvious next step in the sexual revolution is just conservative fearmongering that will never happen—right up until it does and is enthusiastically embraced. This happened with same-sex marriage and with the rush to transition children medically, and polyamory may well be next.

This slippery slope was predictable, and predicted, because, other than the requirement for consent, sexual liberation views all restrictions on the sexual desires of adults as illegitimate. Ironically, in practice this moral framework requires a greater reliance on prejudice to restrain the next logical step of the sexual revolution—a restraint that will fail in its turn. This explains the shift from "How dare you suggest that same-sex marriage will lead to polygamy?" to "We must endorse polygamy (rebranded as polyamory) as the next step in the LGBT rights revolution." The limits of sexual liberalism are purely conventional, rooted in nothing more than feelings shaped by what public opinion is willing to accept. Polygamy was unthinkable, until suddenly it was an obvious next frontier in the sexual revolution.

It is hard for a sexual ethos based only on autonomous consent to condemn on principle, rather than prejudice, even the most freakish sexual behaviors, such as a 2021 attempt by a parent and a child to marry each other.[32] After all, as the lawsuit in their behalf pointed out, they were consenting adults whose union would not (for unspecified reasons) be able to conceive children. The response to such provocations tends more toward "ick" than a principled rejoinder. It is good that people are prejudiced against incest and that most Americans are still prejudiced against polygamy, but these healthy prejudices alone may not hold against the corrosive ethos of sexual liberalism. These prejudices do keep many, perhaps most, advocates of sexual liberation from seeing more than a step or two down the road, even as their principles constantly impel them further than they ever intended to go—and so we see Andrew Sullivan wondering how the movement he dedicated himself to didn't stop when he wanted it to.[33]

The slippery slope has been less a fallacy than a prophecy when it comes to the sexual revolution. And the authoritarian turn ("Bake the cake, bigot") was inevitable because the LGBT movement regarded sexual desire as our essential identity and effaced the differences between men and women. It was not just a redrawing of moral lines but a revolution in what it means to be human, which, as it triumphed, wrote its false anthropology into laws, regulations, and judicial opinions. If the cause of gay rights had been righteous, we might have seen a sort of live-and-let-live result like that wished for by Sullivan. That matters have instead gone so wrong, so quickly, requires a reconsideration of the entire project.

This reevaluation will often be uncomfortable, for the premises of the LGBT movement derive from the sexual revolution as a whole. Same-sex marriage was not the top of the slippery slope; it was just a point where it got steeper. Many people who eagerly signed up for the toboggan ride down the incline are only now wondering about what is at the bottom and worrying over the absence of brakes. These people persuaded themselves that the cultural and sexual revolutions would go just as far as they were comfortable with, and no further.

Even many critics of gender ideology are hesitant to say anything negative about the LGB part of the movement. For example, despite the overall excellence of her book *Feminism Against Progress*, Mary Harrington ignored that gay rights were inseparable from the movements she memorably denounced as "cyborg theology" and "Meat Lego Gnosticism":[34] love is love, embodiment does not matter, and children are luxury consumer goods to be ordered, not persons to beget. While the gay-rights movement did not invent these ideas, it was a major accelerant in their acceptance, and the LGB set the stage for the T and the rest of the alphabet soup.

The slide began with the effort to detach sex and its pleasures from obligation and commitment—the lie that we could and should separate sex from marriage, and marriage from the natural family of mother, father, and children. The desire for sexual pleasure without constraint or commitment is a perennial temptation, but the wealth and technological prowess of our age made it seem more plausible and less harmful than it did in less prosperous times lacking the Pill and penicillin. But money and technology are poor substitutes for virtue and justice, and so we have kept sliding down the slope, finding less pleasure and more suffering than we were promised at the top.

Same-sex marriage accelerated this slide, building on past lies and adding new ones. It also prevents recovery, insofar as it institutionalizes falsehoods about sex, marriage, and family. Truth must be the foundation for rebuilding a healthy sexual and family culture. And that will require rejecting dogmas (now government endorsed and enforced) declaring that men and women are sexually and relationally interchangeable, subject only to the sovereign whim of adult preference. Humans rarely follow a line of reasoning to its fullest unfolding; we are not creatures of logical inexorability. But the logic of the sexual revolution is taking us further than we meant to go, and restraining its latest expansions will require challenging its past triumphs.

However, discussing any limits opens an awkward can of worms for sexual liberalism. Acknowledging the importance of human embodiment and sexual dimorphism, and the consequent need to regulate sexual desire, will require rolling back much more than Lia Thomas' swim career. Thinking seriously about embodiment and the differences between men and women raises a multitude of questions that sexual liberalism thought it had settled on its terms. For instance, if the differences between men and women are real and important, then having two dads is probably not just as good as having a mother and a father. If the differences between men and women matter, then an economic system that treats men and women as interchangeable units of labor may be deeply flawed and anti-human. If the differences between men and women matter, then how they are united matters, which means that a sexual culture ordered toward the indulgence of desire may not be ordered toward human flourishing.

Claiming the Kids

The transgender and polyamorous moments arrived because of the victories of the gay-rights movement, which were built upon the foundation of the broader sexual revolution. Each successive addition has further altered ideas and practices regarding sex, sexuality, and relationships for everyone. For example, in 2019, Nathaniel Frank (director of the What We Know Project discussed in the previous chapter) wrote a *Washington Post* piece boasting that the LGBT movement's "legacy isn't just about making

queer people look more like everyone else. It's also, perhaps more mutinously, about making everyone else look
a bit more queer."[35]

An obvious manifestation of this is that identifying as
LGBT has become fashionable. More people want to identify with rainbow identities than actually want to have
same-sex sexual relationships or to transition medically.[36]
As one writer put it, there is an "odd proliferation of
straight-married women who identify as 'queer,' based on
what seems mainly like a conviction that they're just too
interesting to be plain ol' heterosexual."[37] Young women in
particular have been declaring LGBT identities at much-
increased levels,[38] but many do little to act on them.
Indeed, some sexual identities seem to have been invented
only to include fairly normal female sexuality in the ever-
evolving Pride flag—for example, "demisexuals", who
are defined by needing an emotional connection before
feeling sexual attraction. Claiming this common experience of female sexual desire as an identity is a way for
young women to escape the stigma of being another bland
cisgender, heterosexual, (probably) white female. It also
offers a trendy rainbow-glitter excuse to step away from a
toxic culture of casual sex.

However, when everyone else looks "a bit more queer",
it undermines the LGBT movement's central narrative.
The mantra of "born this way" was a cultural and political
triumph—there was even a song by Lady Gaga—but it was
not true, and this falsehood has had baleful consequences.
The argument that each of us is born with an immutable
sexual orientation and gender identity provided an ersatz
natural-law case for everything from same-sex marriage
to gender transition. But it also ensured that the LGBT
movement was coming for the kids. This is why fights over
"LGBT youth" are now at the center of the culture war.

The gay-rights movement was never just about keeping the government out of the bedrooms of consenting adults, or just about government recognition of their relationships. Rather, the idea that every baby is born with a predetermined sexual orientation and gender identity means that some children are born into the sexual elect of the "LGBTQI+ community". This then suggests that all children ought to learn about sex and gender ideology as soon as possible so that they will be able to discover their authentic selves. In this view, kids need to learn about gay sex and gender transition because some of them are gay, trans, or some other rainbow identity, even if they don't know it yet—and the rest need to learn to be allies. Many activist educators and their political allies are acting on this belief.

Affirming these identities is considered essential to a person's flourishing, for the sexual self is seen as the authentic self. Thus, child drag queens[39] and supposed transgender toddlers[40] have been championed by the LGBT movement for years now. After all, if sexual orientation and gender identity are innate and immutable, there is no reason to fear adults grooming children into LGBT identities. The only reasonable fear is that old-fashioned bigots will pressure children into repressing those identities. Furthermore, if children are born LGBT, it follows that they should be raised by adults who will support them in these intrinsic, immutable identities. Thus, it was inevitable that the LGBT movement would become increasingly hostile toward parents who do not cheer on LGBT identities. After all, a parent who refuses to embrace a child's fundamental identity is obviously not acting in the best interests of the child. The assertion that children must be affirmed in LGBT identities lest they commit suicide provides further justification to take kids away from "unsupportive" parents.

Because it is not immediately clear whether a child will identify as LGBT, all parents who resist LGBT ideology are necessarily suspect. This was made explicit in the Biden administration's "Guide for Foster Parents", published in June 2021, which endorsed the "born this way" thesis, including the notion that a four-year-old may be transgender. The guide declared that "behaviors that openly reject a youth's LGBTQ+ identity must be avoided and not tolerated. This includes ... forcing youth to attend activities (including religious activities ... and family gatherings)."[41] This overt attack on religion and family demonstrates how LGBT dogmas are becoming state orthodoxy.

In 2023, the Biden administration proposed new rules for foster care, which would treat rejecting LGBT ideology as child abuse. These regulations state that "to be considered a safe and appropriate placement, a provider is expected to utilize the child's identified pronouns, chosen name, and allow the child to dress in an age-appropriate manner that the child believes reflects their self-identified gender identity and expression."[42] In short, people who do not accept LGBT ideology and affirm LGBT identities are unfit to be foster parents. Already, states from Oregon to Massachusetts have begun making this their official policy, explicitly excluding Christians and others who oppose LGBT orthodoxy from foster care and adoption. For example, in 2024, two families sued Vermont because the state had stripped them of their foster care licenses when they questioned LGBT orthodoxy. Both families had excellent records, and the state was in "desperate" need of foster families. One of these families, Pastor Bryan Gantt and his wife, Rebecca, had been asked by the state to "adopt a baby about to be born to a homeless woman who was addicted to drugs". The Gantts, whom officials described as offering "the perfect home", agreed, only to have the offer rescinded and their license revoked when their opposition to the LGBT agenda became known.[43] And there is no reason to expect that the precedents established for foster parents will not eventually be extended to all parents. Somehow, "love wins" has become a mandate to keep children from loving families.

The "born this way" mantra was politically and culturally triumphant. But the radical implications of the claim that children are members of the "LGBTQI+ community" from birth ensure continued conflict. Many people who accepted same-sex marriage and played along as Bruce became Caitlyn are balking at preteen drag queens and "trans toddlers". They are right to be appalled, and this revulsion should induce a reevaluation of the "born this way" claim and the movement that pushed it. Something that has gone so wrong must be scrutinized.

Taken at face value, the "born this way" narrative is not a good argument. It is often wrong to act on an innate desire—genuinely wanting something does not make it right. The slogan is better understood as shorthand for a cluster of assumptions along the following lines: Human flourishing depends on being authentically oneself; this requires freedom for identifying and acting on one's sexual orientation and gender identity, which are innate, essential elements of a person that are harmful to repress or attempt to alter.

But regardless of how expanded or complex this line of reasoning becomes, it fails because sexual orientation and gender identity are not innate and immutable from birth. This is not to say that they are fully conscious choices or that they are entirely malleable. Some people feel strong same-sex attractions that they did not choose; some people are genuinely distressed by their biological sex. Nonetheless, the dogmatic claims of "born this way" are at odds with reality. Scientifically, the search for a "gay gene" ended in failure a few years ago after a massive study, reported in *Nature*, was conducted.[44] The best scientific evidence suggests multicausal explanations for how we experience sexual desire and gender, with environmental and social factors playing crucial roles in their development. As one LGBT-sympathetic writer put it following the release of the *Nature* paper, "It's likely that our sexualities and genders are textured by a mix of social experience, the firings off of neurons, hormonal swirls and the transcription of DNA."[45] That is to say, we are not simply "born this way".

Though it lacks the zip of a good slogan, the truth is closer to "born with some possible inclinations this way that can be activated or increased by a mixture of environmental and social factors, as well as individual choice". Because of the complexity of the factors involved, the sources and intensity of various sexual inclinations will vary from person to person. And yes, sexual orientation can sometimes change. As fashion designer Michelle Smith told *Vogue* in 2022, "I identify as pansexual. I grew up very straight, but around the age of 40, my attraction to people changed: I stopped being attracted to someone through their gender and became attracted to people through who they are and their energy."[46] Though her shift from being "very straight" to a "pansexual" in a relationship with another woman shatters the "born this way" narrative, it was nonetheless reported as an affirming tale of self-actualization.[47] Fluidity is acceptable and even praised—if it goes toward making everyone "a bit more queer".

The LGBT movement is starting to admit that "born this way" was, in their view, a noble lie. As Lydia Polgreen wrote for *The New York Times* in 2023, "For gays and lesbians, social acceptance and legal protection came as Americans learned to see sexual orientation as an innate and immutable characteristic.... Believing gay people had no choice but to be gay was a critical way station on the road to accepting homosexuality as just another way of being in the world." But, as she related, her own experience was certainly not that of having been born that way; rather, "like many queer people, I had many different romantic entanglements in my youth, and had I not met my wife in college it is not impossible to imagine that I might have ended up on another path. I certainly did not experience myself as being born any particular way." She then admitted that many people change their sexual orientation and added, "I think most of us know intuitively that sexual orientation is not binary, and is subject to change over the course of our lives."[48]

Polgreen suggested that "born this way" should be discarded now that it has served its purpose. As she explained, "The born-this-way narrative prevails in most mainstream organizations and institutions and dominates much of the discourse. And yet. To many queer people, myself very much included, it feels like an incomplete account of their experiences, a simplification that shortchanges their lives." She concluded that "we ended up with the born-this-way model because of the tension between the seeking of rights for an embattled minority and the broader search for liberation. But this tension is ultimately dialectical—it contains the seeds of its own destruction."[49] Notably, Polgreen wrote this in a piece arguing for medically transitioning children. She presumably believes it is now safe to admit that the real goal of sexual liberation is not to be slotted into the identity one was born with but to be free to choose whatever sexual or gender identity one wants at any given time. Forget "born this way"; what matters is what someone wants today.

Still, the collapse of the "born this way" narrative also collapses the arguments used by LGBT activists and their allies to claim children as part of the "LGBTQI+ community". The truth is that people's identities, including their sexual identities and sense of gender, are not predetermined, and their development is complex and at least partly socially conditioned. Though children are not blank slates, neither are they born with their sexualities fully formed, and what is taught to and modeled for them will be part of their sexual development. Thus, instead of helping children discern intrinsic sexual orientations and gender identities, the educational and cultural efforts of LGBT activists and their allies are shaping children's sexuality and sense of gender.

LGBT activists such as Polgreen know that children are suggestible and malleable and that this includes their developing senses of sexuality and gender. Children are deliberately included among those being made to "look a bit more queer". This is a feature, not a bug, for the many activists who want every kindergarten to teach that boys can become girls and girls can become boys, and who want every middle school to have an LGBT club with teachers actively recruiting for it. They are determined to celebrate and praise kids who come out as part of the rainbow elect, while labeling those who do not as cis-hetero oppressors. They are, in short, acting like recruiters, with activist teachers hiding students' LGBT identities from potentially disapproving parents. Of course, because "born this way" is a lie, the result has been a surge[50] in children and young adults claiming rainbow identities.[51] This increase in the number of young people who identity as LGBT[52] far exceeds what could be explained by more people coming out as stigma declines.[53] According to 2022 research by Gallup, one in five adults from Gen Z identifies as LGBT.[54] These identities are being created, not discerned.

LGBT activists used to insist that they were not interested in recruiting children, and some adults who identify as LGBT still feel that way. But those driving the LGBT movement now really are coming for children, as demonstrated by programs such as school-based LGBT clubs and sex-ed summer camps for elementary school students.[55] Children are being taught to define themselves by desires they may not even have yet. We are told that this is to affirm their intrinsic identities, but it is really about affirming the identities and ideologies of the adults instructing them.

Does Desire Define Us?

"I can't turn off what turns me on."[56] This refrain from the title track of the 2017 album *Masseduction* by St. Vincent encapsulates the attitude and rationale of the LGBT movement: This is what I like; this is who I am. St. Vincent (the stage name of Annie Clark) is a skilled songwriter and performer with an antagonistic view of Christianity, faith in sexual and gender fluidity,[57] and some high-profile sexual relationships with other women, including model Cara Delevingne. Her lyric illuminates how even abandoning the "born this way" narrative does not collapse LGBT identities.

Though the absence of a "gay gene" precludes a simple deterministic explanation for sexual desire, the mysteriousness of its sources does not make it less compelling or apparently essential to who we are. Sexual desire tends to be both intense and unbidden, and its sources are often opaque to us and rarely rationally chosen. Thus, sexual yearning may seem to be an expression of our deepest, most authentic self. Even if we recognize that desire, in general, is shaped by culture, experience, and environment and that it can be manipulated, the intensity of sexual desire—and the longing for relationship that can accompany it—may make it seem especially authentic. And St. Vincent is right: We can't turn off what turns us on. Not easily, anyway, and sometimes not at all.

The idea of sexuality as an identity, rather than as something one does, is largely a modern construct. It may be explained as an attempt to fill a void left by the death of God. Nietzsche's famous, often misunderstood, claim that God is dead is more than disbelief. After all, the madman in Nietzsche's parable announces the death of God to "many of those who did not believe in God [who] were standing around just then".[58] Nietzsche understood the death of God as a psychological and cultural event rather than a triumphant philosophical postulate. This is why, in Nietzsche's tale, those who first disbelieved remain oblivious to the death of God, even though they themselves have killed Him. As the madman poetically puts it, "Lightning and thunder require time; the light of the stars requires time; deeds, though done, still require time to be seen and heard. This deed is still more distant from them than the most distant stars—*and yet they have done it themselves.*"[59] Because the death of God is not mere unbelief but a result of it, those who have killed God are unaware of what they have done. They still live with many of the moral pieties and cultural conditions derived from established Christianity, even though they no longer believe in the source.

But the eventual result of their unbelief is the destruction of the human conception of the world along with its source. The madman who announces the death of God expresses wonder and despair at the deed: "How could we drink up the sea? Who gave us the sponge to wipe away the entire horizon?"[60] The idea of God, even if false, had provided mankind with meaning and coherence and established the world as a home for mankind. The death of God was the death of the Beyond as a wellspring of meaning and order in life. God, or some sort of transcendence, had been considered the source of love, awe, greatness, order, truth, beauty, and everything else that seemed to draw humans beyond themselves. All this was now revealed as mere human invention—an elaborate game of make-believe.

Thus, the death of God unmoored the world from what had been its source. Identity and meaning were detached from anything permanent, leaving people to construct their own identities from the contingencies of human existence. As the madman puts it, "What were we doing when we unchained this earth from its sun? Whither is it moving now? Whither are we moving? Away from all suns? Are we not plunging continually? Backward, sideward, forward, in all directions? Is there still any up or down? Are we not straying as through infinite nothingness? Do we not feel the breath of empty space?"[61] The divine sources of transcendent identity and meaning are gone, along with the murdered God. The cosmos has been shattered; creation is no longer created. There is no higher meaning to life, the universe, and everything. Mankind no longer has a given place within the universe but is revealed as merely a minuscule, purposeless development within it.

The divine source of value and meaning is revealed as a human delusion. Thus, if mankind is not to succumb to nihilism, we need to engage in the conscious creation of new sources of meaning and new identities for ourselves. And we must do this despite our contingency, finitude, suffering, and banality—the last being perhaps the most distressing to Nietzsche. This task of creation demands the Übermensch, the superior, self-overcoming man who can establish new meaning and values. As the madman cries out, "God is dead. God remains dead. And we have killed him. How shall we comfort ourselves, the murderers of all murderers? . . . Is not the greatness of this deed too great for us? Must we ourselves not become gods, simply to appear worthy of it?"[62] But what if we cannot? Are we then stuck waiting for the Übermensch?

Our inability to fill the void left by the death of God explains our culture's odd identity crisis. Our endless discussions of identity as something to construct and deconstruct are rooted in the cultural unfolding of the death of God, which makes it a struggle to claim identities that are more than social constructs or personal idiosyncrasies. We must self-create, and yet we doubt our ability to do so authentically—with good reason, given that the materials we must use are contingent cultural artifacts. Inconsistent and unstable identities prevent us from living with authenticity and integrity, especially in relation to others. Harmony is impossible when our identities are grounded only in contingency and desire. Conflicting identity claims by groups and individuals compete with no prospect of resolution, as there is no source of identity beyond the human—the all-too human.

This anthropological shift is behind the assertion that to challenge people's sexual or gender identity is to question, deny, or attack their humanity and even their existence. This seems grandiose and incoherent to those who still reside in a Christian cosmos, for whom sexual desire or one's feelings about gender are not at the core of one's identity and for whom criticizing sinful acts is not encouraging a genocide of the sinful. But to those whose experiential sense of self is only that which they have constructed from their culture and their own desires, the claim makes sense. If self-creation is the fullest expression of our humanity, then to critique someone's self-constructed identity is to assail his humanity.

It often seems that the opposing sides of our cultural and political conflicts are living in different worlds. They are. Those who still believe they are living in a created cosmos really do inhabit a different psychological world from those living after the death of God. Those whose identity is rooted in the divine order of existence are divided from those whose identity is self-created.

However, the lines are not always clear. Just as the audience in Nietzsche's parable was unaware of the death of God despite their unbelief, there are many today who are unconsciously divided between the two worlds. Facing the full implications of the death of God takes courage and perspicacity that few have even after Nietzsche has led the way. Instead, people often live within a mixture of self-creation, nihilistic despair, and residual religiosity mostly derived from Christianity—self-creation when it flatters and indulges, mixed with sentimental religiosity for comfort. All the while, however, the black snake of nihilism chokes us; we cannot live authentically spiritual lives and cannot replace the murdered God ourselves.

A return to the pre-Christian world is impossible; we might morally repaganize, but a genuine revival of pagan belief and a sense of a pagan cosmos are still far from us. A return to Christian sources of identity is possible but will be demanding. Christian belief, and the transcendence and meaning it provides, will not be separated from Christian ethics, including sexual ethics. These sexual rules are rooted in our responsibilities to one another and our embodiment as male and female. Christianity decisively rejects the attempt to define ourselves by our sexual urges and preferences. Though Christian sexual ethics place an especially difficult task before those who are same-sex attracted, they also provide richer and fuller sources of identity than our sexual inclinations.

In contrast to the liberation of sexual desire, Christianity teaches self-discipline based on love for God and others. The duty of chastity is for all Christians, and all who are not in a Christian marriage should be abstinent, regardless of to whom they are attracted. Churches should nonetheless recognize that those with intense same-sex attractions are called to bear a heavy cross, which may not become lighter over time. It was a mistake for some Christians to treat same-sex attraction as a psychological disorder and to suggest that it could therefore be readily cured through psychotherapy or fixed by efforts to "pray the gay away".

Yes, prayer is powerful. Yes, sexuality is somewhat fluid and can change. Yes, "born this way" was a false narrative. And yes, well-informed therapy can be helpful in understanding, regulating, and changing oneself. But neither God nor psychology will remove all temptations from us, and it is wrong to promise that they will—which is clear if we shift focus from unwanted same-sex attractions to other sexual temptations, such as an addiction to pornography. Easy assurances of "curing" us of our sinful desires are not in keeping with Christianity, which instead directs us to seek the strength to resist temptation and the grace to repent when we do not. Though self-control and humility are often difficult and sacrificial, they direct us toward genuine well-being and fulfillment. Not even the most intense sexual pleasures can satisfy the deepest longings of our hearts. Only love can do that.

And love is more complex than "love is love" sloganeering admits. It is not just that there are different varieties of love (parental love is very different from friendship, for example) but that not all forms of erotic love (which is what is meant by the slogan) are interchangeable. A hookup, however passionate, is not love in the way that a lifelong marriage can be. A genuinely self-giving love must be both rightly ordered and specific, and therefore committed and exclusive. Love cannot flit from person to person without destroying itself. This is why polyamory is a particularly apt illustration of how the sexual revolution encourages us to try to have our cake and eat it too—to have not just pleasure but also the joys of love, while keeping our options open and never really giving all of ourselves to anyone.

In contrast, Christianity insists that sex be reserved for the exclusive, self-giving commitment of lifelong marriage between a man and a woman. This is a difficult task, but our culture may (grudgingly) see the beauty and benefits of the Christian ideal of marriage, especially as the injuries, social and personal, inflicted by the sexual revolution continue to pile up. And Christianity recognizes that marriage is rooted in the reality and purpose of our embodiment; men and women were made for each other, and it is through the union of male and female that we may become participants in the begetting of new human beings who will be able to know God and enjoy Him forever.

This is why the conflict between Christianity and the LGBT movement runs far deeper than just disagreeing over the morality of homosexuality. Rather, it implicates the sources of our fundamental identity and the significance (or lack thereof) of our embodiment. The Christian insistence that men and women are meant for each other in lifelong, monogamous unions is not arbitrary or capricious but embedded within an understanding of the universe as a cosmos—a created order. In the Christian view, sex is bound up with the order of creation, our duties toward others, and our eschatological fulfillment in Christ. The teachings of Christianity direct our often-wayward wills and desires back toward our flourishing and that of others, while also pointing toward our ultimate good—union with God, which is itself described in terms of a marriage, with the Church as the Bride of Christ.

5

Whose Liberation?

Christianity Means What It Says

Despite the evils inflicted by the sexual revolution, Christian sexual ethics remain unpopular; they are denounced as restrictive and exclusionary and dismissed as unrealistic. Yet most of our culture is still too influenced by Christianity to want a return to anything like ancient pagan sexuality. Instead, there is a longing for a more permissive version of Christian sexual ethics, though it is rarely articulated in those terms.

For example, in her 2022 book, *Rethinking Sex: A Provocation*, Christine Emba laid out in painful detail the wreckage of the current relational and sexual landscape, yet she not only stopped short of condemning the sexual revolution but also essentially affirmed it, provided that it could be kinder and gentler. She proposed a sort of moralistic therapeutic Thomism—we should care about our sexual partners and will their good but need not adhere to all (or any) of the commands of Christian sexual ethics. Fornication, sodomy, and all the rest are still on the menu—just be respectful and responsible.

Emba's half-hearted attempt to restrain the sexual revolution may seem reasonable because many of its evils arise in the aggregate. Though it is sometimes possible to point to *this* hookup producing a pregnancy ended by abortion, or *that* affair destroying a family, not every violation of Christian sexual norms leads to such obvious, immediate, or significant harms. Cultures and individual lives can endure some sin—whether greed, fornication, or hatred—without disaster, at least to a point. Furthermore, harmful trends will always have some exceptions (for example, *this* boy succeeded despite being fatherless, while *that* one ruined his life despite being blessed with a loving father).

This resilience is a grace necessary for us to live, for it is impossible to rid the world in general, and ourselves in particular, of all sin. The wages of sin may be death, but payment is often mercifully put off. This divine forbearance may tempt us to dismiss our sins as harmless and to ignore their growing evils. Thus, even many who acknowledge that our sexual and relational culture is a disaster still argue that the commands of Christianity on these matters are too strict and that the rules can be loosened without necessarily leading to all the ill effects we see around us. These half-hearted sexual revolutionaries want to find a way for sexual liberation to be somehow ethical and responsible, for permissiveness not to be followed by cruelty and exploitation—for the slippery slope of sin somehow to offer firm footing. For instance, even as he reported on the wickedness of the online porn business, *New York Times* columnist Nick Kristof insisted that "the issue is not pornography but rape" and that it should "be possible to be sex positive and Pornhub negative".[1] Surely the next batch of fruit from the poison tree will be nourishing.

There are even efforts to incorporate sexual liberalism into Christianity itself. Many people want to retain elements of Christian belief, or to claim a Christian identity, while rejecting its challenging moral teachings, especially about sex. Thus, they deny that Christianity really means what it teaches. The arguments deployed for this purpose are alluring, insofar as they let us off the hook, but they are intellectually empty and spiritually poisonous.

For example, the assertion that the moral teachings of Jesus and the apostles no longer apply—that they were meant only for the particular time and place in which they were given and must be reimagined in accordance with modern circumstances and sensibilities—would undermine all Christian teaching and doctrine. If Jesus was indeed divine, and if the apostles were appointed by Him, then we must conform ourselves and our culture to their teachings, not their teachings to ourselves and our culture. Conversely, if Jesus was not divine, then His words and those of the apostles are easily set aside—but so is all of Christianity, negating the urgency of whether its moral teachings are compatible with the sexual revolution. This argument is therefore irrelevant to both Christians and non-Christians.

An alternate claim meant to reconcile Christianity and the sexual revolution is that the Church has misunderstood Jesus and the apostles and that their condemnations of sexual immorality did not mean what the Church has taken them to mean. In particular, this argument has been deployed to claim that when the apostles condemned homosexuality, they did not mean homosexuality as such, but just exploitative homosexual relationships. This line of reasoning is ahistorical nonsense. For example, Romans clearly equates homosexuality as such to rebellion against God and His created order.

> God gave them up in the lusts of their hearts to impurity, to the dishonoring of their bodies among themselves, because they exchanged the truth about God for a lie and worshiped and served the creature rather than the Creator, who is blessed for ever! Amen.

For this reason God gave them up to dishonorable passions. Their women exchanged natural relations for unnatural, and the men likewise gave up natural relations with women and were consumed with passion for one another, men committing shameless acts with men and receiving in their own persons the due penalty for their error. (1:24–27)

The book of Jude likewise emphasizes the unnaturalness of homosexuality as it reminds readers of the fate of "Sodom and Gomorrah and the surrounding cities, which likewise acted immorally and indulged in unnatural lust" (v. 7). These and other New Testament passages are clear, even if modern readers wish they were not.

It is especially ridiculous to argue that the early Christians misunderstood the cultural context of the apostolic teaching they received regarding homosexuality. They understood their own cultural context just fine, and the apostles were not ambiguous—it is not that the benighted ancient Christians were just unable to imagine modern enlightened sodomy. As Kyle Harper noted in his book *From Shame to Sin: The Christian Transformation of Sexual Morality in Late Antiquity*, "Same-sex love, regardless of age, status, or role, was forbidden without qualification and without remorse."[2] Christian sexual morality, like its Jewish forebearer, emphasized the union of husband and wife as an imperative of the creation order and regarded same-sex coupling as a rebellion against the designs of God, and therefore against His holiness. Whether same-sex attraction was natural in the sense of arising spontaneously from within a person was irrelevant from this perspective, which regarded desire as something to be governed in accordance with the laws of God.

Furthermore, as generations of rabbis and pastors, along with historians such as Harper, have explained, the people of Israel saw sexual and spiritual unfaithfulness as linked. Sexual immorality was symbolic of, and intertwined with, idolatry—just look at the book of Hosea and Ezekiel 16 for examples. And as the Christian faith reached beyond its Jewish origins, avoiding sexual immorality continued to be recognized as essential, including for Gentile converts. Thus, Christian sexual ethics were always a direct challenge to Roman sexual culture. As Harper observed, "For Paul, the sexual disorder of Roman society was the single most powerful symbol of the world's alienation from God.... God's will inheres in the order of creation and is manifest in it. Same-sex love was thus, for the apostle, a particularly egregious violation of the natural order.... It symbolized the estrangement of men and women, at the very level of their innermost desires, from nature and the creator of nature."[3]

This teaching is unpopular today—indeed, the Christian condemnation of homosexuality may now be more reviled than the broader Christian rejection of fornication—but it is undoubtedly the authentic apostolic teaching. Recognizing this, some have attempted to drive a wedge between Jesus and the apostles, asserting that Paul's writings in particular should be regarded as his own doctrine, distinct from and less authoritative than the words of Jesus. This argument takes the general nature of Jesus' recorded condemnations of sexual immorality as an opening to argue that sexual behaviors He did not specifically condemn may be permissible.

This sort of reasoning—"Jesus never said anything about homosexuality; therefore, it is permissible" or "Jesus never said anything about abortion; therefore, it is acceptable"—is not a convincing hermeneutic. A lack of specific condemnation is not an endorsement from Jesus, especially for behaviors considered sinful in the first-century Jewish context in which He preached and which His apostles later did condemn by name. But this claim has been deployed by many, such as Nick Kristof of *The New York Times*. In a 2022 interview, he declared that "two of the main moral issues that evangelicals have been associated with in the last few decades are hostility to abortion and to gay people. Jesus never spoke directly about either.... So why hijack faith to obsess about abortion and same-sex lovers?"[4]

There are many rejoinders to this challenge. One is that evangelicals and other faithful Christians are usually playing culture-war defense; it was sexual liberalism that pushed these issues to the fore. Another reply is that many things that Jesus did not specifically condemn are nonetheless obviously incompatible with His teachings. But the crucial point is that setting Jesus against the apostles leads neither to the biblical Jesus nor to the "historical Jesus" but only to a Jesus manufactured in one's own image. If we cannot trust the writings and teachings of the apostles, then we can trust neither Scripture nor Christian tradition, leaving us with only wispy shades of whoever Jesus was. And yet this ahistorical, anti-Scriptural approach to Jesus still gives no evidence that He rejected the Jewish sexual morality of His time. What Kristof and others like him want is a Jesus who came not to call sinners to repentance but to affirm and approve of them just as they are. They want a Jesus without any difficult teachings or condemnation of sin. But with regard to sex, as with so much else, Jesus showed us that we cannot possibly be free from sin. Forgiveness presumes guilt; we can see our Savior only when we first see our sin.

Though Scripture is sometimes difficult to interpret, these efforts to deny clear Christian teachings about sex are not honest mistakes. Rather, they are bad-faith exegesis by those who want a religion made in their own image.

Christians must resist such attempts to hollow out our faith to accommodate the sexual revolution.

Reflecting on the example of John the Baptist may aid this task, for John began his life as a witness for the importance of unborn life and ended it as a martyr for marriage. Before he was even born, John testified to the sanctity of all unborn human life and thereby also against the violent destruction of such lives. Indeed, John shows why the personhood of humans *in utero* cannot be denied without embracing grave heresy about Jesus. John's ministry proclaiming Jesus began before either was born. According to Luke's account: "When Elizabeth heard the greeting of Mary, the child leaped in her womb; and Elizabeth was filled with the Holy Spirit and she exclaimed with a loud cry, 'Blessed are you among women, and blessed is the fruit of your womb! And why is this granted me, that the mother of my Lord should come to me? For behold, when the voice of your greeting came to my ears, the child in my womb leaped for joy'" (1:41–44). The unborn John's recognition of the unborn Jesus was a miracle that revealed the value of human life in the womb in several ways. First, the passage shows that the fetal John the Baptist and the embryonic Jesus were human persons congruous with their adult selves and that they were already participating in their divine missions. This was a fulfillment of the angel's promise that John would be filled with the Holy Spirit even in the womb.

Second, the recognition of Jesus as Lord early in Mary's pregnancy testifies to His divinity even as He grew within Mary's womb. This divinity from conception is why Christians honor Mary as the *Theotokos*, the God-bearer. This title is affirmed by Catholic, Orthodox, and Reformed Protestant teaching and is attested to by many ancient sources, such as Ambrose of Milan's great Advent hymn, "Veni, Redemptor

Gentium" ("Savior of the Nations, Come"), which declares Jesus' full divinity and full humanity in the womb.[5]

Third, this passage shows the full humanity of all unborn persons. To claim that the unborn are not fully human is necessarily to claim that Jesus was not fully human while in Mary's womb, for the Bible insists that His humanity was like ours in every way but sin. Denying the full humanity of the unborn therefore requires either also denying the full divinity of the unborn Jesus (thereby rejecting the reason for the unborn John's joy and the teaching of the ancient Church) or asserting that Jesus' full divinity was present without His full humanity. Either is grave heresy.

Just as the beginning of John's life shows us the value of unborn human life, the end of John's life illuminates the importance of marriage. John was martyred for bearing witness to the inviolability of marriage. As recorded in the Gospel of Matthew, "Herod had seized John and bound him and put him in prison, for the sake of Herodias, his brother Philip's wife; because John said to him, 'It is not lawful for you to have her'" (14:3–4). John was later executed after Herod promised a favor to Herodias' daughter, which her mother told her to fulfill by asking for John's head.

John could have kept quiet regarding Herod's sexual sins or confined himself to calls to repentance that did not single out the powerful by name. He could have said that Herod's sexual conduct was not actually a serious sin worth worrying about because God does not really care about what people do in the bedroom. He could, after being imprisoned, have recanted in the hope of saving himself. But there is no indication that John wavered or doubted on this matter. Rather, he took his stand for marriage and fidelity, and he held to this position to his death. And Jesus did not tell John that he was wrong or even that this was not worth dying over.

John's martyrdom is a reminder of the importance Christianity assigns to marriage and sexuality. John the Baptist, whom Jesus declared to be the greatest man born of woman, died as a martyr for marriage. And the lurid details of John's death highlight how sin grows when indulged. John's death shows that sin stays hungry—it doesn't settle for what it already has but instead demands more while giving less. Herod did not desire John's execution, but he was so entangled by his sins of lust and pride that he felt compelled to add evil to evil by ordering John's death. Herod began as a king doing what he felt like; he ended in bondage to his own sin.

This progression vindicates the Christian understanding of sin, which sees sin as part of our nature, rather than only a term for discrete acts of wrongdoing. Sin has internal, as well as external, effects. Indeed, the internal results of sin may be intense even while they are outwardly undetectable. Our sins change us even when they do not seem to affect the world around us. Thus, the expanding evils and radicalism of the sexual revolution are due to more than the relentless unfolding of its logic. Our choices, including those related to our sex lives, alter who we are, both individually and collectively. This is why what was dismissed as an absurd and slanderous hypothetical (for example, polyamory as the next frontier in LGBT rights) is now very real. It is why the transgender movement has focused on sterilizing children. Past decisions—personal, political, and cultural—have made us into a people who would consider and even endorse such things.

Furthermore, as the pleasures of sin recede, we find ourselves chasing them with increased recklessness. It is not just that we want more of the same but that we want something *more*. We crave something more intense, more fulfilling, but the same old sin does not deliver it. And so we are tempted to find another stimulus—newer, stronger, stranger—to give us that jolt we crave. The turn toward the deviant and violent in pornography, which is now shaping generations of real-world sexuality, is a paradigmatic example of this. Indulging sinful desires results in sin reshaping our desires.

Sin promises that just a little more will satisfy us, but these blandishments are deceptive, for a selfish life of pleasure seeking cannot fulfill our deepest needs and longings for love and communion with others. Indeed, because sin changes us, selfishness renders people increasingly incapable of desiring and pursuing genuine human goods. Sin thereby creates a vicious cycle in souls and lives as people chase after that which cannot satisfy them. Sin lures us away from the good and toward the empty and unfulfilling. We become morally desensitized: less capable of differentiating good and evil; less repulsed by that which is wicked, ugly, and false; and less drawn to that which is good, true, and beautiful. This is why Christianity has to hold the line, even when it comes to unpopular teachings about sex. Sin is always bad for us and others, and so we should respond to our sins with repentance, rather than hardening our hearts.

Freedom: Indulgence, Reason, or Righteousness?

Sometimes, liberation is just another form of slavery.

At the beginning of Plato's *Republic*, Cephalus tells an anecdote about the poet Sophocles, who, when asked in old age if he could still make love to a woman, replied, "Quiet, man.... I am very glad to have escaped from all that, like a slave who has escaped from a savage and tyrannical master." Cephalus approvingly adds, "When the appetites relax and cease to importune us ... we escape from many mad masters."[6] If desire, sexual and otherwise, is not controlled, it will rule over us.

Plato regarded it as subhuman and beastly for reason to be the slave of the passions, as this subjects the most elevated and noble part of us to that which is the lowest. And this rule by passion is also destructive; many people have thrown away their fortunes, families, reputations, honor—and even their liberty and lives—under the whip of the "mad master" of an overpowering desire. Thus, among the central concerns of the *Republic* is how to escape from the tyranny of our appetites even while they are vigorous, rather than hoping that reason will finally prevail if they wither in old age. The imperative to subordinate desire to reason is a persistent theme in classical philosophy, albeit one that often had little influence on the broader pagan culture.

In contrast to this need for self-control, the sexual revolution declared that to be authentically human means indulging our desires and even defining ourselves by them. It insisted that we should identify with our desires and our consumption: We are what we want. Our culture has therefore been remade to accommodate and encourage an expanding array of sexual preferences and expressions.

Sexual liberalism takes the opposite attitude to that which Cephalus praised in Sophocles. Rather than welcoming aging as a cooling of the passions, the ethos of sexual liberation tells us to devote our resources to remaining forever young—trying not just to remain reasonably fit and healthy as we grow old but also perpetually to have the appearance and the sex drive of youth. For those who need additional stimulus, there are pills. For those, young and old, who are unable or unwilling to find a partner, there is an endless online emporium of porn and webcam sex shows, an expansive sex toy industry, and a nascent AI girlfriend industry. The goal is untrammeled sexual self-indulgence and expression, and so sexual liberation seeks freedom even from the social necessity of finding another person to fulfill one's urges. Rather than teaching us to control our passions, sexual liberalism gives them free rein as it removes obstacles, whether taboos or the need for another person, from their expression. The dream of sexual liberation is freedom not only from the restraints of custom and obligation but even from biology and its limits.

Both Christianity and the classical philosophical tradition see this obsessive indulgence as a form of bondage. The best of the ancient philosophers and Stoics taught that reason should govern desire—their idea of sexual liberation would have meant freedom from the "mad master" that Sophocles was glad to be rid of. True freedom, in this view, consists of placing one's appetites and actions under the control and regulation of reason. Christianity goes further, viewing sexual ethics and self-control not merely as matters of moderation but as ones of holiness and sanctification. For the Christian, authentic sexual liberation is part of the righteous overcoming of sin, including sexual sins.

Thus, our cultural history offers three visions of what could be meant by sexual freedom: the sexual revolution's liberation of desire, the classical tradition of reason's liberation from the tyranny of desire, and the Christian teaching of liberation from sexual sin through sanctification.

Christians may see the classical philosophical vision as elevating, especially compared to the squalid cruelty of common pagan sexuality and the indulgence of modern sexual liberalism. And classical philosophy could be ennobling. But the ancient philosophical traditions had significant limitations, beginning with philosophy's status as a niche pursuit. Unlike Christianity, which converted the masses, philosophy was content to remain a rare private hobby. At most it imagined governing through a philosophic few who had attained power or a powerful few who had become philosophic. There was no ambition to make the teeming masses into philosophical acolytes.

Thus, though ancient philosophers might look down on those who abandoned themselves to sexual desire, they still remained part of the pagan world, with all the cruelty and injustice of its erotic life. Philosophers were often indifferent to the exploitative sexual reality of the culture around them, in which prostitution, the sexual use of slaves, pederasty, infanticide, and more were common. At most, philosophers might disapprove of these practices, but they lacked the Christian horror at, and subsequent reforming zeal toward, them. The philosophers, admirable as they were at times, never seriously challenged the everyday evils that defined pagan sexuality—that task was left for the Christian Church.

This is not to say that pagan sexual morality was a free-for-all, for it was governed by social necessity and hierarchy. Despite their subsequent reputation in some quarters, the Romans were not unbridled hedonists. The bonds and obligations of family were very important to them. They respected marriage and abhorred adultery, at least officially. But a married man having sex with slaves and prostitutes did not count as adultery, and though married love was hoped for and praised, divorce was easy to obtain. The rules governing sex and family life served the needs of the family and city—but also the interests and impulses of those with power, especially men.

Philosophers might urge moderation or even abstinence, but this counsel was for their (few) followers; they had little interest in overturning the entire social order. Furthermore, a philosophic detachment from the pleasures of the flesh did not necessarily mean forgoing them—some indulgence was allowed a reasonable man, so long as he did not become a slave to his desires. Pagan philosophers were, after all, still pagan. They had not experienced the radical change in perspective that Christianity spread through the world.

The Christian sexual revolution was based on a radically different understanding about what it is to be human than the pagan masses, or even the pagan philosophers, had. Christianity goes beyond urging restraints on sexual desire that are rational and socially and personally beneficial. Rather, it views a right ordering of sex not only as an important part of living righteously in the created order of this world but also as a sign of our eschatological fulfillment.

Christianity teaches that we are created male and female and are meant for each other. Sex within this creation order takes on a heightened significance because it is how new persons are begotten, each with the end of knowing and glorifying God forever. This Christian belief in the value of each person was the source of Christian horror at abortion and infanticide. In contrast to the casual pagan exploitation and discarding of the weak, from infants to slaves, in service of sexual pleasure, Christianity demands that we regulate sexuality in the best interests of children, rather than ordering it to adult amusement and advantage. Furthermore, the believer's identification with Christ makes sexual sin a defilement, whereas marriage is an image of the union of Christ and the Church—itself described as the Bride of Christ.

The Christian understanding of sex, and the sexual morality it teaches, is not arbitrary. Rather, it brings together creation, procreation, the eschaton, human unions, and the union of human and divine. Furthermore, just as Christianity introduced a view of sex far more elevated than that of the pagan world it overcame, it also saw sin, including sexual sin, as far more pernicious and intractable than pagans did. The division of self is not just between reason and passion but between sin nature and the sanctification of the believer through divine grace. Freedom from sin is about a reordering of the whole person, a vision that is at best hinted at in ancient philosophy.

Thus, a Christian vision of sexual liberation involves both personal liberation from sin through grace and a redemption of the creation order, specifically turning sexual relations back toward that which was ordained by God. And so Christianity saw and sought to end the exploitation and double standards that the ancient world took for granted. Particularly notable was that Christian sexual teaching applied to everyone. It is not that sexual double standards ceased with the triumph of Christianity over paganism but that Christianity enabled double standards to be identified and denounced as unjust and hypocritical, rather than presumed as a natural expression of how things are.

The Christian sexual revolution meant freeing people from the bondage created by sexual sin and trying to restore the creation order of marriage as the lifelong, faithful union of a man and a woman. Christianity toppled the pagan norms because it offered a better way of life, including sexually, in which freedom consists of self-control, aided by grace, directed toward genuine human flourishing in accord with God's will and our nature. Christian sexual morality protects both the social order and our spiritual well-bring. It honors our nature as men and women, and it guards and elevates marriage, which is the basis of civilization and culture in this world, the vocation to which most of us are called, and a sign of our union with God in the world to come. Marriage is the rightful place of human participation in God's work of creation through procreation, as the physical union of the two halves of the human species is ordered toward the begetting of new human life.

Christian freedom from sin offers not just hope for liberation from the tyranny of desire but also a positive vision that classical philosophy lacked—a partial restoration of the goodness of the created order and the proper place of sex within it. In contrast, much of the sexual revolution is an attempt, seemingly made plausible by technology, to democratize the sexual license that the pagan world allowed for men, especially the rich and powerful. But this is not freedom, only a return to the bondage of sin.

Sex and Social Justice

"I have sex just because I like it. Sex is fun."[7]

Well, yes, but is it worth killing for? This is the obvious response to *New York Times* editor Mara Gay's justification for abortion, which said the quiet part out loud: Abortion enables people to have the fun of sex without the duty of caring for the babies conceived by that fun.

Her outlook illustrates why the sexual revolution is incompatible with genuine social justice. The point of appealing to social justice (as opposed to justice in general) is to emphasize how our actions intersect with the lives of others. Social justice, rightly understood, is rooted in the truth that we are not isolated, atomistic individuals. Rather, we need others to survive and thrive, and we are therefore emmeshed in relational and cultural webs of dependence and duty, gratitude and obligation. Right relations with others depend on recognizing this and acting with an awareness of how our deeds affect others, starting with those who are closest to us—our family, friends, and neighbors.

And so social justice necessarily includes our sex lives. Sex is, after all, interpersonal, and its consequences are far-reaching, with a multitude of relational implications.

Furthermore, sex is foundational to society, for it is how the next generation comes into being. A commitment to social justice cannot be indifferent to sex or regard it as merely a private matter. Our sexual choices, and the relational decisions tied to them, cannot be divested of responsibility toward others—and these responsibilities cannot be reduced merely to the question of consent. The evils inflicted by sexual liberation show that a right understanding and ordering of human sexuality is essential to social justice, for a disordered sexual culture harms us all.

That sex is fun does not negate the imperative to act justly, both individually and as a society. We restrict and regulate, by social convention and law, many things that are fun. But the intensity of sexual desire tempts us to overlook the evils done in its behalf. Both individuals and entire cultures can be blind to the wrongs done for the sake of sex. For example, it took the advent of Christianity to perceive the victims of the pagan sexual world and to seek justice for them. The Christian war on Roman sexual culture—the casual sexual exploitation of slaves and prostitutes (and slavery and prostitution were thoroughly entwined), the exposure of infants, presumptive male infidelity—was a fight for social justice.

The sexual cruelties of pagan antiquity may be obvious to us, but our sexually liberated culture has its own injustices that are often overlooked. Children in particular are victimized by the effects of sexual liberalism—from the children aborted because their conception was inconvenient to the children growing up without mothers or fathers because the sexual grass looked greener elsewhere. The relational instability created by the sexual revolution has been devastating for children, with grave effects on all of society. Our culture would be very different if we put the interests and needs of children before the adult pursuit of sexual pleasure. Everyone knows this, but few want to hear about it, let alone do anything about it.

The response to economist Melissa Kearney's 2023 book, *The Two-Parent Privilege*, demonstrates our culture's unwillingness to address how adult relational and sexual choices harm children. Kearney's argument is simple—being raised by married parents is, on average, better for kids, so marriage should be encouraged for the sake of children in particular and society in general. But as Nick Kristof put it in a *New York Times* piece discussing the book, "There is a deep discomfort in liberal circles about acknowledging these realities." He framed his column as a plea to his fellow liberals to face these uncomfortable facts, a plea he felt he had to surround "with a shower of caveats" to comfort his readers as they faced a difficult truth.[8]

The reasons for this gingerly approach may be seen in the review *The Washington Post* published. The reviewer, Becca Rothfeld, did not want to accept that having married parents is better for children. Thus, she complained about the book's "reactionary mores" and sought in vain for a way to discredit its data. Having struggled to propose a plausible alternative to Kearney's findings, Rothfeld concluded, "If marriage benefits children because it affords them more emotional support, why should we 'work to restore and foster' the nuclear family, which privatizes affection and attention, instead of working to foster a new norm of communal child-rearing? Is there any reason to conclude that marriage is the best solution, except that it is the solution that already (although perhaps not for much longer, if current trends continue apace) exists?"[9]

Get ye to a commune, children.

Of course, schemes for "communal child-rearing" do not work. They have never worked, for reasons that have been explained again and again ever since Aristotle demolished

Plato's flights of fancy about having wives and children in common (whether Plato meant for his "city in speech" to be taken seriously as a practical model has remained a subject of debate). A "new norm of communal child-rearing" especially will not work in a continental democratic republic with well over three hundred million inhabitants. That Rothfeld retreated to such nonsense demonstrates her reluctance to admit that our current culture of adult sexual autonomy hurts children by depriving them of stable relationships with their parents.

Child-rearing should include extended family, friends, fellow congregants, and so on, but though such support is excellent, it does not replace having a mother and a father. Furthermore, help and support in raising children will largely be based on the presence of strong nuclear families. Stable marriages are a source of, and support for, solid bonds with extended family members and others in a community, whereas a lack of parental commitment will preclude or imperil such connections. The nuclear family is the indispensable basis for healthy communities because marriage provides a foundation upon which other relationships may rely.

The data is not really in dispute: Broken families break people and communities. And there is no substitute for family, even if *Washington Post* writers wish there were. Stable marriages are the best anti-child-poverty program,[10] the best educational program,[11] and even the best anti-crime program.[12] We know that the absence of fathers is a major predictor of criminal behavior; boys hurt by paternal abandonment are more likely to grow up to hurt others.[13] Those concerned with real social justice should consider how many men in prison would not be there if their fathers had committed to raising them, as well as how many victims would never have been robbed, raped, beaten, or killed. Those concerned about the bottom line ought to reflect on how much of the wealth and technological progress of the last decades has been spent mitigating the effects of the sexual revolution. Intact families are better and cheaper than prisons and welfare programs. Furthermore, we cannot spend our way out of all the consequences of family collapse.

All this is obvious, but there is still resistance to admitting it, for that often means accepting culpability in the social injustice caused by the sexual revolution. The evils and deprivations inflicted on children in the name of adult sexual liberation may be the clearest examples, but there are, as described in the preceding chapters, many more harms, from loneliness to porn addiction to the self-hatred and mutilation encouraged by gender ideology. This is why Christianity, as it calls us to the fellowship with God and other people that we were meant for, does not ignore sexuality. Christian sexual ethics, though often difficult to adhere to, are for our good and the good of others. Christianity provides moral and relational resources to resist both pleasant-seeming temptations and the apparently expedient evils they encourage.

Just as the early Church recognized and challenged the evils and exploitation at the core of pagan sexual culture, the Church today must not shy away from addressing the evils of the sexual revolution and from preaching and modeling a better way. Sin persists, of course, within even the best families and congregations, for all believers are limited and imperfect. Worse still is the peril of false teachers and treacherous leaders who prey, including sexually, upon those they should protect. However, these failures and betrayals should not dissuade Christians from proclaiming the truth about marriage, family, and sexuality, for it is desperately needed by both the Church and the world.

The evils the sexual revolution has inflicted upon our culture, communities, and families can seem overwhelming. Resisting them personally, and in our families and churches, is hard enough, let alone rolling them back in the broader culture. But we are called not to do everything all at once but to do what we can where God has placed us. In particular, Christians need to recognize that it is up to us to teach a crumbling culture how we are to live amid the wreckage of the sexual revolution.

Christians can offer a superior vision of human flourishing. But instantiating it requires practical wisdom, instruction, and assistance, as well as a recognition of the extent of the sexual and relational wasteland. Churches need to consider how they can help young men and women become ready for marriage, pair off and get married, and then succeed in their marriages—and a weekend of premarital counseling is not nearly enough. Church leaders need to think hard about how to help young men and women form and maintain godly relationships in a culture where all the old scripts and skills have been lost. For example, even many basic relational skills, such as how to ask a woman out on a date, are now mysterious to many young men, and they are finding it hard to muddle through. If older men and Church leaders don't help them, they will be left to learn how to be men and how to relate to women from the likes of TikTok, YouTube, and Reddit.

Efforts to promote marriage will make demands on the always-limited time and resources of churches, but they are necessary because marriage is essential to the life of the Church. Marriage is the vocation to which most Christians are called, and churches need to help make it a plausible option for most young Christians. Plus, chastity is a harder sell to those who, following the culture, do not expect to get married until around thirty, if at all.

Another challenge is the need for Christians to act according to the teachings of Christianity. This requires grace and self-discipline, as well as repentance when we fail. It also demands courage to proclaim unpopular beliefs about sex. But, and perhaps more painful still, retaining a Christian witness amid a hostile culture requires churches to discipline their members. This was essential for the early Church, and it cannot be ignored now. For example, far too many churches, especially evangelical churches, that profess doctrinal orthodoxy on sexual matters are unwilling to take seriously Jesus' warning in Matthew 19 about the adulterous nature of divorce and remarriage. Jesus was clear, but many churches and pastors do not act as if they believe this admonition. Rather, they implicitly (and sometimes explicitly) endorse easy divorce and remarriage even though it compromises the gospel and imperils souls. Discipline is rarely easy, but it is necessary for the good of the Church and its witness to the world.

There is also much for Christians to do in their positions as citizens and public officials. Some of this is a continuation of long-standing efforts—for instance, restricting abortion remains a paramount political imperative for Christians. But Christians must also adapt and respond to new threats and opportunities. For example, though curtailing pornography seemed like a lost cause for years, laws that restrict pornography by requiring meaningful age verification now appear to be both effective and supported by bipartisan majorities. Such laws protect children and discourage adult consumption—and they are political winners. Furthermore, while direct political conflict over the sexual revolution is unavoidable on some matters (for example, abortion and gender ideology), there are also many ways in which Christians can strike against the material basis and effects of the sexual revolution. Public policy should encourage good and right ways of living, by, for instance, rewarding stable marriages. Thus, Christians should try to make the tax code more family friendly and to influence housing policy so that it is better suited to the needs of families, especially young ones with children. A great array of tasks await, from the public to the private, and there is room for a diversity of opinions on many points—for example, though Christians must be united in opposition to the sexual revolution, they may reasonably disagree over the best tax or housing policies.

Theological work must also be done, especially among Protestants. For instance, as Katelyn Walls Shelton observed for *World Opinions*, a dire need exists for Protestants to undertake something like a theology of the body, and that project has only just begun.[14] Many evangelicals who have tried to hold the line on Christian sexual ethics have nonetheless struggled to articulate a systematic reason for their beliefs beyond fidelity to Scripture. And despite some exceptions, there is a general lack of serious evangelical reflection on subjects such as contraception and in vitro fertilization (IVF). There are intellectual tasks, as well as political and ministry projects, to be done. Catholics, in contrast, have a strong intellectual tradition but have struggled to inspire parishioners to adhere to it or to enforce Church discipline even in many cases of public and egregious violations.

From the polls to the pews, Christians must resist the evils of the sexual revolution and offer something better—an understanding of sex that contributes to real social justice. In these efforts, there will be space for some reasonable disagreement among faithful Christians. However, upholding the truths of Christian sexual ethics against the sexual revolution must be a point of unity. There can be no social justice in defiance of God's law, which is given for our good as we live together.

What Sex Is For

Christianity provides the answers about relationships and sex that the world needs. As the Baptist theologian Andrew Walker put it, "We are getting to a place where the gospel is not only what reconciles us to God, but what will be the only pathway to authentic living in a world that runs on cynicism and deception."[15] Christian teachings about marriage and sex are rooted in the order of creation. It is therefore a dereliction of the love we owe to our neighbors to stop proclaiming these truths, for they are beneficial for, and applicable to, everyone. For example, having lots of sexual partners before marriage correlates with less relational stability and less relational and sexual satisfaction.[16] Likewise, cohabitating before marriage does not make a happy marriage more likely; rather, it is correlated with decreased relational stability and satisfaction.[17] Following Christian teaching that sex is meant only for marriage turns out to be good for marriages,[18] which are, in turn, good for us personally and socially.

Despite such vindication, some Christians are uncomfortable with treating Christian truths as, well, true when it comes to public policy. They have internalized the idea that we are not to "impose" our morality (especially sexual morality) on others and that we are instead to accept the "neutrality" of liberalism, in which everyone is free to do what is right in his own eyes.

But when it comes to sex, this supposed neutrality has been a catastrophe that has ruined lives and relationships by the millions, in part because sexual liberalism's refusal to judge between desires leaves its adherents stuck. Even if they recognize the disaster of the current relational marketplace, they are barred as a matter of principle from making moral judgments about it. For example, without a normative understanding of what is good in a relationship (including sex), why should a woman's desire for romance, or even simple kindness, matter more than a man's porn-induced kinks? Furthermore, theoretical neutrality between competing desires favors, in practice, desires that are simple and strong over those that are more complex and diffuse. In such cases, intensity and immediacy tend to win out, and so relational needs are subordinated to sexual wants. Thus, liberalism's purported neutrality about the nature of the good and the good life is not actually neutral, for it denigrates self-control, commitment, and kindness while promoting selfish indulgence.

Indeed, there can be no neutrality between truth and falsehood, and the truth is that Christian sexual ethics are essential to social justice and human flourishing. Of course, there must be prudence in how these truths are implemented—we cannot mandate all virtue and prohibit all vice. Nonetheless, Christianity is correct that sex was meant for marriage and that this limitation was established for our good. Like the rest of our appetites, our sexual desires are often out of control. This is why Jesus and the apostles warned repeatedly about sexual sin, which, like all sin, is enslaving and harmful. However, the Christian understanding of what sex is for not only protects us, prohibiting actions that are harmful, but also directs us toward a fuller, richer life.

Christianity goes beyond urging sexual self-control for the sake of personal and social benefits. It teaches that sex is bound up with deep truths, which is why marriage is repeatedly used as a symbol of the union of Christ and the

Church. Christianity recognizes that a right ordering of sex is not only an important part of living righteously in the created order of this world but also a sign of our eschatological fulfillment.

Jesus affirmed that monogamous marriage between a man and a woman is part of God's creation order. Matthew records His words to the Pharisees: "Have you not read that the one who made them at the beginning 'made them male and female,' and said, 'For this reason a man shall leave his father and mother and be joined to his wife, and the two shall become one flesh'? So they are no longer two, but one flesh" (19:4–6, NRSVCE). The one-flesh description applies both to the physical intimacy of sex and to its generative nature, in which the gametes of a man and a woman are united in the conception of a new human life—their flesh literally uniting to become one in a new person. Rather than viewing children as an optional (and often unwanted) side effect of sex, Christianity sees children as a fulfillment of our sexual natures, for sex is generative by design. Sex is perhaps the preeminent example of human participation in, and furtherance of, divine creation, as through it we take on the responsibilities, sorrows, and joys of begetting new persons.

Paul's first letter to the tumultuous church in Corinth further illuminates the significance Christianity sees in sex. After condemning sexual immorality and instructing the church to discipline members who are guilty of it, Paul explained why our bodies, and specifically our sex lives, matter spiritually. The apostle expounded upon how the believer's identification with Christ and indwelling by the Holy Spirit make sexual immorality a defilement:

> The body is not meant for [sexual] immorality, but for the Lord, and the Lord for the body. And God raised the Lord

and will also raise us up by his power. Do you not know that your bodies are members of Christ? Shall I therefore take the members of Christ and make them members of a prostitute? Never! Do you not know that he who joins himself to a prostitute becomes one body with her? For, as it is written, "The two shall become one." But he who is united to the Lord becomes one spirit with him. Shun [sexual] immorality. Every other sin which a man commits is outside the body; but the [sexually] immoral man sins against his own body. Do you not know that your body is a temple of the Holy Spirit within you, which you have from God? You are not your own; you were bought with a price. So glorify God in your body. (6:13–20)

Our bodies are God's workmanship, for His glory and our good. We are embodied and are meant to glorify God in our embodiment. Our bodies shall, like Christ's, be resurrected and transformed, for they are intrinsic to our nature. And our current bodies, though tainted and cursed by sin, are still identified with Christ and indwelt by the Holy Spirit. Therefore, the one-flesh union ordained by God for marriage becomes a loathsome defilement outside marriage. Sex goes beyond intimacy to unity. Thus, for a believer, who is identified with Christ, to be sexually unified outside the marriage relationship God ordained and blessed is to dishonor and disgrace Christ. This spiritual significance is part of why sexual sins matter even if other immediate negative consequences are avoided.

Then, in the next chapter, Paul informed the Corinthian believers that celibate devotion to God and the Church is a special gift that is to be honored but that those who are not called to this vocation ought to marry lest they be tempted into sexual immorality. Yet the Apostle's description of married sex goes beyond presenting it as just a licit outlet for those not called to holy celibacy. He wrote,

Because of the temptation to [sexual] immorality, each
man should have his own wife and each woman her own
husband. The husband should give to his wife her conju-
gal rights, and likewise the wife to her husband. For the
wife does not rule over her own body, but the husband
does; likewise the husband does not rule over his own
body, but the wife does. Do not refuse one another except
perhaps by agreement for a season, that you may devote
yourselves to prayer; but then come together again, lest
Satan tempt you through lack of self-control. (7:2–5)

Paul, like Jesus, described marriage as intrinsically heterosexual and monogamous. He insisted that spouses are to
be faithful to each other. He presented sex in a Christian
marriage as a reciprocal unitive self-giving: The husband
gives himself to the wife and the wife to her husband. This
physical, one-flesh union of the marriage bed is integral to
the self-giving of Christian marriage, in which husband and
wife forsake not only all others but also their former independent selves. This is a sharp contrast to the sexual revolution, which tells us always to look out for ourselves and our
desires first and to hold back from total commitment.

This faithfulness is essential to fulfill both the unitive and
generative purposes of sex. Without faithfulness, there is no
true unity in sex; rather, there is only, at most, a temporary convergence of selfish interests. And it is faithfulness
that supports the children conceived through sex and ame-
liorates some of the asymmetries of human reproduction.
Faithfulness enables children to be welcomed as the physical instantiation of love, rather than the by-product of lust.
Faithfulness thereby allows sex to have significance beyond
the immediate physical act. In turn, this commitment, with
its unity and potential fruitfulness, allows Christian marriage
to be a fitting image of the union of Christ and the Church.

The Apostle concluded this passage by offering advice in which he emphasized the worth of celibacy devoted to the work of God but also reiterated that there is nothing shameful about Christian marriage. Marriage might be a lesser good than holy celibacy, but it is not a lesser evil—because it is not an evil. Marriage is more than a concession to desire; it is a positive good established by God. Indeed, Paul even advised that, if possible, marriages to pagans should be preserved, in the hopes of converting the nonbelieving spouse and for the sake of any children.

Other New Testament passages containing instruction and advice for Christian households also presume that marriage is a faithful union between a man and a woman.[19] Each has duties to the other, as do children and parents. Ephesians 5 is a particularly rich passage, with the comparison of marriage to the relationship between Christ and the Church. The Apostle explained,

> He who loves his wife loves himself. For no man ever hates his own flesh, but nourishes and cherishes it, just as Christ does the Church, because we are members of his body. "For this reason a man shall leave his father and mother and be joined to his wife, and the two shall become one flesh." This is a great mystery, and I mean in reference to Christ and the Church; however, let each one of you love his wife as himself, and let the wife see that she respects her husband. (vv. 28–33)

This comparison to Christ and the Church is explicitly made to the physical, one-flesh union of husband and wife, not just the wedding ceremony or the nonsexual aspects of married life. The complete union of Christian marriage is a reason for a man to love his wife, and it is also an image of Christ's love for the Church and union with it, which in turn provides yet more reasons for husbands to love their wives. This expresses a deep spiritual mystery yet also provides practical instruction on Christian living.

First, Christianity recognizes that men and women are different and that these differences between the sexes are essential, rather than incidental. Instead of simply telling husbands and wives each to love and respect each other, Paul emphasizes different points for each sex. Christians should not shy away from this, for it is necessary to acknowledge the importance of our embodied existence as men and women. Though this truth cuts against the current culture, it will also come as a relief to many who are sick of having to pretend that men and women are essentially interchangeable. Rather than apologize, Christians should celebrate the reality and importance of our being as male and female.

This, then, gives Christians the weighty task of rightly understanding and acting upon these differences. After all, the pagans saw the differences between men and women—and often used them as an excuse for evil, as exemplified by their sexual double standards for men and women. Christians must avoid such injustices even as we resist a culture that denies the importance of male and female embodiment. That Christians have made mistakes on this matter in the past is cause for humility but not cultural conformity—indeed, many of the past errors were themselves due to cultural conformity (for example, those who elevated middle-class Victorian ideals of homemaking into a Scriptural command). Christians should beware of fleeing from these past mistakes only to fall headlong into the follies of our age, such as the pretense that two men living together are a sufficient substitute for a mother and a father.

Second, this passage shows why sex takes on both more and less significance within Christian marriage. It takes on more significance insofar as it is the consummation of a sacred union representing Christ and the Church, a union that is maximally physically intimate and ordered toward the begetting of new immortal persons. At the same time, though the commitment of marriage provides a relational space of comfort and familiarity that results (on average) in higher sexual satisfaction, it removes the pressure of trying to make sexual pleasure the highest good in a relationship. The Christian marriage is ordered toward something grander than the maximization of sexual pleasure.

Third, by specifically identifying sex within a Christian marriage as an image of Christ's union with the Church, the Apostle highlights that marital sex is good and honorable. The efforts by various radically ascetic Christian movements to denigrate the physical union of husband and wife are rebutted by the Apostle's inspired imagery. But, though the physical union of marriage is a good part of the creation order, it may still be degraded, even in a Christian marriage. Marriage is not a license for any and every sexual behavior. Paul's imagery reminds us that, in particular, a husband's sexual relationship with his wife must exhibit the attributes of Christ's love for the Church; it must be faithful and self-giving, based on a love for and identification with the beloved, rather than an objectification of her.

This vision of marriage highlights the difference between Christian sexual ethics and those of the sexual revolution. The sexual revolution is about getting what one can for oneself, often heedless of the cost to others. Christian sexual teaching is about protecting and loving others, even when this requires restraining oneself. Sex is not disassociated from the rest of life and society but is embedded and regulated within it in a way that is ordered toward the temporal and eternal goods of all. Christians know that even Eros must bow before Christ.

CONCLUSION

Authentic Humans, Authentic Human Flourishing

The Givenness of Life

Entertainment is easy. Living is hard.

We have never had so many ways to amuse ourselves. We carry devices in our pockets that provide immediate access to more music, movies, books, and games than we could consume in countless lifetimes. The production of new content far exceeds our capacity to keep up with it, without even taking into account our unparalleled broadcasting of sports and other live spectacles. And there is so much more waiting for us outside our smartphones and other streaming devices. The options for experiences and travel and shows and games and so on have never been greater. And while some of it is pricey, much is almost free—all those musicians on YouTube, for instance.

Yet despite all these amusements, ours is not a happy culture. Rather, it is lonely, anxious, and depressed. The terms in which we describe entertainment—as content to be consumed—suggest why. Consumption is not really living. It does not fulfill us, for it is an endless feeding that does not satisfy. It grows wearying—a parade of sensations, few leaving any real impression, let alone providing lasting fulfillment. It is the life of Phil, Bill Murray's character in the movie *Groundhog Day*: eating, drinking, reveling, and seducing, but ultimately trapped and despairing, proving Rita right when she quotes Walter Scott to him:

> The wretch, concentred all in self,
> Living, shall forfeit fair renown,
> And, doubly dying, shall go down
> To the vile dust, from whence he sprung,
> Unwept, unhonour'd, and unsung.[1]

What Phil needed was not more experiences and consumption but love. Phil needed to become a person who loved others, who genuinely willed their good and was not just out for himself. He tried pretending to be a nice guy to seduce Rita, but it was only when he became a new man, and no longer sought to seduce her, that he was free—one of the most consequential decisions during filming was that Phil and Rita would not have sex on the night when he was finally freed from the eternal return of Groundhog Day.

Living well requires love, not just consumption. And sexual consumption (and that is how the sexual revolution has taught us to think of sex: as something to be consumed) is not the same as love. The sexual revolution conceded this, insofar as it deliberately separated sex from any pretense of love. To the extent that it tolerated love, it was defined as the heady rush of early romance. But commitment, real till-death-do-us-part commitment, is, in the calculus of sexual liberalism, an intolerable giving up of control over one's life and the pursuit of pleasure.

Sexual liberalism teaches us to identify with our desires, rather than our relationships and responsibilities. According to the sexual revolution, we are meant, so far as we are meant for anything, to be autonomous pleasure-seekers. We should always be free to move on and to reinvent ourselves.

In contrast, Christianity teaches us that we need committed love to flourish. Christianity thereby offers a better way of life, in which freedom consists not of revolting against our nature but of accepting the givenness of our being and striving to live with self-control aided by grace and directed toward genuine human flourishing. This flourishing comes through love for other people and commitment to them, even at the cost of suffering ourselves. We are to find our identities through love expressed in right relations with others: first God and then our neighbors.

The Christian way of life is often laborious, difficult, and self-denying, but it is genuine living rather than a mere existing. For example, watching porn is easy; forming and maintaining a marriage is difficult. But the latter offers a far more fulfilling life, including sexually. That which is best in life requires perseverance. And the labor this requires is often redeemed by the purpose. The work we put into being fully human is a large part of what makes us fully human. Just as sin changes us, so, too, does doing what is right. In *Groundhog Day*, Phil could do whatever he felt like, with no lasting consequences, yet he came to find it pointless and empty. It was only as he gradually became a new person that he was able to find joy and meaning in loving others.

Human flourishing requires accepting both the need to labor and the limits of what we can accomplish. The work of changing oneself also makes manifest the givenness of life. It is through turning potentiality into actuality that we encounter the limits of our being. We cannot, it turns out, be whatever we want to be, and we certainly cannot be everything we want to be all at once. It is only by accepting our limits and foreclosing many other options that we can actually become something worthwhile. It is precisely in this that we are able to become fully alive, rather than remaining stuck in an amused but anxious and lonely potentiality, too afraid of missing out on some other possibility to ever do or become anything much.

This is evident in the work of raising children. Having a baby is often the best of times and the worst of times, both a fulfillment of our most fervent wishes and almost unbearably exhausting. Newborn days are often a months-long sleep-deprived blur, in which moments of bliss (the inner glow of holding one's child) alternate with moments of near insanity (as he wakes up every hour during the night). Joy in the morning? Yes, but also more weariness than before going to bed the previous night.

Despite all the work it entails, the timeless miracle of meeting a new human life is a unique fulfillment. Yes, we know there is a new human person growing in the womb—there are the kicks and hiccups and, thanks to the achievements of modern science, images via ultrasound. Yet finally meeting one's child face-to-face is still astounding beyond full expression in words. It may be a transformative moment because it is such a clear reminder that people are the point of it all, that it is through love that fulfillment may be found. And this love is particular, a dedication to this individual child who has been given to us. We do not receive generic children; we are instead bound to specific persons with all their distinctiveness. The joys and fulfillment of parenting require commitment to the particular, and therefore the closing of many other alternatives, including sexually—being a good father means being committed to the mother of one's children.

Moments such as meeting one's child for the first time are difficult to describe because our language and thoughts have become defined by the mastery of objects, an approach seemingly validated by the triumphs of modern science. But a baby is not a thing or a product. Rather, a baby is a person—an immortal being radiant with transcendence. The language of subjects and objects is especially ill-suited for the attempt to capture the full truth of the person, who always exceeds definition. And yet some of our expressions are truer than we realize. For instance, the problem with the cliché that a child is a gift is not that it is wrong but that, because it is a cliché, we often glance past the profundity of its truth. The gift of life is inseparable from the givenness of life. We are begotten by our parents, not made by them. Existence is given to us; we cannot preview our life before living it, nor select our attributes as we would an avatar on the character-creation screen at the start of a video game. We cannot choose our parents, we cannot choose whether we are male or female (much as the gender ideologues wish otherwise), and so on.

In contrast, we have more control over the circumstances of our children's lives, and we want the best for their lives. But within the natural and good impulse to care for our children, there are temptations that diminish the respect owed to their personhood. There are helicopter parents, tiger moms, and an extensive array of products promising a competitive edge for the children who use them. Alongside this attitude of competitive child-rearing, we are encouraged to view our progeny as products—to be planned for, carefully ordered when desired, and discarded if not up to spec. Biotechnology is knocking on the door of designer children, but the dehumanizing, dystopian ramifications of this mindset are already here. There are the discarded embryos from IVF, the evils of surrogacy, and the abortions of children deemed defective, less desirable, or inconveniently timed.

Excessive efforts to control the givenness of our children's lives expose our doubts that life is a good gift in itself. They reveal a vision of human flourishing that measures success in terms of fame and fortune, possessions and pleasures. Our work, in this view, is a means to these things—the point of labor is to enable more and better consumption and to attain more status. But though these things may be good in their place, they can easily become idols that divert our attention from that which is best in this life, such as beauty, friendship, and love. The ordinary life well lived is characterized not by an abundance of possessions and accomplishments but by virtuous living in loving relationships and community.

These relationships, in turn, give us glimpses of a destiny beyond this life. The joy of a child's laugh may offer a brief flash of the inexhaustible glory of eternity. More than the good things of this life, what we should desire for ourselves and our children is to have the life of God that transcends death. We must teach them that they are of value in themselves, regardless of what they do or do not achieve, and that their fullest life and happiness will be found in loving God and then in loving others.

Such a life will often be strenuous and painful. Marriage and parenthood are hard. They are also glorious. They do not offer the comfortable complacence of those who live to be entertained. They can, however, give peace and rest that cannot be found in a life of consumption, for relationships and love are not consumed in their enjoyment. Communion with others is not a finite resource. Rather, it is able to expand—growing both deeper and broader—as it is enjoyed. Thus, though other delights and pleasures plateau, only the inexhaustibility of persons can satisfy us.

Love and Vulnerability

Christians have been promised much trouble in this world, and we get it. The early Church grew on the blood of its martyrs, and the Church has been persecuted and assailed through the centuries. Though Christians in the West to-day are not persecuted unto death, many believers around the world are. And we in the West are still subject to the sufferings that our flesh is heir to, as well as mental tur-moil and anguish. We are mortal, and even the best social arrangements will fall far short of perfection. Evil persists in the world, and even in the lives of Christians as they are still being sanctified. Thus, Christians must balance a confi-dence in the beneficence of Christian moral teachings with a humility about our own sinfulness and a recognition of the troubles of the world.

Christianity is not the health and wealth dispensary proclaimed by prosperity-gospel preachers. God does not promise us money, success, and healing if we just believe more fervently—and throw some cash into the prosperity preacher's collection as a sign of our faith. That is not the gospel of Christ but heresy, one that also comes in sub-tler forms. It is, for example, tempting to exaggerate the benefits of a righteous life, including when it comes to sex. But following the commands of God is not a surety of happiness and freedom from suffering. Chastity—abstinence outside marriage and fidelity within it—does not ensure a great sex life. Yes, it avoids many evils and produces, on average, more marital and sexual satisfac-tion, but it is not a sure formula for sexual delight, for Christianity offers no such promises for any of the goods or pleasures of this life.

Nor does God promise that we will be safe from the emotional storms of this life. Christianity is not stoicism, offering peace through indifference to this world, and it does not promise freedom from grief, sorrow, anxiety, and other such afflictions. It promises no permanent happi-ness in this life, for such an assurance would simply be an emotional version of the prosperity gospel, offering mental health and wealth instead of material riches. Christianity tells us that we will suffer; all those psalms of lament and exhortations to endure trials and tribulations are in the Bible for a reason.

Yet Christianity still leads us toward authentic, joyful living. One reason for this is that Christian moral teachings direct us away from many harmful and self-destructive behaviors. The world would be a much better place if more people tried to live according to Christian moral teachings, including those about sex. But that is not the whole of it. Christianity provides more than moral advice to ameliorate the evils of the world and to avoid self-destruction. The deeper reason Christians can anticipate trouble while still confidently proclaiming that they follow a better way of life is because they know that the way of love is also a way of suffering. As C. S. Lewis wrote,

> To love at all is to be vulnerable. Love anything and your heart will certainly be wrung and possibly be broken. If you want to make sure of keeping it intact, you must give your heart to no one ... avoid all entanglements; lock it up safe in the casket or coffin of your selfishness. But in that casket—safe, dark, motionless, airless—it will change. It will not be broken; it will become unbreakable, impenetrable, irredeemable. The alternative to tragedy, or at least to the risk of tragedy, is damnation. The only place outside Heaven where you can be perfectly safe from all the dangers and perturbations of love is Hell.[2]

Love extends our affections beyond ourselves, and therefore it adds to our potential sources of pain. Love makes our well-being dependent on others. Because love draws our concerns outside ourselves and our physical comforts and pleasures, loving others necessarily means that our happiness is intertwined with that of others. We rejoice when they rejoice, but we also mourn when they mourn, for their misfortunes become our own. Love makes us hostages to the wills and whims of others; those whom we love have the power to make us miserable if they betray or reject us.

In the end, love leads to mourning; death awaits as the conclusion of even the most fortunate and joyous relationships. A good marriage is one that culminates with a wife in tears at her husband's deathbed, or vice versa. Children bury parents, siblings bury each other, friends miss those who have died before them. It is impossible to love others without putting oneself at risk of being hurt.

And so there are those who flee from love, who strive to avoid entanglements and keep their hearts secure. They occupy themselves with safe, selfish pleasures and amusements or retreat to the idyls of imagination. Examples abound: Some are worldly men and women; others are dreamers such as the philosopher Jean-Jacques Rousseau, whose longing for love was overwhelmed by his terror at the psychological vulnerability it required.[3]

Our culture offers and encourages such retreats from love, and we should expect more with advances in AI and virtual reality. There are plenty of pursuits and pleasures to distract ourselves with. As for our physical longing for others, the sexual revolution has relentlessly pursued the separation of sexual pleasure and love. It promised that we could have pleasure without having to make any commitments, that there was no need to swear to love or be faithful. It told us to share our bodies readily and our hearts grudgingly, if at all—ditto for our bank accounts, as some things are just too personal and intimate to offer to anyone else. But we cannot be happy without love, and so we are increasingly alone, depressed, and anxious—and for all this, often still heartbroken. Nor will AI girlfriends be an adequate answer; better fake companionship (emotional or sexual) will no more satisfy our real needs than better video games have.

In contrast to the world's retreats from, and artificial substitutes for, love, Christianity insists that we must follow the way of love despite the vulnerability it creates. Those who want the fulfillments of love must be willing to sacrifice and suffer, for no genuine love for others can be guaranteed to be free from pain. Only through openness to the wounds of love are we able to realize the fulfillments of love and communion with God and neighbor that we were meant for. Only through love are we able to live authentically human lives.

Embracing the way of love is for our good even in this life and its sufferings. And it is through letting go of our lives by extending beyond ourselves that we can experience joys and fulfillments that are impossible for those who remain in self-protective selfishness—regardless of how avariciously they pursue pleasure. We are fulfilled by finding our identities through love and right relations with others, not by the constant indulgence of appetites.

This truth provides a glimpse of how marriage is a source of grace and an image of Christ and His Church. Jesus Christ spent a life in humble service to establish His Church, finally dying for her. Nothing that He asks of us in protecting and preserving marriage is more difficult to endure than what He has already undergone for our sake. Christianity does not pretend to offer freedom from suffering; rather, it claims to transform it. It teaches that suffering can be sanctified and redeemed, that it can become part of the glory and beauty of the divine renewal of creation. In this fallen world, we are conceived to die and born to suffer, but that is not the end of the story. Christians declare that God is love. And to say that God is love means that God is, in some way, vulnerable. God's love for us is also a divine vulnerability, which was made manifest in the Incarnation. "God so loved the world that he gave his only-begotten Son" (Jn 3:16), who entered into this world to redeem it and to draw it to Himself by taking suffering upon Himself.

The bodily suffering and sacrifice of Jesus call us in turn to be willing to sacrifice our bodies and our bodily desires in service to God and for the good of others. The mysteries of Incarnation, Crucifixion, and Resurrection are the ultimate rebuttals to the notion that God does not care about what we do with our bodies. We are saved though the Body and Blood of Jesus. Bodies matter, for we are saved because God had a body. And God has a body. God will have a body, world without end, amen.

And so do and shall we. Christianity does not proclaim only a spiritual immortality, with souls shedding vestigial bodies to enter a realm of pure spiritual bliss. Rather, it assures us also of a bodily resurrection. This is sometimes hard to believe, but it is at the center of the Christian creed. From its earliest days, the Church has testified to Christ's physical Resurrection and proclaimed the hope that we will likewise be raised from death. We are not promised heaven as a state of incorporeal bliss but the Kingdom of God in a new heaven and a new earth. The physical universe shall be renewed in glory, along with the children of God. Instead of a promise to eliminate suffering in this life, Christianity promises a renewed, eternal life, which is made available to us through the suffering and vulnerability of love.

The Romance of Marriage and Family

"Marriage is a duel to the death, which no man of honour should decline."[4]

Like many of G. K. Chesterton's aphorisms, this line illuminates—and then perplexes. It is a wonderful utterance by a character in *Manalive*, and many readers will feel that it gets something right. Yet, on further reflection, it is confusing. Who are the duelists? If they are husband and wife, then the saying takes on a decidedly un-Chestertonian grimness—he cannot have meant to praise the ugly conflicts that mar some marriages. And even if we take him to mean romantic sparring, that would still be exhausting and myopic if indulged to the extent suggested. Spouses may at times flirtatiously contend, but marriage also has a lot of mundane work: doing laundry, making dental appointments, washing the dishes, and so on. To describe that joint effort as a duel would seem to miss the point. Furthermore, Chesterton surely did not mean that unmarried men, including the celibate priests of his Catholic faith, are all dishonorable.

Nonetheless, Chesterton's line resonates as more than a prettily turned but nonsensical phrase in one of his fantastic tales. This is because for men marriage is indeed a duel to the death—not against one's wife but for her. Our traditional marriage vows are quite as romantic as any oaths a storybook knight ever took. "For richer and for poorer, in sickness and in health, forsaking all others, till death do us part"—these vows are a defiance of all the world, if it comes to that. The duel is not with one's wife but with potentially everything and everyone else, including oneself. The quest to faithfully live up to one's vows is arduous at times and joyous at others, but the measure is not distributed equally. Adhering to these promises may bring terrible suffering.

Such is the risk of love. The traditional Christian marriage vows are explicit on this point: One is promising to remain married for worse, for poorer, and in sickness, if that is what comes. Prudence can mitigate some risks, but marriage nonetheless remains an acceptance of lifelong vulnerability if one takes these vows seriously. To quote *Manalive* again, "Imprudent marriages! ... where in earth or heaven are there any prudent marriages? Might as well talk about prudent suicides."[5] A commitment unto death is not prudent, if one is only looking out for oneself.

And marriage is a death of the autonomous self because it establishes a lifelong "we" over the solitary "I" of the individual. The physical union of marriage that the Bible describes as becoming one flesh is only part of the merger that is marriage, in which the self is not abolished but is irrevocably committed to another person. It may be terrifying to give up sole control of one's life in this way, and many will refuse to do so. One can have pleasure while maintaining control and safety, but one cannot have love. And pleasure without love will grow stale. Those who will not risk their hearts will end up making themselves heartless. This is why the traditional wedding vows recognize that they promise eventual heartbreak, for if hearts are not hardened over the years, then one, at least, will be broken when death parts them.

Yet those in love continue to get married, not only out of social custom or for the benefits that romantic and family stability provide to society but also because their love compels them to do so. There is something about being in love that induces us to make promises of lasting fidelity, as if we know that such faithfulness offers a better way of life, whatever the risks may be. It is commitment that allows a relationship to move from potentiality to actuality. The self that sacrifices its autonomy upon the marriage altar will find itself more fully realized in that marriage. It is only by foreclosing the other options of what we might become that we can really set about the business of becoming something;

only by forsaking all others can we fully realize our relationship with one.

But, on this point, there is a pitfall lurking in our culture: the idea of a soulmate or "the One". This is a quasi-spiritual notion: There is one person you are meant to be with, and if you marry that person, you will be happy in marriage—and conversely, if you marry someone else, you will be unhappy. This view, which some Christians have echoed, may seem to alleviate concerns about the risks of commitment, but it only makes matters worse. The notion of "the One" is alluring because it suggests that romance and marriage with the soulmate will be easy, but this assurance of ease provides an excuse for laziness (moral and otherwise) in a relationship and for abandoning the marriage when troubles inevitably come.

Furthermore, the person who seems to be one's soulmate at the age of twenty or twenty-five or thirty might be a dreadful match later on. A perfect fit for one's immature self will preclude growth into maturity, as it leaves no room for development (the rock band Rush was right in singing that "the spaces in between leave room for you and I to grow"[6]). The idea of a soulmate fails to account for the dynamism and development necessary to sustain and delight in a lifelong relationship. It can also become an idol that leads us astray from our marriage vows. J. R. R. Tolkien observed the dangers of this false idea in a letter to his son Michael, warning,

> When the glamour wears off, or merely works a bit thin, they think they have made a mistake, and that the real soul-mate is still to find. The real soul-mate too often proves to be the next sexually attractive person that comes along. Someone whom they might indeed very profitably have married, if only—. Hence divorce, to provide the "if

only." And of course they are as a rule quite right: they did make a mistake. Only a very wise man at the end of his life could make a sound judgment concerning whom, amongst the total possible chances, he ought most profitably to have married!... But the "real soul-mate" is the one you are actually married to.[7]

One should, of course, choose one's partner in life carefully, but we should not assume we will find ease and perfect compatibility if only we find the right person. Furthermore, we might add to Tolkien's admonition the following: Even if there were someone perfect for you, what on earth would make you think you deserve that person? Or that you would even like a perfect soulmate? What you might want in a soulmate is probably quite different from what would be good for you. Someone truly perfect for you would not let you jog along comfortably but would want you to be a better person, and many of us will not welcome this correction, regardless of how gently we are prodded toward improvement. Nor do God's providential designs have our ease and comfort in this life as their highest end. The notion of the soulmate ignores the realities of human sinfulness, which could corrupt and destroy even soulmate relationships, if they existed in something like the form they take in the popular imagination.

The foolish idea of soulmates provides no escape from the vulnerability of love and the risks of lifelong commitment in marriage. There is in reality only an initial choice (thoughtful, one hopes) and then the lifelong attempt to live up to one's vows in the teeth of tragedy, suffering, or just the comfortable boredom of life in the prosperity of the modern world. It is fashionable to mock as bland the ordinary men and women living out their married lives together, but they are often engaged in a quest far more challenging and romantic than anything the bohemian libertine will attempt.

Marriage is an act of defiance against all the difficulties of life, from the catastrophic to the mundane. In marriage, men and women promise themselves to each other and tell fate to go to hell. The ancient vows that solemnize a marriage are some of the greatest assertions of human agency, and therefore of human dignity, possible. Our freedom is realized not in the possibility that we might do anything but in doing what we have said we will do. Human freedom is consummated in the voluntary self-limitation of the promise made and fulfilled. In the making and keeping of promises, we assert ourselves against the world and the future as acting agents, not mere reactive beings responding to circumstance. The power of oaths in legend and law is due to their assertion of free human choice and will within the cosmos.

As Hannah Arendt observed, it is the making and keeping of promises, along with forgiveness, that put an end to reaction and allow us to begin something new.[8] Seen from this perspective, marriage vows are not an ending that establishes a static state but a beginning that allows something new to grow and flourish. Through faithfulness, we assert our freedom and dignity as acting agents while uniting the two halves of the human race in a union that continues it.

Most of us are called to the vocation of marriage, and Christianity recognizes and rejoices in the pragmatic benefits and blessing of marriage and family life, which are part of the created order. That marriage is ordinary does not mean it is bland or boring; rather, marriage and family offer some of the deepest challenges, as well as joys and fulfillments, in this life. We are made for relationships and therefore find ourselves in self-giving. Christians understand marriage in terms of both the beginning and the beyond—marriage is integral to life in the creation order we live in now, and it reflects the union with God and fellowship with His people we are destined for in eternity.

Meanwhile, we must recognize that the devil's promises in the sexual revolution have proven empty. They may be alluring, but they are destructive in this life, and that destruction echoes in the life that is to come. But there is a better way to live, with true love for God and our fellow man. Instead of the selfishness of the sexual revolution, we can live out the faithful love of marriage vows made and kept. God's promises are true, and by His grace, ours can be too.

ACKNOWLEDGMENTS

Books do not spring forth fully formed from an author's head—at least this one didn't. I have been aided in many ways by many people, and it is only right and just to publicly thank some of them here.

I owe a debt to the team at Ignatius Press, who have taken this from a long Word document to a book. In particular, Laura Shoemaker shepherded me through the early process, and then Kathy Mosier and Abigail Tardiff expertly edited the manuscript, including heroically cleaning up my messy citations.

I am also deeply grateful to the Ethics and Public Policy Center for offering me a place at the best think tank in D.C. Not only has the generosity of its supporters enabled this book to be written, but I have many wonderful colleagues, several of whom are quoted in this book. I especially want to thank Mitch Muncey, who provided essential advice and assistance, and Ryan Anderson, who for years has been a friend, mentor, and leader.

I have written on these subjects for years and am thankful for the scholars, activists, editors, and publications I have worked with over the years for having the courage to address these issues. In particular, Jay Richards and Mollie Hemmingway generously provided important feedback as the book developed, and Carl Olson offered crucial encouragement and help.

Because I have written on these subjects before, bits and pieces of old columns naturally made their way into this volume. I would especially like to thank *Public Discourse* and *World Opinions* for allowing me to borrow from articles they hold the copyrights to. A list of these articles is appended on page 219.

As thankful as I am for editors, colleagues, and comrades-in-arms, I am even more so for my family: for my lovely children, who are always a blessing beyond what I deserve—and were especially so as I was trying to write—and for my wife, Julie, who, along with her many other responsibilities, gracefully bears the burden of being my editor of first resort.

Finally, in the words of Jude: "To him who is able to keep you from falling and to present you without blemish before the presence of his glory with rejoicing, to the only God, our Savior through Jesus Christ our Lord, be glory, majesty, dominion, and authority, before all time and now and for ever. Amen" (vv. 24–25).

NOTES

Introduction

1. C. S. Lewis, *The Screwtape Letters* (Macmillan, 1954), 49.

2. Suzy Weiss, "First Comes Love. Then Comes Sterilization", *Free Press*, October 25, 2021, https://bariweiss.substack.com/p/first-comes-love-then -comes-sterilization; Anna Brown, "Growing Share of Childless Adults in U.S. Don't Expect to Ever Have Children", Pew Research Center, November 19, 2021, https://www.pewresearch.org/fact-tank/2021/11/19/growing-share-of -childless-adults-in-u-s-dont-expect-to-ever-have-children/; Damien Cave, Emma Bubola, and Choe Sang-Hun, "Long Slide Looms for World Population, with Sweeping Ramifications", *New York Times*, May 22, 2021, updated May 24, 2021, https://www.nytimes.com/2021/05/22/world/global -population-shrinking.html.

3. Alex Williams, "To Breed or Not to Breed?", *New York Times*, November 20, 2021, updated June 22, 2023, https://www.nytimes.com/2021/11/20 /style/breed-children-climate-change.html.

4. Frank Bruni, "I Live Alone. Really, I'm Not That Pathetic", *New York Times*, December 9, 2022, https://www.nytimes.com/2022/12/09/opinion /living-alone-single.html.

5. See, for example, Sam Peltzman, "The Socio Political Demography of Happiness", Working Paper No. 331 (George J. Stigler Center for the Study of the Economy and the State, University of Chicago, October 2, 2023), https:// papers.ssrn.com/sol3/papers.cfm?abstract_id=4508123.

6. Musa al-Gharbi, "How to Understand the Well-Being Gap Between Liberals and Conservatives", *American Affairs*, March 21, 2023, https:// americanaffairsjournal.org/2023/03/how-to-understand-the-well-being-gap -between-liberals-and-conservatives/.

7. Brad Wilcox, Hal Boyd, and Wendy Wang, "How Liberals Can Be Happier", *New York Times*, November 25, 2021, https://www.nytimes.com /2021/11/25/opinion/liberals-happiness-thanksgiving.html.

8. Kate Julian, "Why Are Young People Having So Little Sex", *Atlantic*, December 2018, https://www.theatlantic.com/magazine/archive/2018/12/the -sex-recession/573949/.

9. W. Bradford Wilcox and Wendy Wang, "Sacred Sex", *First Things*, February 15, 2024, https://www.firstthings.com/web-exclusives/2024/02/sacred -sex.

189

10. Julian, "So Little Sex".

11. Julian, "So Little Sex".

12. Nona Willis Aronowitz, "I Still Believe in the Power of Sexual Freedom", *New York Times*, August 16, 2022, https://www.nytimes.com/2022/08/16/opinion/sex-women-feminism-rules.html.

13. Michelle Goldberg, "Why Sex-Positive Feminism Is Falling Out of Fashion", *New York Times*, September 24, 2021, https://www.nytimes.com/2021/09/24/opinion/sex-positivity-feminism.html.

14. Michelle Goldberg, "A Manifesto Against Sex Positivity", *New York Times*, March 21, 2022, https://www.nytimes.com/2022/03/21/opinion/manifesto-against-sex-positivity.html.

15. Goldberg, "Manifesto".

16. Aronowitz, "I Still Believe".

17. Lewis, *Screwtape*, 49–50.

18. Stefan Zweig, *Society of the Crossed Keys: Selections from the Writings of Stefan Zweig*, trans. Anthea Bell (Pushkin Press, 2014), 71.

19. Zweig, *Crossed Keys*, 62.

20. Zweig, *Crossed Keys*, 82.

21. "Unrelated Adults in the Home Associated with Child-Abuse Deaths", The University of Chicago Medicine, November 7, 2005, https://www.uchicagomedicine.org/forefront/news/2005/november/unrelated-adults-in-the-home-associated-with-child-abuse-deaths.

22. Kyle Harper, "The First Sexual Revolution", *First Things*, January, 2018, https://www.firstthings.com/article/2018/01/the-first-sexual-revolution.   This article is a condensation of Harper's excellent book *From Shame to Sin: The Christian Transformation of Sexual Morality in Late Antiquity*, cited below.

23. The Free Press, "WATCH: Has the Sexual Revolution Failed? A Free Press Debate", *The Free Press*, October 4, 2023, https://www.thefp.com/p/debate.

Chapter 1: From Liberation to Loneliness

1. Milly Veitch, "'The Sincerity Radiates from Her': Drew Barrymore Is Praised for Raw and Vulnerable Interview with Brooke Shields About Childhood Exploitation", *Daily Mail*, April 13, 2023, https://www.dailymail.co.uk/tvshowbiz/article-11968345/Drew-Barrymore-praised-raw-interview-Brooke-Shields-childhood-exploitation.html.

2. Marta Jary, "Paris Hilton Reveals That Despite Her Reputation as a Man-Eater She Felt Lovemaking Was a Chore", *Daily Mail*, March 11, 2023, https://www.dailymail.co.uk/tvshowbiz/article-11847783/Paris-Hilton-reveals-asexual-20s-faked-orgasms-sex-over.html; and Tom Leonard, "Paris Hilton Was the Poor Little It-Girl Whose Infamous Sex Tape Lent Her a Tawdry Glamour", *Daily Mail*, March 14, 2023, https://www.dailymail.co.uk/debate/article-11860519/TOM-LEONARD-Paris-Hilton-written-book-paints-victim-predatory-men.html.

3. For a partial list, see Kevin D. Williamson, "The Left's Sexual Counter-revolution", *National Review Plus Magazine*, November 27, 2017, https://www.nationalreview.com/magazine/2017/11/27/hollywood-sexual-revolution-harvey-weinstein/.

4. Josh Boswell, "Exclusive: 'There Was Rape on a Regular Basis'", *Daily Mail*, February 1, 2022, https://www.dailymail.co.uk/news/article-10443917/The-mini-Playboy-mansions-women-trafficked-drugged-raped.html.

5. Christine Emba, *Rethinking Sex: A Provocation* (Sentinel, 2022), xii–xiii.

6. Katherine Kersten, "False Feminism: How We Got from Sexual Liberation to #MeToo", *First Things*, February 2019, https://www.firstthings.com/article/2019/02/false-feminism.

7. Nicholas H. Wolfinger, "Is the Sex Recession Over?", *Single Life* (blog), Institute for Family Studies, May 23, 2023, https://ifstudies.org/blog/is-the-sex-recession-over.

8. Richard Fry, "Young Adults in the U.S. Are Reaching Key Life Milestones Later Than in the Past", Pew Research Center, May 23, 2023, https://www.pewresearch.org/short-reads/2023/05/23/young-adults-in-the-u-s-are-reaching-key-life-milestones-later-than-in-the-past/.

9. Kate Julian, "Why Are Young People Having So Little Sex", *Atlantic*, December 2018, https://www.theatlantic.com/magazine/archive/2018/12/the-sex-recession/573949/.

10. Elizabeth Bruenig, "Modern Porn Education Is Totally Unprepared for Modern Porn", *Atlantic*, July 18, 2021, https://www.theatlantic.com/ideas/archive/2021/07/porn-education-totally-unprepared-modern-porn/619464/.

11. Peggy Orenstein, "The Troubling Trend in Teenage Sex", *New York Times*, April 12, 2024, https://www.nytimes.com/2024/04/12/opinion/choking-teen-sex-brain-damage.html.

12. Orenstein, "Troubling Trend".

13. Orenstein, "Troubling Trend".

14. Ezra Marcus, "The 'E-Pimps' of OnlyFans", *New York Times Magazine*, May 16, 2022, https://www.nytimes.com/2022/05/16/magazine/e-pimps-onlyfans.html.

15. Sirin Kale, "OnlyFans: A Day in the Life of a Top(less) Creator", *1843*, January 6, 2020, https://www.1843magazine.com/people/onlyfans-a-day-in-the-life-of-a-topless-creator.

16. Kale, "OnlyFans".

17. Charlotte Shane, "OnlyFans Isn't Just Porn ;)", *New York Times Magazine*, May 18, 2021, https://www.nytimes.com/2021/05/18/magazine/onlyfans-porn.html.

18. Gabrielle Drolet, "The Year Sex Work Came Home", *New York Times*, April 10, 2020, https://www.nytimes.com/2020/04/10/style/camsoda-onlyfans-streaming-sex-coronavirus.html; and Shane O'Neill, "How Cam Models Practice Sexual Distancing", video, *New York Times*, April 10, 2020,

https://www.nytimes.com/video/style/100000007078360/onlyfans-camsoda
-coronavirus.html.

19. Louise Perry, *The Case Against the Sexual Revolution* (Polity, 2022), 99.

20. Raven Saunt, "I Earned MILLIONS from Doing Porn", *Daily Mail*, May 19, 2023, https://www.dailymail.co.uk/femail/article-12103601/I-earned
-MILLIONS-doing-porn-adult-film-career-ruined-life.html.

21. Rachel Sugar, Jack Denton, Laura Thompson, and Adriane Quinlan, "How Much Does It Cost to Live Like This?", *Curbed*, May 22, 2023, https://www.curbed.com/article/cost-of-living-nyc-calculator.html.

22. Faith Karimi, "These Women Wanted a Symbolic Expression of Self-Love. So They Married Themselves", *CNN*, May 21, 2023, https://www.cnn
.com/2023/05/28/us/sologamy-self-marriage-women-cec/index.html.

23. A cynic might say that this is because a successful relationship is a financial loss for the dating app that sets it up—dating apps have a strong incentive to keep people on the dating market.

24. Kaktussimba, "Situationship", Urban Dictionary, February 14, 2022, https://www.urbandictionary.com/define.php?term=Situationship. Another user defined a "situationship" as what happens when people "take part in a relationship, but out of fear of making things serious or messy, do not label it, leading to said relationship, ironically, becoming more serious and messier. *A Situationship is emotional trauma in a gift box.*" The_Simple_Freak, "Situationship", November 2, 2021.

25. Emba, *Rethinking Sex*, 80–81.

26. Mary Harrington, *Feminism Against Progress* (Regnery Publishing, 2023), 92.

27. Perry, *Sexual Revolution*, 49.

28. Elizabeth Bruenig, "I Became a Mother at 25, and I'm Not Sorry I Didn't Wait", *New York Times*, May 7, 2021, https://www.nytimes.com/2021/05/07
/opinion/motherhood-baby-bust-early-parenthood.html.

29. Caleb Howe, "*NY Times* Columnist Writes About Motherhood for Mother's Day and Twitter Melts Down", *Mediaite*, May 10, 2021, https://www.mediaite.com/politics/ny-times-columnist-writes-about-motherhood
-for-mothers-day-and-twitter-melts-down/.

30. Anastasia Berg and Rachel Wiseman, "The Success Narratives of Liberal Life Leave Little Room for Having Children", *New York Times*, June 10, 2024, https://www.nytimes.com/2024/06/10/opinion/natalism-liberalism
-parenthood.html.

31. "Having a Baby After Age 35: How Aging Affects Fertility and Pregnancy", ACOG (The American College of Obstetricians and Gynecologists), accessed November 8, 2024, https://www.acog.org/womens-health/faqs/having
-a-baby-after-age-35-how-aging-affects-fertility-and-pregnancy.

32. Mayo Clinic Staff, "Pregnancy After 35: Healthy Pregnancies, Healthy Babies", Healthy Lifestyle, Mayo Clinic, July 15, 2022, https://www

.mayoclinic.org/healthy-lifestyle/getting-pregnant/in-depth/pregnancy/art
-20045756.

33. Megan McArdle, "Overruling 'Roe' Likely Wouldn't Generate the Female Backlash That Feminists Expect", *Washington Post*, December 3, 2021, https://www.washingtonpost.com/opinions/2021/12/03/overruling-roe-likely-wouldnt-generate-female-backlash-that-feminists-expect/.

34. Zach Goldbert (@ZachG932), "Some of you asked for it, so here is the last chart broken down by gender", Twitter (now X), April 11, 2020, https://twitter.com/ZachG932/status/1249764370458062850.

35. See Erika Bachiochi, "The Justice Mothers Are Due", *Plough*, May 12, 2023, https://www.plough.com/en/topics/culture/holidays/mothers-day/the-justice-mothers-are-due.

36. Vivek H. Murthy, "Surgeon General: We Have Become a Lonely Nation. It's Time to Fix That", *New York Times*, April 30, 2023, https://www.nytimes.com/2023/04/30/opinion/loneliness-epidemic-america.html.

37. Daniel de Visé, "A Record Share of Americans Is Living Alone", *The Hill*, July 10, 2023, https://thehill.com/blogs/blog-briefing-room/4085828-a-record-share-of-americans-are-living-alone/.

38. Charles M. Blow, "The Married Will Soon Be the Minority", *New York Times*, October 20, 2021, https://www.nytimes.com/2021/10/20/opinion/marriage-decline-america.html.

39. Janet Adamy, "Why Americans Are Having Fewer Babies", *Wall Street Journal*, May 26, 2023, https://www.wsj.com/articles/why-americans-are-having-fewer-babies-3be7f6a9.

40. Ross Douthat, "The Case for One More Child: Why Large Families Will Save Humanity", *Plough*, November 18, 2020, https://www.plough.com/en/topics/life/parenting/the-case-for-one-more-child.

41. Alexandra DeSanctis, "Children Do Better When Raised in Intact, Two-Parent Homes", *National Review*, June 17, 2021, https://www.nationalreview.com/corner/children-do-better-when-raised-in-intact-two-parent-homes/.

Chapter 2: Abortion Hardens the Hearts It Doesn't Stop

1. For reference, the structure of DNA, with all its explanatory power for our understanding of biology, had been discovered only two decades before *Roe*. In another illuminating example, home pregnancy tests weren't yet available in 1973, so absent a trip to the doctor for a lab-mediated test, a woman might not even be sure she was pregnant for some time.

2. Ryan T. Anderson, "The Way Forward After *Dobbs*", *First Things*, October 2024, https://www.firstthings.com/article/2024/10/the-way-forward-after-dobbs.

3. DuPont Clinic (@DupontClinic), "Abortion is good in all trimesters. Your reason is the right reason, don't let anyone tell you differently", Twitter (now X), September 14, 2022, https://twitter.com/DupontClinic/status/1570009026494070784.

4. Planned Parenthood (@PPFA), "For every abortion story you hear, remember there are countless never told. Every reason is the right reason, and your story matters", Twitter (now X), March 21, 2023, https://x.com/PPFA/status/1638193899339481091.

5. Elaine Godfrey, "The Abortion Absolutist", *Atlantic*, May 12, 2023, https://www.theatlantic.com/politics/archive/2023/05/dr-warren-hern-abortion-post-roe/674000/.

6. Maggie Shannon, "A Safe Haven for Late Abortions", *New Yorker*, February 5, 2024, https://www.newyorker.com/magazine/2024/02/12/a-safe-haven-for-late-abortions.

7. John McCormack, "Jen Psaki Isn't Telling the Truth About Late-Term Abortion", *National Review*, August 28, 2023, https://www.nationalreview.com/2023/08/jen-psaki-isnt-telling-the-truth-about-late-term-abortion/.

8. Judith Jarvis Thomson, "A Defense of Abortion", *Philosophy and Public Affairs* 1, no. 1 (1971): 47–66.

9. Joseph Bottum, "The Events Leading Up to My Execution", in *Why I Turned Right*, ed. Mary Eberstadt (Threshold Editions, 2007), 157–58.

10. Thomas Chatterton Williams (@thomaschattwill), "Hard to imagine anything more dystopian than being forced to give birth", Twitter (now X), May 4, 2022, https://twitter.com/thomaschattwill/status/1521835539179126784.

11. Søren Kierkegaard, *Repetition* and *Philosophical Crumbs*, trans. M. G. Piety (Oxford University Press, 2009), 60.

12. See, for example, John Finnis, "Abortion Is Unconstitutional", *First Things*, April 2021, https://www.firstthings.com/article/2021/04/abortion-is-unconstitutional.

13. For example, Margaret Renkl, "What Mothers Really Need", *New York Times*, May 2, 2022, https://www.nytimes.com/2022/05/02/opinion/mothers-day-abortion-rights-republicans.html.

14. Governor J. B. Pritzker (@GovPritzker, "I'm proud to proclaim today as Abortion Provider Appreciation Day in Illinois", Twitter (now X), March 10, 2023, https://twitter.com/GovPritzker/status/1634290790976442368.

15. Alexi Giannoulias, Secretary of State, *2023 Illinois Register: Rules of Governmental Agencies* 47, no. 16 (April 21, 2023), 5828, https://www.ilsos.gov/departments/index/register/volume47/register_volume47_16.pdf.

16. Erika Bachiochi, "Sex-Realist Feminism", *First Things*, April 2023, https://www.firstthings.com/article/2023/04/sex-realist-feminism.

17. Sarah Vine, "Sarah Vine: America's Abortion Shambles Is a Dystopian Warning for Us in Britain", *Daily Mail*, June 25, 2022, updated June 26, 2022, https://www.dailymail.co.uk/debate/article-10953129/SARAH-VINE-Americas-abortion-shambles-dystopian-warning-Britain.html.

18. That this ideal of equality serves the interests of big business more than of women as women is another indicator of how abortion has destroyed solidarity on the American Left. See Alexandra DeSanctis, "Why Big Business Loves Abortion", *National Review Plus Magazine*, October 3, 2022, https://

www.nationalreview.com/magazine/2022/10/03/why-big-business-loves
-abortion/.

19. Jeff Nelson, "Britney Spears Reveals She Had an Abortion Because
Justin Timberlake 'Didn't Want to Be a Father' (Exclusive)", *People*, October 17, 2023, https://people.com/britney-spears-justin-timberlake-pregnancy
-abortion-exclusive-8362622.

20. C. S. Lewis, *The Screwtape Letters* (Macmillan, 1954), 64.

21. Leah Libresco Sargeant, "Dependence: Toward an Illiberalism of
the Weak", *Plough*, December 7, 2020, https://www.plough.com/en/topics
/justice/culture-of-life/dependence.

22. John Locke, *The Second Treatise of Government* (Liberal Arts Press, 1952), 4.

23. Erika Bachiochi, "The Rights of Women: A Natural Law Approach",
New Digest, January 2, 2024, https://thenewdigest.substack.com/p/the-rights
-of-women-a-natural-law.

24. David Walsh, *The Priority of the Person: Political, Philosophical, and Historical Discoveries* (University of Notre Dame Press, 2020), 87.

Chapter 3: The Abolition of Man and Woman: From Self-Creation to Castration

1. *The Kevin Roberts Show*, "Q&A with Detransitioner on Puberty Blockers and Gender Surgery", The Heritage Foundation, January 12, 2023, https://
www.youtube.com/watch?v=_udq4M4nKqE.

2. Alex Hammer, "Detransitioning Woman, 18, Suing Kaiser Permanente
for 'Pushing Her' into Gender-Changing Surgery", *Daily Mail*, June 18, 2023,
updated June 19, 2023, https://www.dailymail.co.uk/news/article-12207743
/Detransitioning-woman-18-suing-Kaiser-Permanente-pushing-gender
-changing-surgery.html.

3. Carl R. Trueman, "Mary Harrington Takes on the Machine", *Fairer
Disputations*, April 28, 2023, https://fairerdisputations.org/mary-harrington-takes
-on-the-machine/.

4. For a discussion of this, see Nathanael Blake, "How Transgender Ideology
Takes Children Hostage", *National Review*, June 10, 2021, https://www.national
review.com/2021/06/how-transgender-ideology-takes-children-hostage/.

5. *Kevin Roberts Show*, "Q&A with Detransitioner".

6. *Kevin Roberts Show*, "Q&A with Detransitioner".

7. Jonathon Van Maren, "Is Violent Porn Making Girls Identify as Transgender?", *The European Conservative*, February 7, 2024, https://european
conservative.com/articles/commentary/is-violent-porn-making-girls
-identify-as-transgender/.

8. *Kevin Roberts Show*, "Q&A with Detransitioner".

9. *Kevin Roberts Show*, "Q&A with Detransitioner".

10. *Kevin Roberts Show*, "Q&A with Detransitioner".

11. Hammer, "Detransitioning Woman".

12. Soren Aldaco, "Gender Expectations Made Me Think I Was Trans", *Dallas Morning News*, August 3, 2023, https://archive.ph/2023.08.03-135940 /https://www.dallasnews.com/opinion/commentary/2023/08/05/gender -expectations-made-me-think-i-was-trans/#selection-1939.0-1939.12.

13. Aldaco, "Gender Expectations".

14. *Kevin Roberts Show*, "Q&A with Detransitioner".

15. James Reinl, "EXCLUSIVE: LA's TikTok Doctor for Trans Kids as Young as Seven Admits That Puberty Blockers and Hormones CAN Cause Bone Disease and Infertility", *Daily Mail*, June 28, 2023, https://www.daily mail.co.uk/news/article-12242933/LA-TikTok-doc-trans-kids-admits-puberty -blockers-hormones-cause-disease-infertility.html.

16. Gerald Posner, "The Truth About 'Puberty Blockers'", *Wall Street Journal*, June 7, 2023, https://www.wsj.com/articles/the-truth-about-puberty -blockers-overdiagnosis-gender-dysphoria-children-933cd8fb.

17. Christopher F. Rufo, "Thrown to the Wolves", *City Journal*, June 21, 2023, https://www.city-journal.org/article/transgender-ideology-and-the -corruption-of-medicine.

18. Christina Jewett, "Drug Used to Halt Puberty in Children May Cause Lasting Health Problems", *Stat*, February 2, 2017, https://www.statnews.com /2017/02/02/lupron-puberty-children-health-problems/.

19. Tomasz Tabernacki, David Gilbert, Stephen Rhodes, Kyle Scarberry, Rachel Pope, Megan McNamara, et al., "The Burden of Chronic Pain in Transgender and Gender Diverse Populations: Evidence from a Large US Clinical Database", *European Journal of Pain*, September 20, 2024, https://online library.wiley.com/doi/full/10.1002/ejp.4725.

20. Katie Glenn, "Hormone Therapy for Gender Dysphoria May Raise Cardiovascular Risks", American College of Cardiology, February 23, 2023, https://www.acc.org/About-ACC/Press-Releases/2023/02/22/20/29 /Hormone-Therapy-for-Gender-Dysphoria-May-Raise-Cardiovascular-Risks.

21. Dorte Glintborg, Jens-Jakob Kjer Møller, Katrine Hass Rubin, Øjvind Lidegaard, Guy T'Sjoen, Mie-Louise Julie Ørsted Larsen, et al., "Gender-Affirming Treatment and Mental Health Diagnoses in Danish Transgender Persons: A Nationwide Register-Based Cohort Study", *European Journal of Endocrinology* 189, no. 3 (2023): 336–45, https://academic.oup.com/ejendo /article-abstract/189/3/336/7261571?redirectedFrom=fulltext.

22. Megan Brock, "Surgeon Who Performs Transgender Vaginoplasties: Complications 'Can Be Pretty Bad'", *The Daily Signal*, February 14, 2024, https://www.dailysignal.com/2024/02/15/in-unearthed-video-prominent -surgeon-admits-complications-of-trans-genital-surgery-can-be-pretty-bad/.

23. Kay S. Hymowitz, "The Transgender Children's Crusade", *City Journal*, Spring 2023, https://www.city-journal.org/article/the-transgender-childrens -crusade.

24. Mia Ashton, "Trans Teen Died from Vaginoplasty Complications During Landmark Dutch Study Used to Justify Child Sex Changes", *PM.* (*The*

Post Millennial), April 24, 2023, https://thepostmillennial.com/trans-teen-died
-from-vaginoplasty-complications-during-landmark-dutch-study-used-to-justify
-child-sex-changes.

25. Billboard Chris (@BillboardChris), "This is psychiatrist Kellyn Lakhardt, of Kaiser Permanente in Oakland, California. He admits they have done penile inversion surgeries on 16-year-old boys, having started the process at 15, and they have cut off the breasts of a 12-year-old girl", Twitter (now X), June 16, 2023, https://twitter.com/BillboardChris/status/1669740026488565760.

26. Lisa Selin Davis, "Yes, Kids Are Getting Gender Surgeries", *BROAD-view*, April 19, 2022, https://lisaselindavis.substack.com/p/yes-kids-are-getting
-gender-surgeries?s=w; and Christopher F. Rufo (@realchrisrufo), "The media line that 'hospitals don't do genital surgeries on minors' is a brazen lie. Researchers have long confirmed that 'vaginoplasties are being performed on minors by surgeons in the United States.' They even titled their paper 'Age Is Just a Number.'", Twitter (now X), August 19, 2022, https://twitter.com
/realchrisrufo/status/1560515684421242881.

27. Libby Emmons, "'Gender Affirming' Surgeon Admits Children Who Undergo Transition Before Puberty NEVER Attain Sexual Satisfaction", *PM. (The Post Millennial)*, May 1, 2022, https://thepostmillennial.com/gender
-affirming-surgeon-admits-children-who-undergo-transition-before-puberty
-never-attain-sexual-satisfaction.

28. James Reinl, "Pink-Haired Portland Surgeon Who Performs Sex-Change Surgery on Trans CHILDREN Admits They Face Lifetime of Infertility, Incontinence and Sexual Dissatisfaction", *Daily Mail*, July 14, 2023, https://
www.dailymail.co.uk/news/article-12299393/Portland-surgeon-dubbed-Dr
-Frankenstein-reveals-drawbacks-genital-ops-trans-adolescents.html.

29. James Reinl, "Trans Indigenous Canadian Slams Doctors for Denying Her Euthanasia Request", *Daily Mail*, July 28, 2023, https://www.dailymail
.co.uk/news/article-12349523/Trans-indigenous-Canadian-slams-doctors
-denying-euthanasia-request-saying-death-free-agony-surgically-built-vagina
.html.

30. Jay W. Richards (@DrJayRichards), "How contrary to standard medical practice is it to recommend the social transition-to-sterilization pipeline for kids, as the AAP and the HHS now do? Let's compare it to something like prostate cancer—which will kill ~35,000 American men this year", Twitter (now X), February 5, 2023, https://twitter.com/DrJayRichards
/status/1622258129323835393.

31. Mridula Nadamuni, Anthony V. D'Amico, Jenny L. Donovan, and Freddie C. Hamdy, "Decision Making in Prostate Cancer", *New England Journal of Medicine* 389, no. 14 (October 4, 2023), https://www.nejm.org/doi
/full/10.1056/NEJMclde2307619.

32. Madeleine Kearns, "The 'Trans' Child as Experimental Guinea Pig", *National Review Plus Magazine*, April 22, 2019, https://www.nationalreview
.com/magazine/2019/04/22/the-trans-child-as-experimental-guinea-pig/.

33. See Ryan T. Anderson, *When Harry Became Sally: Responding to the Transgender Moment* (Encounter Books, 2018), 119, 123, 125.

34. Chad Felix Greene, "The Explosion in Queer Sexuality Among Kids Is Not a Natural Trend", *The Federalist*, March 1, 2021, https://thefederalist.com/2021/03/01/the-explosion-in-queer-sexuality-among-kids-is-not-a-natural-trend/.

35. Abigail Shrier, "Inside Planned Parenthood's Gender Factory", *The Truth Fairy*, February 8, 2021, https://abigailshrier.substack.com/p/inside-planned-parenthoods-gender.

36. Aaron Sibarium, "Planned Parenthood Is Helping Teenagers Transition After a 30 Minute Consult. Parents and Doctors Are Sounding the Alarm.", *Washington Free Beacon*, October 4, 2023, https://freebeacon.com/latest-news/planned-parenthood-is-helping-teenagers-transition-after-a-30-minute-consult-parents-and-doctors-are-sounding-the-alarm/.

37. Robin Respaut and Chad Terhune, "Putting Numbers on the Rise in Children Seeking Gender Care", *Reuters*, October 6, 2022, https://www.reuters.com/investigates/special-report/usa-transyouth-data/.

38. Caitlin Tilley, "EXCLUSIVE: Number of 'Top' Surgeries Performed on Trans Children Has Risen 13-FOLD in Last Decade", *Daily Mail*, December 6, 2022, https://www.dailymail.co.uk/health/article-11392117/Trans-child-surgery-risen-13-TIMES-decade-hospitals.html.

39. Azeen Ghorayshi, "How a Small Gender Clinic Landed in a Political Storm", *New York Times*, August 23, 2023, https://www.nytimes.com/2023/08/23/health/transgender-youth-st-louis-jamie-reed.html.

40. Ari Blaff, "*New York Times* Confirms St. Louis Gender Clinic Whistleblower's Claim That Adolescents Were Rushed into 'Affirming' Care", *National Review*, August 23, 2023, https://www.nationalreview.com/news/new-york-times-confirms-st-louis-gender-clinic-whistleblowers-claim-that-adolescents-were-rushed-into-affirming-care/.

41. Lisa Littman, "Parent Reports of Adolescents and Young Adults Perceived to Show Signs of a Rapid Onset of Gender Dysphoria", *PLOS One*, August 16, 2018, https://journals.plos.org/plosone/article?id=10.1371/journal.pone.0202330.

42. Riittakerttu Kaltiala, Elias Heino, Mauri Marttunen, and Sari Fröjd, "Family Characteristics, Transgender Identity and Emotional Symptoms in Adolescence: A Population Survey Study", National Library of Medicine, February 8, 2023, https://www.ncbi.nlm.nih.gov/pmc/articles/PMC9963798/.

43. James Reinl, "'It Turned Out to Be a Big Mistake'", *Daily Mail*, June 21, 2023, https://www.dailymail.co.uk/news/article-12219343/Gen-Zs-trans-poster-child-Milo-2016-MTV-reemerges-tearfully-regretting-hormone-jabs.html.

44. "Special Issue: Gender Revolution", *National Geographic*, January 2017, https://www.nationalgeographic.com/magazine/issue/january-2017.

45. Megan K. Stack, "When Parents Hear That Their Child 'Is Not Normal and Should Not Exist'", *New York Times*, February 18, 2023, https://www.nytimes.com/2023/02/18/opinion/trans-gender-missouri.html.

46. Henry Olsen, "California Wants to Teach Kindergarteners About Gender Identity. Seriously.", *Washington Post*, May 13, 2019, https://www.washingtonpost.com/opinions/2019/05/13/california-wants-teach-kindergartners-about-gender-identity-seriously/?utm_term=.307d38a5ed30.

47. Alan Blinder, "Lia Thomas Wins an N.C.A.A. Swimming Title", *New York Times*, March 17, 2022, https://www.nytimes.com/2022/03/17/sports/lia-thomas-swimmer-wins.html.

48. Joe Kinsey, "OutKick Exclusive: Penn Trans Swimmer's Teammate Speaks Out as Lia Thomas Smashes More Records", *OutKick*, December 10, 2021, https://www.outkick.com/outkick-exclusive-penn-trans-swimmers-teammate-speaks-out-as-lia-thomas-smashes-more-records/.

49. Madeleine Kearns, "Parents of Female Swimmers Speak Out: 'Shame on the NCAA'", *National Review*, March 19, 2022, https://www.nationalreview.com/2022/03/parents-of-female-swimmers-speak-out-shame-on-the-ncaa/.

50. Shawn Cohen, "EXCLUSIVE: 'We're Uncomfortable in Our Own Locker Room.'", *Daily Mail*, January 27, 2022, https://www.dailymail.co.uk/news/article-10445679/Lia-Thomas-UPenn-teammate-says-trans-swimmer-doesnt-cover-genitals-locker-room.html.

51. James Reinl, "U-Penn Women Swimmers Had to Undress Next to '6-foot-4 Biological Male' Lia Thomas", *Daily Mail*, July 27, 2023, updated August 4, 2023, https://www.dailymail.co.uk/news/article-12345937/U-Penn-women-swimmers-undress-6-foot-4-biological-male-Lia-Thomas-18-times-week-told-reeducated-complained-Congress-hears-bombshell-testimony.html.

52. Jake Nisse, "Lia Thomas' Former UPenn Swimming Teammate Paula Scanlan Said She Had 'NIGHTMARES for Weeks' After Sharing Locker Room with the Transgender Athlete", *Daily Mail*, August 1, 2023, updated August 31, 2023, https://www.dailymail.co.uk/sport/othersports/article-12363207/Lia-Thomas-former-UPenn-swimming-teammate-Paula-Scanlan-said-NIGHTMARES-weeks-sharing-locker-room-transgender-athlete.html.

53. Cheryl Cooky, "Lia Thomas' NCAA Championship Performance Gives Women Sports a Crucial Opportunity", *Think*, March 21, 2022, https://www.nbcnews.com/think/opinion/we-should-be-celebrating-lia-thomas-we-did-jackie-robinson-ncna1292521.

54. "Fairness in Women's Sports: Connecticut", Alliance Defending Freedom, accessed November 12, 2024, https://adfmedialegalfiles.blob.core.windows.net/files/SouleOnePageSummary.pdf.

55. "Fairness in Women's Sports"; see also "Soule v. Connecticut Association of Schools", Alliance Defending Freedom, accessed November 12, 2024, https://adflegal.org/case/soule-v-connecticut-association-schools.

56. Genevieve Gluck, "Male Powerlifter Sets New Women's Record During 2023 Western Canadian Championship", *Reduxx*, August 14, 2023, https://reduxx.info/male-powerlifter-sets-new-womens-record-during-2023 -western-canadian-championship/; and Genevieve Gluck, "Trans-Identified Males Racking Up Wins in Women's Fencing as Trans Activist Officials Claim They Are Fine with Female Athletes Being at a 'Disadvantage'", *Reduxx*, September 12, 2023, https://reduxx.info/trans-identified-males-racking-up -wins-in-womens-fencing-as-trans-activist-officials-claim-they-are-fine-with -female-athletes-being-at-a-disadvantage/.

57. Maggie Hroncich, "Female Athletes Sidelined as Biological Male Advances to Olympics to Compete in Women's Weightlifting", *Federalist*, June 21, 2021, https://thefederalist.com/2021/06/21/female-athletes-sidelined-as -biological-male-advances-to-olympics-to-compete-in-womens-weightlifting/.

58. "Canadian Cycling Suspends Danika Schroeter", *Cycling News*, July 21, 2006, https://www.cyclingnews.com/news/canadian-cycling-suspends-danika -schroeter/.

59. "Non-Binary Biological Male Counselors Allowed to Sleep in Fifth-Grade Girls' Cabins at Science Camp", *PM. (The Post Millennial)*, February 20, 2022, https://thepostmillennial.com/non-binary-biological-male-counselors -allowed-to-sleep-in-fifth-grade-girls-cabins-at-science-camp?utm _campaign=64499.

60. Alliance Defending Freedom, "Court Ruling Protects Anchorage Faith-Based Women's Shelter", press release, December 21, 2021, https://adflegal .org/press-release/court-ruling-protects-anchorage-faith-based-womens-shelter.

61. Mary Harrington (@moveincircles), "Remarkably consistent data from prisons across the Anglosphere showing around 50% of trans-identified male prisoners are sex offenders", X, September 13, 2023, https://twitter.com /moveincircles/status/1702031513926205774; expanded upon in a Substack post: Mary Harrington, "The Statistic No One's Allowed to Study", *Mary Harrington*, September 14, 2023, https://reactionaryfeminist.substack.com/p /how-many-sex-offenders?r=1czei.

62. Genevieve Gluck, "EXCLUSIVE DETAILS: Indiana Department of Corrections Ordered to Arrange Transgender Baby Killer's 'Gender Surgeries' After ACLU-Backed Lawsuit", *Reduxx*, September 18, 2024, https://reduxx .info/exclusive-details-indiana-department-of-corrections-ordered-to -arrange-transgender-baby-killers-gender-surgeries-after-aclu-backed-lawsuit/.

63. Alliance Defending Freedom, "Court Ruling".

64. Caroline Downey, "Male Child Molester Housed in Women's Prison Under Investigation for Sexually Harassing Female Cellmate", *National Review*, August 26, 2024, https://www.nationalreview.com/news/male-child -molester-house-in-womens-prison-under-investigation-for-sexually-harassing -female-inmate.

65. Caroline Downey, "Meet the Trans-Identifying Male Felons of the Washington State Women's Prison", July 20, 2024, https://www.national

review.com/news/meet-the-trans-identifying-male-felons-of-the-washingtons
-womens-prison/.

66. Anna Slatz, "EXCLUSIVE: Rapist Quietly Transferred to Washington Women's Prison", *Reduxx*, December 15, 2022, https://reduxx.info/exclusive-rapist-quietly-transferred-to-washington-womens-prison/.

67. Anna Slatz, "'The Worst One Yet': Violent Male Pedophile Moved to Washington Women's Prison", *Reduxx*, March 24, 2023, https://reduxx.info/the-worst-one-yet-violent-male-pedophile-moved-to-washington-womens-prison/.

68. Caroline Downey, "Trans Double Murderer Moved Back to Men's Prison Due to 'Safety Concerns'", *National Review*, July 3, 2024, https://www.nationalreview.com/news/trans-double-murderer-moved-back-to-mens-prison-due-to-safety-concerns.

69. James Reinl, "The Crafty Way a 6ft 2in 'Trans' Inmate Fooled Authorities", *Daily Mail*, June 11, 2024, https://www.dailymail.co.uk/news/article-13518499/trans-detainee-rape-women-inmates-women-California-psychologist.html.

70. Brittany Bernstein, "Lawsuit Accuses California of Endangering Female Prisoners by Forcing Them to Share Housing with Biological Males", *National Review*, November 17, 2021, https://www.nationalreview.com/news/lawsuit-accuses-california-of-endangering-female-prisoners-by-forcing-them-to-share-housing-with-biological-males/.

71. Genevive Gluck, "'This Is a Nightmare': Female Inmate Speaks Out Against Trans-Identifying Male Transfers", *Reduxx*, May 27, 2022, https://reduxx.info/this-is-a-nightmare-female-inmate-speaks-out-against-trans-identifying-male-transfers/.

72. Genevieve Gluck, "EXCLUSIVE: Female Inmate at NJ Women's Prison Alleges Brutal Assault by Trans-Identified Male Transfer", *Reduxx*, May 29, 2023, https://reduxx.info/exclusive-female-inmate-at-nj-womens-prison-alleges-brutal-assault-by-trans-identified-male-transfer/.

73. Ruth Bashinsky, "Transgender Rikers Inmate Serving Time in Women's Wing of Jail", *Daily Mail*, April 26, 2022, https://www.dailymail.co.uk/news/article-10755219/Transgender-Rikers-inmate-incarcerated-assault-housed-womens-wing-RAPES-female-inmate.html.

74. Caroline Downey, "Judge Rules Loudoun County Teen Sexually Assaulted Female Student in Girls' Bathroom", October 26, 2021, https://www.nationalreview.com/news/judge-rules-loudoun-county-teen-sexually-assaulted-female-student-in-girls-bathroom/.

75. Andy Ngo, "Sex Offending Suspect Claims Transgender Harassment in Wi Spa Case", *New York Post*, September 2, 2021, https://nypost.com/2021/09/02/charges-filed-against-sex-offender-in-wi-spa-casecharges-filed-against-sex-offender-in-notorious-wi-spa-incident/.

76. Jennifer (@babybeginner), "They are trying to memory hole this and many people never heard of it", X, August 2, 2023, https://twitter.com/babybeginner/status/1686793192509964288.

77. Mary Margaret Olohan, "EXCLUSIVE: Women Speak Out Against YMCA 'Transgender' Bathroom Policies", *Daily Signal*, August 28, 2023, https://www.dailysignal.com/2023/08/28/exclusive-women-speak-out-against-ymcas-transgender-bathroom-policies/.

78. Joshua Q. Nelson, "Trans Woman Showered with Four Wisconsin High School Girls, Violated Their Privacy, Letter to District Claims", *Fox News*, April 21, 2023, https://www.foxnews.com/media/trans-woman-showered-four-wisconsin-high-school-girls-violated-their-privacy-letter-district-claims.

79. Anna Slatz, "Trans Student Charged After Reportedly Assaulting Two Female Students in School Washroom", *Reduxx*, December 12, 2022, https://reduxx.info/trans-student-charged-after-reportedly-assaulting-two-female-students-in-school-washroom/.

80. Christina Buttons, "New Lawsuit Accuses California School District of Constitutional Violation for 'Parental Secrecy Policy' of Gender Transition", *Daily Wire*, January 12, 2023, https://www.dailywire.com/news/new-lawsuit-accuses-california-school-district-of-constitutional-violation-for-parental-secrecy-policy-of-gender-transition.

81. Eliza Mondegreen, "What Happens to Parents When Kids Come Out as Trans", *Fairer Disputations*, August 18, 2023, https://fairerdisputations.org/what-happens-to-parents-when-kids-come-out-as-trans/.

82. Jay Keck, "My Daughter Thinks She's Transgender", *USA Today*, August 12, 2019, updated August 13, 2019, https://www.usatoday.com/story/opinion/voices/2019/08/12/transgender-daughter-school-undermines-parents-column/1546527001/.

83. Sophie Mann, "Virginia Mom Sues School District Claiming Staff Kept Daughter Sage Blair's Transition to Male a Secret", *Daily Mail*, September 4, 2023, https://www.dailymail.co.uk/news/article-12479157/mom-trans-teen-sage-blair-sues-school.html.

84. Natasha Anderson, "Catholic Father Sues Elementary School After His Daughter, 12, Tried to Kill Herself", *Daily Mail*, January 26, 2022, updated January 27, 2022, https://www.dailymail.co.uk/news/article-10445195/Catholic-father-files-lawsuit-daughter-attempts-suicide-gender-identity.html.

85. Josh Boswell, "EXCLUSIVE: 'I Knew the Hormones Wouldn't Work. Why Did They Play with Her Life?'", *Daily Mail*, March 22, 2022, updated March 30, 2022, https://www.dailymail.co.uk/news/article-10612285/California-mom-claims-LA-school-encouraged-daughter-transition-blame-suicide.html.

86. Christopher F. Ruso, "Radical Gender Lessons for Young Children", *City Journal*, April 21, 2022, https://www.city-journal.org/article/radical-gender-lessons-for-young-children.

87. M.D. Kittle, "Wisconsin School District: Parents Are Not 'Entitled to Know' If Their Kids Are Trans", *Federalist*, March 8, 2022, https://thefederalist.com/2022/03/08/wisconsin-school-district-parents-are-not-entitled-to-know-if-their-kids-are-trans/.

88. Jason Rantz, "Rantz: WA Laws Now Allow Teen Gender Reassignment Surgery Without Parental Consent", 770 KTTH, January 10, 2022, https://mynorthwest.com/3296653/rantz-washington-laws-permit-teen-gender-reassignment-surgery-parental-consent/.

89. Secretary Miguel Cardona (@SecCardona), "Teachers know what is best for their kids because they are with them every day", Twitter (now X), May 10, 2023, https://twitter.com/SecCardona/status/1659652692107468811.

90. Julia Johnson, "Blackburn Seeks Actions After Doctor Touts Profits of Transgender Surgeries on Video", *Washington Examiner*, September 22, 2022, https://www.washingtonexaminer.com/restoring-america/community-family/blackburn-doctor-profits-transgender-surgeries-video.

91. Matt Walsh (@MattWalshBlog), "Vanderbilt opened its trans clinic in 2018", Twitter (now X), September 20, 2022, https://twitter.com/MattWalshBlog/status/1572313523232931840.

92. Jay Richards, "In the Genital Mutilation Market, Business Is Booming", *Federalist*, October 14, 2022, https://thefederalist.com/2022/10/14/in-the-sex-reassignment-surgery-market-business-is-booming/.

93. Tilley, "Number of 'Top' Surgeries".

94. Jason D. Wright, Ling Chen, Yukio Suzuki, Koji Matsuo, and Dawn L. Hershman, "National Estimates of Gender-Affirming Surgery in the US", *JAMA Network Open*, August 23, 2023, https://jamanetwork.com/journals/jamanetworkopen/fullarticle/2808707.

95. Aaron Sibarium, "How a Left-Wing Activist Group Teamed Up with Big Pharma to Push Radical Gender Ideology on American Hospitals", *Washington Free Beacon*, May 15, 2023, https://freebeacon.com/latest-news/how-left-wing-activist-group-teamed-up-with-big-pharma-to-push-radical-gender-ideology-on-american-hospitals/.

96. Matt Walsh (@MattWalshBlog), "1/ BREAKING: The largest 'trans healthcare' providers in the U.S. are rubber-stamping letters approving gruesome, life-altering surgeries", Twitter (now X), June 7, 2023, https://twitter.com/MattWalshBlog/status/1666496308150951954.

97. Christopher F. Rufo, "Oregon's Castration Machine", *City Journal*, July 5, 2023, https://www.city-journal.org/article/oregon-health-science-universitys-castration-machine.

98. Ava Kofman, "The Perils and Promises of Penis-Enlargement Surgery", *New Yorker*, June 26, 2023, https://www.newyorker.com/magazine/2023/07/03/the-perils-and-promises-of-penis-enlargement-surgery.

99. "The Inequality of the Equality Act: Concerns from the Left" (video), The Heritage Foundation, January 29, 2019, https://www.heritage.org/event/the-inequality-the-equality-act-concerns-the-left.

100. Jackson Thompson, "SJSU Volleyball Players Fleeing Program After Season Filled with Trans Athlete Drama", *New York Post*, December 20, 2024, https://nypost.com/2024/12/20/sports/sjsu-volleyball-players-fleeing-program-after-season-filled-with-trans-athlete-drama/.

101. "Konen v. Spreckels Union School District", Center for American Liberty, January 19, 2022, https://libertycenter.org/cases/konen/.

102. "Wisconsin Court Rules to Protect Parents' Rights", Alliance Defending Freedom, October 3, 2023, https://adflegal.org/press-release/wisconsin-court-rules-protect-parents-rights.

103. "Luka Hein v. UNMC Physicians", Center for American Liberty, September 13, 2023, https://libertycenter.org/hein-v-unmc/.

104. Hayley Milon Bour, "'I Want You to Call Me Max Now:' A Family Embraces Life with a Transgender Child", *Loudoun Now*, July 15, 2021, https://loudounnow.com/2021/07/15/i-want-you-to-call-me-max-now/.

105. Eric Orwoll, M.D., "Safety of Testosterone-Replacement Therapy in Older Men", *New England Journal of Medicine* 389, no. 2, https://www.nejm.org/doi/full/10.1056/NEJMe2305946.

106. Diane Chen, Johnny Berona, Yee-Ming Chan, Diane Ehrensaft, Robert Garofalo, Marco A. Hidalgo, et al., "Psychosocial Functioning in Transgender Youth after 2 Years of Hormones", *New England Journal of Medicine* 388, no. 3, https://www.nejm.org/doi/full/10.1056/NEJMoa2206297.

107. See, for example, Alejandra Caraballo (@Esqueer), "Largest study of its kind published in the New England Journal of Medicine shows that trans teen's mental health significantly improves after receiving gender affirming care", Twitter (now X), January 20, 2023, https://web.archive.org/web/20230120164934/https://twitter.com/Esqueer_/status/1616462370687033356.

108. Tyler O'Neil, "EXCLUSIVE: Medical Group Pokes Holes in 'Fatally Flawed' Study Claiming to Prove Kids Benefit from Transgender Hormones", *Daily Signal*, February 1, 2023, https://www.dailysignal.com/2023/02/01/exclusive-medical-group-pokes-holes-fatally-flawed-study-claiming-prove-kids-benefit-transgender-hormones/; and Jesse Singal, "The New, Highly Touted Study on Hormones for Transgender Teens Doesn't Really Tell Us Much of Anything", *Singal-Minded*, February 7, 2023, https://jessesingal.substack.com/p/the-new-highly-touted-study-on-hormones.

109. Jesse Singal, "On Scientific Transparency, Researcher Degrees of Freedom, and That NEJM Study on Youth Gender Medicine (Updated)", *Singal-Minded*, January 31, 2023, https://jessesingal.substack.com/p/on-scientific-transparency-researcher.

110. Jo Yurcaba, "Hormone Therapy Improves Mental Health for Transgender Youths, a New Study Finds", *NBC News*, January 19, 2023, https://www.nbcnews.com/nbc-out/out-health-and-wellness/hormone-therapy-improves-mental-health-transgender-youths-new-study-fi-rcna66306.

111. Kiara Alfonseca and Nicole Wetsman, "Gender-Affirming Care for Trans Youth Improves Mental Health: Study", *ABC News*, January 18, 2023, https://abcnews.go.com/Health/gender-affirming-care-trans-youth-improves-mental-health/story?id=96510337.

112. "Final Report", The Cass Review, accessed November 12, 2024, https://cass.independent-review.uk/home/publications/final-report/.

113. Azeen Ghorayshi, "U.S. Study on Puberty Blockers Goes Unpublished Because of Politics, Doctor Says", *New York Times*, October 23, 2024, https://www.nytimes.com/2024/10/23/science/puberty-blockers-olson-kennedy.html.

114. "America's Best-Known Practitioner of Youth Gender Medicine Is Being Sued", *Economist*, December 6, 2024, https://www.economist.com/united-states/2024/12/06/americas-best-known-practitioner-of-youth-gender-medicine-is-being-sued.

115. Nathaniel Frank, "The Pentagon Is Wrong. Gender Transition Is Effective.", *New York Times*, April 9, 2018, https://www.nytimes.com/2018/04/09/opinion/pentagon-transgender.html.

116. Frank, "The Pentagon Is Wrong". See also "What We Know", Cornell University, accessed November 12, 2024, https://whatweknow.inequality.cornell.edu/.

117. Stephanie L. Budge, Sabra L. Katz-Wise, Esther N. Tebbe, Kimberly A. S. Howard, Carrie L. Schneider, and Adriana Rodriguez, "Transgender Emotional and Coping Processes: Facilitative and Avoidant Coping Throughout Gender Transitioning", *The Counseling Psychologist* 41, no. 4 (2013): 601–47, https://journals.sagepub.com/doi/10.1177/0011000011432753.

118. Michal Avrech Bar, Tal Jarus, Mineko Wada, Leora Rechtman, and Einav Noy, "Male-to-Female Transitions: Implications for Occupational Performance, Health, and Life Satisfaction", *Canadian Journal of Occupational Therapy* 83, no. 2, https://journals.sagepub.com/doi/10.1177/0008417416635346.

119. Louis Bailey, Sonja J. Ellis, and Jay Mcneil, "Suicide Risk in the UK Trans Population and the Role of Gender Transition in Decreasing Suicidal Ideation and Suicide Attempt", *Mental Health Review Journal* 19, no. 4 (2014): 209–20, https://www.researchgate.net/publication/281441727_Suicide_risk_in_the_UK_Trans_population_and_the_role_of_gender_transition_in_decreasing_suicidal_ideation_and_suicide_attempt.

120. Colton M. St. Amand, Kara M. Fitzgerald, Seth T. Pardo, and Julia Babcock, "The Effects of Hormonal Gender Affirmation Treatment on Mental Health in Female-to-Male Transsexuals", *Journal of Gay and Lesbian Mental Health* 15, no. 3: 281–99, https://www.researchgate.net/publication/233068152_The_Effects_of_Hormonal_Gender_Affirmation_Treatment_on_Mental_Health_in_Female-to-Male_Transsexuals.

121. Emily Sarah, Tae L. Hart, Suzanne Dibble, and Lori Kohler, "Female-to-Male Transgender Quality of Life", *Quality of Life Research* 15, no. 9 (2006): 1447–57, https://www.researchgate.net/publication/7025219_Female-to-male_transgender_quality_of_life.

122. Tiffany R. Glynn, Kristi E. Gamarel, Christopher W. Kahler, Mariko Iwamoto, Don Operario, and Tooru Nemoto, "The Role of Gender Affirmation in Psychological Well-Being Among Transgender Women", *Psychology of Sexual Orientation and Gender Diversity* 3, no. 3 (2016): 336–44, https://www.ncbi.nlm.nih.gov/pmc/articles/PMC5061456/.

123. Cecilia Dhejne, Katarina Gorts Oberg, Stefan Arver, and Mikael Landén, "An Analysis of All Applications for Sex Reassignment Surgery in Sweden, 1960–2010: Prevalence, Incidence, and Regrets", *Archives of Sexual Behavior* 43, no. 8 (2014), https://www.researchgate.net/publication/262734734_An_Analysis _of_All_Applications_for_Sex_Reassignment_Surgery_in_Sweden_1960 -2010_Prevalence_Incidence_and_Regrets.

124. Cecilia Dhejne, Paul Lichtenstein, Marcus Boman, Anna L. V. Johansson, Niklas Långström, and Mikael Landén, "Long-Term Follow-Up of Transsexual Persons Undergoing Sex Reassignment Surgery: Cohort Study in Sweden", *PLOS One*, February 22, 2011, https://journals.plos.org/plosone /article?id=10.1371/journal.pone.0016885.

125. Griet De Cuypere, Els Elaut, Gunter Heylens, and Georges Van Maele, "Long-Term Follow-Up: Psychosocial Outcome of Belgian Transsexuals After Sex Reassignment Surgery", *Sexologies* 15, no. 2 (2006), https:// www.researchgate.net/publication/247335377_Long-term_follow-up_Psycho social_outcome_of_Belgian_transsexuals_after_sex_reassignment_surgery.

126. Tim C. van de Grift, Els Elaut, Susanne C. Cerwenka, Peggy T. Cohen-Kettenis, Griet De Cuypere, and Hertha Richter-Appelt, "Effects of Medical Interventions on Gender Dysphoria and Body Image: A Follow-Up Study", *Psychosomatic Medicine* 79, no. 7 (2017): 815–23, https://www.ncbi .nlm.nih.gov/pmc/articles/PMC5580378/.

127. L. Nelson, E. J. Whallett, and J. C. McGregor, "Transgender Patient Satisfaction Following Reduction Mammaplasty", *Journal of Plastic Reconstructive and Aesthetic Surgery* 62, no. 3 (2008): 331–34, https://www.researchgate.net /publication/5764417_Transgender_patient_satisfaction_following_reduction _mammaplasty.

128. Dhejne et al., "Long-Term Follow-Up".

129. Marci L. Bowers, "What Decades of Providing Trans Health Care Have Taught Me", *New York Times*, April 1, 2023, https://www.nytimes .com/2023/04/01/opinion/trans-healthcare-law.html.

130. Alex Marzano-Lesnevich, "Who Should Be Allowed to Transition?", *New York Times*, March 4, 2022, https://www.nytimes.com/2022/03/04 /opinion/trans-laws-doctors-healthcare.html.

131. Valeria P. Bustos, S. Samyd, Andres Mascaro, Gabriel Del Corral, Antonio J. Forte, Pedro Ciudad, et al., "Regret After Gender-Affirmation Surgery: A Systematic Review and Meta-Analysis of Prevalence", *Plastic and Reconstructive Surgery—Global Open* 9, no. 3 (2021), https://journals.lww.com /prsgo/fulltext/2021/03000/regret_after_gender_affirmation_surgery__a.22.aspx.

132. Bustos et al., "Regret After Gender-Affirmation Surgery".

133. Chantal M. Wiepjes, Nienke M. Nota, Christel J. M. de Blok, Maartje Klaver, Annelou L. C. de Vries , S. Annelijn Wensing-Kruger, et al., "The Amsterdam Cohort of Gender Dysphoria Study (1972–2015): Trends in Prevalence, Treatment, and Regrets", *Journal of Sexual Medicine* 15, no. 4 (2018): 582–90, https://pubmed.ncbi.nlm.nih.gov/29463477/.

134. Lisa Selin Davis, "The Beginning of the End of 'Gender-Affirming Care'?", *Free Press*, July 30, 2022, https://www.thefp.com/p/the-beginning-of-the-end-of-gender.

135. Eleanor Hayward, "Tavistock Gender Clinic 'to Be Sued by 1,000 Families'", *Times* (London), August 11, 2022, https://www.thetimes.co.uk/article/tavistock-gender-clinic-to-be-sued-by-1-000-families-lbsw6k8zd.

136. Michael Biggs, "The Dutch Protocol for Juvenile Transsexuals: Origins and Evidence", *Journal of Sex and Marital Therapy* 49, no. 4 (2023): 348–68, https://www.tandfonline.com/doi/full/10.1080/0092623X.2022.2121238.

137. E. Abbruzzese, Stephen B. Levine, and Julia W. Mason, "The Myth of 'Reliable Research' in Pediatric Gender Medicine: A Critical Evaluation of the Dutch Studies—and Research That Has Followed", *Journal of Sex and Marital Therapy* 49, no. 6 (2023): 673–99, https://www.tandfonline.com/doi/full/10.1080/0092623X.2022.2150346.

138. Sarah Ketchen Lipson, Julia Raifman, Sara Abelson, and Sari L. Reisner, "Gender Minority Mental Health in the U.S.: Results of a National Survey on College Campuses", *American Journal of Preventative Medicine* 57, no. 3 (2019): 293–301, https://www.ajpmonline.org/article/S0749-3797(19)30219-3/fulltext.

139. Leo Sapir, "Reckless and Irresponsible", *City Journal*, March 17, 2023, https://www.city-journal.org/article/reckless-and-irresponsible.

140. Rikki Schlott, "Detransitioner Suing American Academy of Pediatrics: 'I Don't Want This to Happen to Other Young Girls'", *New York Post*, December 13, 2023, https://nypost.com/2023/12/13/news/detransitioner-suing-american-academy-of-pediatrics/, ellipses and brackets in original.

141. Jeremiah Keenan, "'Doctor' Advises Threatening Suicide to Get Transgender Treatments for Kids", *Federalist*, April 1, 2019, https://thefederalist.com/2019/04/01/doctor-advises-threatening-suicide-get-transgender-treatments-kids/.

142. Aaron Sibarium, "The Hijacking of Pediatric Medicine", *Washington Free Beacon*, December 7, 2022, https://freebeacon.com/coronavirus/the-hijacking-of-pediatric-medicine/.

143. Matt Donnelly, "Oscar-Nominated 'Umbrella Academy' Star Elliot Page Announced He Is Transgender", *Variety*, December 1, 2019, https://variety.com/2020/tv/news/elliot-page-transgender-ellen-page-juno-umbrella-academy-1234843023/.

144. Brent Lang, "Elliot Page Will Continue to Star in 'Umbrella Academy,' Netflix Changes Credits on His Past Films", *Variety*, December 1, 2020, https://variety.com/2020/tv/news/elliot-page-umbrella-academy-netflix-1234843387/.

145. Ryan T. Anderson, "When Amazon Erased My Book", *First Things*, February 23, 2021, https://www.firstthings.com/web-exclusives/2021/02/when-amazon-erased-my-book.

146. Yael Halon, "Author Accuses Target of Caving to 'Woke Activists' by Briefly Pulling Book Deemed 'Transphobic' on Twitter", *Fox News*,

November 16, 2020, https://www.foxnews.com/media/abigail-shrier-book
-deemed-transphobic-target-pulls.

147. Nathanael Blake (@NBlakeEPPC), "Vimeo has taken down Dead
Name, which is an excellent documentary I reviewed for @FDRLST",
Twitter (now X), January 23, 2023, https://twitter.com/NBlakeEPPC/status
/1617539355245162500.

148. "Cross v. Loudoun County School Board", Alliance Defending Freedom, accessed November 13, 2024, https://adflegal.org/case/cross-v-loudoun
-county-school-board.

149. Jennifer Sieland, "Female Public Transit Employees Reportedly Threatened with Termination for Expressing Concerns About Trans Colleague",
Reduxx, January 3, 2023, https://reduxx.info/female-public-transit-employees
-reportedly-threatened-with-termination-for-expressing-concerns-about-trans
-colleague/.

150. Genevieve Gluck, "Woman Fired After Raising Concerns About
Transgender Serial Killer Living in a Senior Shelter", *Reduxx*, December 7,
2022, https://reduxx.info/woman-fired-after-raising-concerns-about-transgender
-serial-killer-living-in-a-senior-shelter/.

151. Allan Josephson, "What a Federal Appeals Court Gets—but the University of Louisville Doesn't—on Transgender Issues", *Daily Signal*, September 19, 2024, https://www.dailysignal.com/2024/09/19/what-federal-appeals
-court-gets-university-louisville-doesnt-transgender/.

152. Christina M. Roberts, David A. Klein, Terry A. Adirim, Natasha
A. Schvey, and Elizabeth Hisle-Gorman, "Continuation of Gender-affirming
Hormones Among Transgender Adolescents and Adults", *Journal of Clinical
Endocrinology and Metabolism* 107, no. 9 (2022): e3937–e3943, https://pubmed
.ncbi.nlm.nih.gov/35452119/#full-view-affiliation-1.

153. Elizabeth Hisle-Gorman, Natasha A. Schvey, Terry A. Adirim, Anna
K. Rayne, Apryl Susi, Timothy A. Roberts, et al., "Mental Healthcare Utili-
zation of Transgender Youth Before and After Affirming Treatment", *Journal
of Sexual Medicine* 18, no. 8 (2021): 1444–54, https://pubmed.ncbi.nlm.nih.gov
/34247956/.

154. Jesse Singal, "When Children Say They're Trans", *Atlantic*, July/
August 2018, https://www.theatlantic.com/magazine/archive/2018/07/when
-a-child-says-shes-trans/561749/.

155. "When Children Say They're Trans, Continued", *Atlantic*, accessed
November 4, 2024, https://www.theatlantic.com/category/when-children-say
-theyre-trans-continued/.

156. Helena, "By Any Other Name", *Prude Posting*, February 19, 2022,
https://lacroicsz.substack.com/p/by-any-other-name?utm_campaign=post&utm
_source=url&s=r.

157. Laurel Duggan, "'We Were Wrong': Pioneer in Child Gender
Dysphoria Treatment Says Trans Medical Industry Is Harming Kids", *Daily
Caller*, March 11, 2023, https://dailycaller.com/2023/03/11/pioneer-in-child

-gender-dysphoria-treatment-says-trans-medical-industry-is-harming
-kids/.

158. Erica Anderson, "Opinion: When It Comes to Trans Youth, We're
in Danger of Losing Our Way", *San Francisco Examiner*, January 3, 2022, updated
June 16, 2022, https://www.sfexaminer.com/archives/opinion-when-it-comes
-to-trans-youth-we-re-in-danger-of-losing-our-way/article_833f674f-3d88
-5edf-900c-7142ef691f1a.html.

159. Abigail Shrier, "Top Trans Doctors Blow the Whistle on 'Sloppy'
Care", *Free Press*, October 4, 2021, https://bariweiss.substack.com/p/top-trans
-doctors-blow-the-whistle?r=7bjvz&utm_campaign=post&utm_medium=web
&utm_source=&s=r.

160. Madeleine Kearns, "Dr. Zucker Defied Trans Orthodoxy. Now He's
Vindicated.", *National Review*, October 25, 2018, https://www.nationalreview
.com/2018/10/transgender-orthodoxy-kenneth-zucker-vindicated/.

161. Molly Hayes, "Doctor Fired from Gender Identity Clinic Says He
Feels 'Vindicated' After CAMH Apology, Settlement", *Globe and Mail*, October 7, 2018, https://www.theglobeandmail.com/canada/toronto/article-doctor
-fired-from-gender-identity-clinic-says-he-feels-vindicated/.

162. Littman, "Parent Reports".

163. Joy Pullmann, "Explosive Ivy League Study Repressed for Finding
Transgender Kids May Be a Social Contagion", *Federalist*, August 31, 2018,
https://v2-9mdnszte.thefederalist.com/2018/08/31/explosive-ivy-league
-study-repressed-for-finding-transgender-kids-may-be-a-social-contagion/.

164. Jonathan Kay, "An Interview with Lisa Littman, Who Coined the
Term 'Rapid Onset Gender Dysphoria'", *Quillette*, March 19, 2019, https://
quillette.com/2019/03/19/an-interview-with-lisa-littman-who-coined-the
-term-rapid-onset-gender-dysphoria/.

165. Jesse Singal, "The New Study on Rapid-Onset Gender Dysphoria Published in 'Pediatrics' Is Genuinely Worthless", *Singal-Minded*, August 5, 2022,
https://jessesingal.substack.com/p/the-new-study-on-rapid-onset-gender.

166. "Tingley v. Ferguson", Alliance Defending Freedom, accessed
November 14, 2024, https://adflegal.org/case/tingley-v-ferguson.

167. Mia Hughes, "The WPATH Files: Pseudoscientific Surgical and
Hormonal Experiments on Children, Adolescents, and Vulnerable Adults",
Environmental Progress, March 4, 2024, https://environmentalprogress.org
/big-news/wpath-files.

168. Caroline Downey, "Leading Trans Medical Org Members Privately
Voiced Concerns About Risks of Child Transition, Documents Reveal",
National Review, March 6, 2024, https://www.nationalreview.com/news
/leading-trans-medical-org-members-privately-concerned-about-risks-of
-child-transition-internal-docs-reveal/.

169. Azeen Ghorayshi, "Biden Officials Pushed to Remove Age Limits for
Trans Surgery, Documents Show", *New York Times*, June 25, 2024, https://
www.nytimes.com/2024/06/25/health/transgender-minors-surgeries.html.

170. Ghorayshi, "Biden Officials".

171. "WPATH Blocked Publication of Its Own Gender Research", *UnHerd*, accessed November 14, 2024, https://unherd.com/breaking_news/wpath -blocked-publication-of-its-own-gender-research/.

172. "Research into Trans Medicine Has Been Manipulated", *Economist*, July 27, 2024, https://www.economist.com/united-states/2024/06/27 /research-into-trans-medicine-has-been-manipulated.

173. Aaron Sibarium, "Top Transgender Health Group Said Hormones, Surgeries Were 'Medically Necessary' So That Insurance Would Cover Them, Documents Show", *Washington Free Beacon*, July 23, 2024, https://freebeacon .com/courts/top-transgender-health-group-said-hormones-surgeries-were -medically-necessary-so-that-insurance-would-cover-them-documents-show/.

174. John Ely, "Eunuch Is a Gender, Says Prominent Pro-Trans Advocacy Group", *Daily Mail*, September 19, 2022, https://www.dailymail.co.uk /health/article-11227887/Eunuch-gender-says-prominent-pro-trans-advocacy -group.html.

175. Genevieve Gluck, "Top Trans Medical Association Collaborated with Castration, Child Abuse Fetishists", *Reduxx*, May 17, 2022, https://reduxx .info/top-trans-medical-association-collaborated-with-castration-child-abuse -fetishists/.

176. Genevieve Gluck, "Top Academic Behind Fetish Site Hosting Child Sexual Abuse Fantasy, Push to Revise WPATH Guidelines", *Reduxx*, May 21, 2022, https://reduxx.info/top-academic-behind-fetish-site-hosting-child-sexual -abuse-fantasy-push-to-revise-wpath-guidelines/.

177. Gluck, "Top Trans Medical Association".

178. Gluck, "Top Trans Medical Association".

179. Gluck, "Top Academic".

180. Gluck, "Top Academic".

181. Juliana Chan Erikson, "Trans Advocates Add New Gender Identity: The Eunuch", *World*, October 24, 2022, https://wng.org/roundups/trans -advocates-add-new-gender-identity-the-eunuch-1666638882.

182. Genevieve Gluck, "EXCLUSIVE: Cal State 'Gender' Academic Inspired Pedophilic Fantasy on Castrating, Enslaving Young Boys", *Reduxx*, July 8, 2024, https://reduxx.info/exclusive-california-gender-academic-inspired -pedophilic-fantasy-on-castrating-enslaving-young-boys/.

183. Gallagher Plastic Surgery, website of Dr. Sidhbh Gallagher, accessed November 14, 2024, https://gallagherplasticsurgery.com/.

184. James Reinl, "EXCLUSIVE: Miami Sex-Change Surgeon Who Dubs Herself 'Dr Teetus Deletus' Is Reported to Consumer Watchdog for 'Deceptively' Luring 'Vulnerable' Teens into Transgender Operations", *Daily Mail*, October 13, 2022, https://www.dailymail.co.uk/news/article-11303919 /Florida-sex-change-surgeon-dubs-Dr-Teetus-Deletus-REPORTED -consumer-watchdog.html.

185. Sidhbh Gallager MD, "drsidhbhgallagher", Instagram page, accessed November 14, 2024, https://www.instagram.com/drsidhbhgallagher/?hl=en.

186. Alec Schemmel, "Miami Surgeon Performs 'Top Surgery' for 15-Year-Old Transgender Kids, Report Says", *NBC15 News*, September 28, 2022, https://mynbc15.com/news/nation-world/miami-surgeon-performs-top-surgery-for-15-year-old-transgender-kids-report-says.

187. Genevieve Gluck (@WomenReadWomen), "Plastic surgeon Dr. Sidhbh Gallagher is promoting the eunuch gender", Twitter (now X), April 13, 2023, https://twitter.com/identity/status/1646564740242743298.

188. Pamela Paul, "Free to Be You and Me. Or Not.", *New York Times*, December 4, 2022, https://www.nytimes.com/2022/12/04/opinion/free-to-be-you-and-me-anni.html.

189. Megan Twohey and Christina Jewett, "They Paused Puberty, but Is There a Cost?", *New York Times*, November 14, 2022, https://www.nytimes.com/2022/11/14/health/puberty-blockers-transgender.html.

190. David Walter Banks, "What Lia Thomas Could Mean for Women's Elite Sports", *New York Times*, May 29, 2022, updated June 15, 2022, https://www.nytimes.com/2022/05/29/us/lia-thomas-women-sports.html.

191. Katie J. M. Baker, "When Students Change Gender Identity, and Parents Don't Know", *New York Times*, January 22, 2023, https://www.nytimes.com/2023/01/22/us/gender-identity-students-parents.html.

192. Daneila Valdes and Kinnon MacKinnon, "Take Detransitioners Seriously", *Atlantic*, January 18, 2023, https://www.theatlantic.com/ideas/archive/2023/01/detransition-transgender-nonbinary-gender-affirming-care/672745/.

193. Helen Lewis, "The Push for Puberty Blockers Got Ahead of the Research", *Atlantic*, December 16, 2024, https://www.theatlantic.com/ideas/archive/2024/12/why-supreme-court-puberty-blockers/680998/.

194. Lydia Polgreen, "Republicans Are Forgetting One Crucial Truth About People and Their Bodies", *New York Times*, April 14, 2023, https://www.nytimes.com/2023/04/14/opinion/transgender-wisconsin-schools.html.

195. Mary Harrington, *Feminism Against Progress* (Regnery Publishing, 2023), 17.

196. Emily St. James, "What's So Scary About a Transgender Child?", *Vox*, September 29, 2022, https://www.vox.com/policy-and-politics/23281683/trans-kids-transition-medicine-surgery.

197. St. James, "What's So Scary?".

198. Jack Turban, "I'm a Psychiatrist. Here's How I Talk to Transgender Youth and Their Families About Gender Identity", *New York Times*, July 8, 2024, https://www.nytimes.com/2024/07/08/opinion/gender-identity-communication.html.

199. Turban, "I'm a Psychiatrist".

200. St. James, "What's So Scary?".

201. J. Michael Bailey and Ray Blanchard, "Gender Dysphoria Is Not One Thing", 4thWaveNow, December 7, 2017, https://4thwavenow.com /2017/12/07/gender-dysphoria-is-not-one-thing/comment-page-1/.

202. Max Eden, "My Gender Is 'Rock'", *City Journal*, September 19, 2023, https://www.city-journal.org/article/gender-ideology-in-k-12-schools.

203. Wesley J. Smith, "'Gender Hybrid' Children?", *National Review*, August 16, 2023, https://www.nationalreview.com/corner/gender-hybrid-children/.

204. Andrea Long Chu, "Freedom of Sex: The Moral Case for Letting Trans Kids Change Their Bodies", *New York Magazine*, March 11, 2024, https://nymag.com/intelligencer/article/trans-rights-biological-sex-gender -judith-butler.html.

205. Chu, "Freedom of Sex".

206. Chu, "Freedom of Sex".

207. Chu, "Freedom of Sex".

208. Andrea Long Chu, "My New Vagina Won't Make Me Happy", *New York Times*, November 24, 2018, https://www.nytimes.com/2018/11/24 /opinion/sunday/vaginoplasty-transgender-medicine.html.

209. Reduxx (@ReduxxMag), "*New York Magazine* has published an essay by a trans-identified male academic calling for 'trans kids' to be provided with 'sex-changing medical care, regardless of age'", X, March 12, 2024, https:// twitter.com/ReduxxMag/status/1767556892295835839.

210. Ryan T. Anderson, "*The New York Times* Reveals Painful Truths About Transgender Lives", *Public Discourse*, November 25, 2018, https://www .thepublicdiscourse.com/2018/11/47220/.

211. Chu, "Freedom of Sex".

212. Ryan T. Anderson, *When Harry Became Sally: Responding to the Transgender Moment* (Encounter Books, 2018), 159.

Chapter 4: The Wrongs of Gay Rights

1. "Gay-Pride Parade Sets Mainstream Acceptance of Gays Back 50 Years", *Onion*, April 25, 2001, https://www.theonion.com/gay-pride-parade -sets-mainstream-acceptance-of-gays-bac-1819566014.

2. Lauren Rowello, "Yes, Kink Belongs at Pride. And I Want My Kids to See It.", *Washington Post*, June 29, 2021, https://www.washingtonpost.com /outlook/2021/06/29/pride-month-kink-consent/.

3. Elizabeth Spiers (@espiers), "I've never boxed in my life but if I did I'd be fine with boxing a trans woman in my weight class", Twitter (now X), May 24, 2023, https://twitter.com/espiers/status/1661458777978073091. See also Brianna Lyman, "Female Dem Pollster Offers to Box Biological Male to Disprove Transphobia", *Daily Caller*, May 26, 2023, https://dailycaller .com/2023/05/26/elizabeth-spiers-boxing-transphobia/.

4. Caroline Lowbridge, "The Lesbians Who Feel Pressured to Have Sex and Relationships with Trans Women", *BBC*, October 26, 2021, https://www .bbc.com/news/uk-england-57853385.

5. Jordan Boyd, "Naked Men Freely Expose Themselves to Kids at Pride Because the Right Bought the Left's 'Tolerance' Lie", *Federalist*, June 26, 2023, https://thefederalist.com/2023/06/26/naked-men-freely-expose-themselves -to-kids-at-pride-because-the-right-bought-the-lefts-tolerance-lie/.

6. Libs of TikTok (@Libsoftiktok), "Fully naked men expose their gen-italia in front of children at Seattle pride parade", Twitter (now X), June 25, 2023, https://twitter.com/libsoftiktok/status/1673059174211633152.

7. Libs of TikTok (@Libsoftiktok), "Bud Light was a sponsor of a Toronto pride event where completely naked people marched around in front of children", June 25, 2023, https://twitter.com/libsoftiktok/status /1673099249930608641.

8. Anders Hagstrom, "NYC Drag Marchers Chant 'We're Coming for Your Children' During Pride Event", *Fox News*, June 25, 2023, https://www .foxnews.com/us/nyc-drag-marchers-chant-were-coming-your-children -during-pride-event.

9. "Jack Phillips", Alliance Defending Freedom, accessed November 15, 2024, https://adflegal.org/client/jack-phillips.

10. Becket, "Massachusetts Bans Faithful Catholics from Adopting Chil-dren", press release, August 8, 2023, https://www.becketlaw.org/media /breaking-massachusetts-bans-faithful-catholics-from-adopting-children/.

11. "Bates v. Pakseresht", Alliance Defending Freedom, accessed Novem-ber 15, 2024, https://adflegal.org/case/bates-v-pakseresht.

12. Nathanael Blake, "The Left Has Chosen to Prioritize Sex over Solidar-ity, with Tragic Consequences", *Federalist*, June 13, 2022, https://thefederalist .com/2022/06/13/the-left-has-chosen-to-prioritize-sex-over-solidarity-with -tragic-consequences/.

13. R. Albert Mohler, Jr., "A Direct Threat to Christian Education—the Human Rights Campaign Demands That the Biden Administration Deny Accreditation to Christian Colleges and Schools", Albert Mohler, November 18, 2020, https://albertmohler.com/2020/11/18/a-direct-threat -to-christian-education-the-human-rights-campaign-demands-that-the-biden -administration-deny-accreditation-to-christian-colleges-and-schools.

14. John Hirschauer, "Samaritan's Purse, Excluded from NYC for the Sake of 'Inclusion'", *National Review*, May 6, 2020, https://www.nationalreview .com/2020/05/samaritans-purse-excluded-from-nyc-for-the-sake-of-inclusion.

15. Andrew Sullivan, "Gay Rights and the Limits of Liberalism", *The Weekly Dish*, June 23, 2023, https://andrewsullivan.substack.com/p/gay-rights -and-the-limits-of-liberalism.

16. See, for example, Joe Biden (@JoeBiden), "Let's be clear: Transgender equality is the civil rights issue of our time. There is no room for compromise when it comes to basic human rights", Twitter (now X), January 25, 2020, https://x.com/JoeBiden/status/1221135646107955200?mx=2.

17. Hans Fiene (@Hans Fiene), "Either there is a fundamental difference in how our society treats natural sex and unnatural sex or all sex will be celebrated.

You can't tear down the Hoover Dam and expect Lake Mead to only move 6 inches", Twitter (now X), March 24, 2023, https://x.com/HansFiene /status/1661438858670612480.

18. Valeriya Safronova, "Interested in Polyamory? Check Out These Places", *New York Times*, May 16, 2023, https://www.nytimes.com/2023/05/16/style /polyamory-somerville.html.

19. Safronova, "Interested in Polyamory?".

20. Safronova, "Interested in Polyamory?". Study linked in *New York Times* piece: Rhonda N. Balzarini, Christoffer Dharma, Taylor Kohut, Bjarne M. Holmes, Lorne Campbell, and Justin J. Lehmiller, "Demographic Comparison of American Individuals in Polyamorous and Monogamous Relationships", *Journal of Sex Research* 56, no. 6 (2019): 681–94, https://pubmed.ncbi .nlm.nih.gov/29913084/ https://www.ncbi.nlm.nih.gov/pmc/articles/PMC 5958351/.

21. Safronova, "Interested in Polyamory?".

22. Safronova, "Interested in Polyamory?".

23. Alexander Alter, "How a Polyamorous Mom Had 'a Big Sexual Adventure' and Found Herself", *New York Times*, September 16, 2024, https://www .nytimes.com/2024/01/13/books/molly-roden-winter-more-book-open -marriage.html.

24. Jason Bilbrey, "I Was Content with Monogamy. I Shouldn't Have Been.", *New York Times*, June 21, 2024, https://www.nytimes.com/2024/06/21 /style/modern-love-polyamory-i-was-content-with-monogamy.html.

25. Daniel Bergner, "Lessons from a 20-Person Polycule", *New York Times Magazine*, April 15, 2024, https://www.nytimes.com/interactive/2024/04/15 /magazine/polycule-polyamory-boston.html.

26. Jennifer Wilson, "How Did Polyamory Become So Popular?", *New Yorker*, December 25, 2023, https://www.newyorker.com/magazine/2024 /01/01/american-poly-christopher-gleason-book-review-more-a-memoir-of -open-marriage-molly-roden-winter.

27. Allison P. Davis, Alistair Kitchen, Alyssa Shelasky, Anya Kamenetz, and Bindu Bansinath, "A Practical Guide to Modern Polyamory: How to Open Things Up, for the Curious Couple", *The Cut*, accessed November 15, 2024, https://www.thecut.com/_pages/clr9h4wp8oooooikblq8dqnoe.html.

28. New York Magazine (@NYMag), "It's not just you; everyone is talking about being open. But even though it's become more discussed, it isn't such a simple thing to do well", X, January 16, 2024, https://x.com/NYMag /status/1747228468742418449.

29. Clare Thorp, "Couple to Throuple: How Polyamory Is Becoming a 'New Normal'", *BBC*, February 9, 2024, https://www.bbc.com/culture /article/20240209-couple-to-throuple-how-polyamory-is-becoming-a-new -normal.

30. Nicholas Rice, "What Is a Throuple—and How to Know When the Relationship Type Is Right for You, According to an Expert", *People*, April

21, 2024, https://people.com/what-is-a-throuple-how-to-know-when-the
-relationship-type-is-right-for-you-expert-8636145.

31. "Marriage", Gallup, accessed November 15, 2024, https://news.gallup
.com/poll/117328/marriage.aspx.

32. Kathianne Boniello, "New York Parent Seeks OK to Marry Their Own
Adult Child", *New York Post*, April 10, 2021, https://nypost.com/2021/04/10
/new-york-parent-seeks-ok-to-marry-their-own-adult-child/.

33. Andrew Sullivan, "The Queers Versus the Homosexuals", *The Weekly
Dish*, May 19, 2023, https://andrewsullivan.substack.com/p/the-queers-versus
-the-homosexuals.

34. Mary Harrington, *Feminism Against Progress* (Regnery Publishing,
2023), 141, 169.

35. Nathaniel Frank, "A Match Made in Heaven", *Washington Post*, June 21,
2019, https://www.washingtonpost.com/news/posteverything/wp/2019/06
/21/feature/a-match-made-in-heaven/.

36. Nicholas H. Wolfinger, "Bisexual America", *Institute for Family Studies*,
June 5, 2023, https://ifstudies.org/blog/bisexual-america.

37. Kat Rosenfield, "The Death of Intimacy: Sex Positivity Has Created
a Cult of Celibacy", *UnHerd*, January 22, 2022, https://unherd.com/2022/01
/the-death-of-intimacy/.

38. Cassidy Morrison, "Number of Gen Z Who Say They Are Gay or Bisex-
ual Doubles to 22%—with Women Twice as Likely as Men to Be LGBTQ+",
Daily Mail, https://www.dailymail.co.uk/health/article-13192251/Number-Gen
-Z-say-gay-bisexual-doubles-22-women-twice-likely-men-LGBTQ.html.

39. David Marcus, "Video Emerges of Drag Kid 'Desmond Is Amazing'
Pretending to Snort Ketamine", *Federalist*, February 17, 2020, https://the
federalist.com/2020/02/17/video-emerges-of-drag-kid-desmond-is-amazing
-pretending-to-snort-ketamine/.

40. "Transgender Children and Youth: Understanding the Basics",
Human Rights Campaign, accessed November 15, 2024, https://www.hrc.org
/resources/transgender-children-and-youth-understanding-the-basics.

41. Child Welfare Information Gateway, "Supporting LGBTQ+ Youth:
A Guide for Foster Parents", Factsheets for Families, June 2021, https://www
.childwelfare.gov/resources/supporting-lgbtq-youth-guide-foster-parents/.

42. Child Welfare Information Gateway, "Supporting LGBTQ+ Youth".

43. "Vermont to Foster Parents: Promote Gender Ideology or Lose Your
License", Alliance Defending Freedom, June 4, 2024, https://adflegal.org/press
-release/vermont-foster-parents-promote-gender-ideology-or-lose-your-license/.

44. Jonathan Lambert, "No 'Gay Gene': Massive Study Homes in on
Genetic Basis of Human Sexuality", *Nature* 573 (2019): 14–15, https://www
.nature.com/articles/d41586-019-02585-6.

45. Joanna Wuest, "The New Genomics of Sexuality Moves Us Beyond
'Born This Way'", *Psyche*, February 24, 2021, https://psyche.co/ideas/the
-new-genomics-of-sexuality-moves-us-beyond-born-this-way.

46. Michelle Smith, as told to Christian Allaire, "'I Want All Genders to Feel Welcome in My Clothes'", *Vogue*, June 14, 2022, https://www.vogue.com/article/michelle-smith-on-embracing-her-pansexuality.

47. Erica Tempesta, "'I Grew Up Very Straight ... My Attraction to People Changed': Ex-Milly Designer Michelle Smith on Coming Out as Pansexual in Her 40s", *Daily Mail*, June 15, 2022, https://www.dailymail.co.uk/femail/article-10920209/Ex-Milly-designer-Michelle-Smith-discusses-coming-pansexual-40s.html.

48. Lydia Polgreen, "Born This Way? Born Which Way?", *New York Times*, December 1, 2023, https://www.nytimes.com/2023/12/01/opinion/politics/life-without-regret.html.

49. Polgreen, "Born This Way?".

50. Madeleine Kearns, "Trans and Teens: The Social-Contagion Factor Is Real", *National Review Plus Magazine*, February 2, 2023, https://www.nationalreview.com/magazine/2023/02/20/trans-and-teens-the-social-contagion-factor/.

51. Eric Kaufmann, "Born This Way? The Rise of LGBT as a Social and Political Identity: CSPI Report No. 6", Center for the Study of Partisanship and Ideology, May 30, 2022, https://www.cspicenter.com/p/born-this-way-the-rise-of-lgbt-as-a-social-and-political-identity.

52. Meredith Deliso, "More Americans Identify as LGBT Than Ever Before: Poll", *ABC News*, February 24, 2021, https://abcnews.go.com/US/americans-identify-lgbt-poll/story?id=76097305.

53. Cara Murez, "Big Rise in U.S. Teens Identifying as Gay, Bisexual", *U.S. News*, June 15, 2021, https://www.usnews.com/news/health-news/articles/2021-06-15/big-rise-in-us-teens-identifying-as-gay-bisexual.

54. Erin Doherty, "The Number of LGBTQ-Identifying Adults Is Soaring", *Axios*, February 19, 2022, https://www.axios.com/lgbtq-generation-z-gallup-24551003-3bfa-414a-bbef-ff663368c4b5.html.

55. Caroline Downey, "LGBTQ Activists Host Gender-Inclusive Sex-Ed Summer Camp for Elementary Schoolers", *National Review*, March 8, 2022, https://www.nationalreview.com/news/lgbtq-activists-host-gender-inclusive-sex-ed-summer-camp-for-elementary-schoolers/.

56. St. Vincent, vocalist, "Masseducation", by Jack Antonoff and Annie Clark, track 3 on *Masseducation*, Loma Vista Recordings, released October 13, 2017.

57. Jonah Weiner, "The Dream World of St. Vincent", *Rolling Stone*, June 23, 2014, http://www.rollingstone.com/music/news/the-dream-world-of-st-vincent-20140623.

58. Friedrich Nietzsche, *The Gay Science*, trans. Walter Kaufmann (Vintage Books, 1974), 181.

59. Nietzsche, *Gay Science*, 182.

60. Nietzsche, *Gay Science*, 181.

61. Nietzsche, *Gay Science*, 181.

62. Nietzsche, *Gay Science*, 181.

Chapter 5: Whose Liberation?

1. Nicholas Kristof, "The Children of Pornhub", *New York Times*, December 4, 2020, https://www.nytimes.com/2020/12/04/opinion/sunday/pornhub -rape-trafficking.html.

2. Kyle Harper, *From Shame to Sin: The Christian Transformation of Sexual Morality in Late Antiquity* (Harvard University Press, 2013), 85.

3. Harper, *From Shame to Sin*, 94.

4. Nicholas Kristof, "A Christmas Conversation About Christ", *New York Times*, December 24, 2022, https://www.nytimes.com/2022/12/24/opinion /a-christmas-conversation-about-christ.html; see also Nicholas Kristof, "Er, Can I Ask a Few Questions About Abortion?", *New York Times*, October 28, 2020, https://www.nytimes.com/2020/10/28/opinion/abortion-america-politics .html.

5. See Gregory DiPippo, "St. Ambrose's Christmas Hymn *Veni, Redemptor Gentium*", New Liturgical Movement, December 30, 2016, https://www .newliturgicalmovement.org/2016/12/st-ambroses-christmas-hymn-veni.html.

6. Plato, *Republic*, trans. G. M. A. Grube (Hackett Publishing Company, 1992), 4.

7. Mara Gay, "The Republican War on Sex", *New York Times*, July 2, 2022, https://www.nytimes.com/2022/07/02/opinion/abortion-ban-sex.html.

8. Nicholas Kristof, "The One Privilege Liberals Ignore", *New York Times*, September 13, 2023, https://www.nytimes.com/2023/09/13/opinion/single -parent-poverty.html.

9. Becca Rothfeld, "'The Two-Parent Privilege' Gets Caught in the Trap of Convention", review of *The Two Parent Privilege* by Melissa S. Kearney, *Washington Post*, October 14, 2023, https://www.washingtonpost.com/books /2023/10/14/two-parent-privilege-melissa-kearney-review/.

10. John Hood, "Family Structure Shapes Economic Outcomes", *Carolina Journal*, October 16, 2023, https://www.carolinajournal.com/opinion /family-structure-shapes-economic-outcomes/.

11. Nicholas Zill, "The College Completion Gap and How to Close It", *Institute for Family Studies*, August 2, 2023, https://ifstudies.org/blog /the-college-completion-gap-and-how-to-close-it.

12. Jason L. Riley, "The Biggest Root Cause of Crime Is Fatherlessness", *Wall Street Journal*, December 12, 2023, https://www.wsj.com/articles/the -biggest-root-cause-of-crime-is-fatherlessness-single-motherhood-5cdfe763.

13. Rob Henderson, "Does Poverty Create Psychopathic Behavior? No, but Family Instability Appears To", *Institute for Family Studies*, July 13, 2021, https://ifstudies.org/blog/does-poverty-create-psychopathic-behavior-no -but-family-instability-appears-to.

14. Katelyn Walls Shelton, "Toward a Protestant Theology of the Body", *World Opinions*, September 28, 2024, https://wng.org/opinions/toward-a -protestant-theology-of-the-body-1695873170.

15. Andrew Walker (@andrewtwalk), "We are getting to a place where the gospel is not only what reconciles us to God, but what will be the only

pathway to authentic living in a world that runs on cynicism and deception", Twitter (now X), April 1, 2023, https://twitter.com/andrewtwalk/status /1642272824097218561.

16. Jason S. Carroll and Brian J. Willoughby, "The Myth of Sexual Experience", *Institute for Family Studies*, April 18, 2023, https://ifstudies.org/blog /the-myth-of-sexual-experience-.

17. Brad Wilcox and Alysse ElHage, "Cohabitation Doesn't Help Your Odds of Marital Success", *Institute of Family Studies*, April 27, 2023, https:// ifstudies.org/blog/cohabitation-doesnt-help-your-odds-of-marital-success.

18. Jesse Smith and Nicholas H. Wolfinger, "Testing Common Theories on the Relationship Between Premarital Sex and Marital Stability", *Institute for Family Studies*, March 6, 2023, https://ifstudies.org/blog/testing-common -theories-on-the-relationship-between-premarital-sex-and-marital-stability.

19. See Ephesians 5–6; Colossians 3; 1 Timothy 3; and Titus 1.

Conclusion: Authentic Humans, Authentic Human Flourishing

1. Sir Walter Scott, "The Lay of the Last Minstrel", in *The Poems and Plays of Sir Walter Scott*, ed. Ernest Rhys (E.P. Dutton & Co., n.d.), 1:401.

2. C.S. Lewis, *The Four Loves* (Hardcourt Brace Jovanovich, 1960), 169.

3. Nathanael Blake, "The Solitary Lover: Rousseau's Fear of Love", *Anamnesis*, no. 6 (2017).

4. G.K. Chesterton, *Manalive* (Thomas Nelson and Sons, 1912), 340.

5. Chesterton, *Manalive*, 95.

6. "Entre Nous", by Neil Peart, Geddy Lee, and Alex Lifeson, produced by Rush and Terry Brown, track 4 on Rush, *Permanent Waves*, Anthem Records, 1980.

7. J.R.R. Tolkien, *The Letters of J.R.R. Tolkien*, ed. Humphrey Carpenter (Houghton Mifflin, 2000), 51.

8. Hannah Arendt, *The Human Condition*, 2nd ed. (University of Chicago Press, 1958), 236–47.

PREVIOUSLY PUBLISHED MATERIAL

I thank *World Opinions* and *Public Discourse* (the online journal of the Witherspoon Institute of Princeton, N.J.) for allowing me to draw from much of my previously published writing.

The introduction includes material from "Indulged, Miserable, and Yet 'Liberated'?" *World Opinions*, August 29, 2022, https://wng.org/opinions/indulged-miserable-and-yet -liberated-1661774137.

Chapter 1 includes material from "The Problems of Putting Off Children", *Public Discourse*, May 2, 2022, https://www .thepublicdiscourse.com/2022/05/82029/.

Chapter 2 includes material from "Liberal Individualism Is Undermining Itself", *Public Discourse*, November 13, 2022, https://www.thepublicdiscourse.com/2022/11/85563/.

Chapter 3 includes material from "Sending the Wounded to the Front", *Public Discourse*, February 27, 2023, https://www .thepublicdiscourse.com/2023/02/87212/; "What We Don't Know: Does Gender Transition Improve the Lives of People with Gender Dysphoria?", *Public Discourse*, April 30, 2019, https://www.thepublicdiscourse.com/2019/04/51524/; "The Materialist Magicians of Transgenderism", *World Opinions*, November 18, 2022, https://wng.org/opinions/the -materialist-magicians-of-transgenderism-1668774959; and "A Tyrannical Assault on Parental Rights", *World Opinions*, September 11, 2023, https://wng.org/opinions/a-tyrannical-assault -on-parental-rights-1694431236.

Chapter 4 includes material from "OK, Groomer: Why Some in the LGBT Movement Are Focusing on Kids", *Public Discourse*, March 28, 2022, https://www.thepublicdiscourse .com/2022/03/81314/; and "Self-Creation or God's Creation?

Mistaken Identities and Nietzsche's Madman", *Public Discourse*, June 20, 2018, https://www.thepublicdiscourse.com/2018/06/21585/.

Chapter 5 includes material from "John the Baptist Was a Witness for Life and a Martyr for Marriage", *Public Discourse*, June 21, 2023, https://www.thepublicdiscourse.com/2023/06/89446/.

The conclusion includes material from "Baby Is a Punk Rocker: On the Givenness of Life", *Public Discourse*, December 28, 2020, https://www.thepublicdiscourse.com/2020/12/73008/; "We Were Parents", *Public Discourse*, March 31, 2019, https://www.thepublicdiscourse.com/2019/03/50630/; and "The Romance of Ordinary Marriage", *Public Discourse*, March 8, 2018, https://www.thepublicdiscourse.com/2018/03/20926/.

INDEX